Y0-BZM-071

Studies in the Textual Tradition of Terence

The textual tradition of the Latin dramatist Publius Terentius Afer (second century BC) is unusually rich and complex. Over six hundred manuscripts containing some or all of Terence's six comedies have survived, but only one codex and three small fragments date from antiquity. All the rest were copied in the Middle Ages and the Renaissance when Terence was very popular. Recently scholars have been devoting considerable study to the role of his works and the commentaries on them in the cultural and intellectual development of the Middle Ages and the Renaissance. However, little attention has been given to an examination and re-examination of the manuscripts in order to determine which are the most useful for establishing a reliable text of the plays.

In this study John N. Grant examines afresh the manuscript tradition of the comedies, looking in particular at a branch of the medieval manuscripts which has been neglected in the past. He establishes the primacy of one manuscript, the value of which has hitherto been disputed, and points out the importance of others which have been known but have been neglected by past editors of Terence. In addition, through a careful study of the cycle of illustrations that appear in some medieval manuscripts he brings under scrutiny the history of the transmission of the text in late antiquity. He shows that, contrary to the generally held view, the date of the original cycle of illustrations from which those in the medieval manuscripts are derived cannot be used to provide a chronological keystone for the lost ancient manuscripts which were the ancestors of the surviving witnesses.

An appendix with a selection of readings from over 150 manuscripts will be of value to those interested in investigating further the relationships among the extant manuscripts.

This study lays the foundation for a new edition of the plays of Terence.

JOHN N. GRANT is Professor of Classics, University of Toronto.

PHOENIX

Journal of the Classical Association of Canada
Revue de la Société canadienne des études classiques
Supplementary Volume xx
Tome supplémentaire xx

JOHN N. GRANT

Studies in the Textual Tradition of Terence

UNIVERSITY OF TORONTO PRESS
Toronto Buffalo London

Toronto Buffalo London
Printed in Canada
ISBN 0-8020-2574-9

Printed on acid-free paper

Canadian Cataloguing in Publication Data

Grant, John N. (John Neilson), 1940–
Studies in the textual tradition of Terence

(Phoenix. Supplementary volume, ISSN 0079–1784; 20)
Bibliography: p. 238
Includes index.
ISBN 0–8020–2574–9

1. Terence – Criticism, Textual. I. Title. II. Series: Phoenix.
Supplementary volume (Toronto, Ont.); 20.

PA6768.G73 1986 872'.01 C86–093638–4

This book has been published with
the help of a grant from
the Canadian Federation for the Humanities,
using funds provided by the Social Sciences and
Humanities Research Council of Canada.

TO LILIAN

CONTENTS

PREFACE

When Publius Terentius Afer died in 159 BC, he left to posterity six *fabulae palliatae*, plays which were his adaptations of examples of Greek New Comedy, four written by Menander and two by Apollodorus of Carystus. In the decades after Terence's death productions of his plays continued,[1] and it is probable that even in the first century BC they were not absent from the Roman stage, even though at this time popular dramatic taste inclined to the mime. In his literary epistle to Augustus, Horace lists the early Latin dramatists as illustrations of how ancient literary figures were overestimated by his contemporaries: 'These (ie Ennius, Naevius, Pacuvius, Afranius, Plautus, Caecilius and Terence) are the dramatist-poets whom mighty Rome learns by heart and watches in a theatre so packed it seems small' (*Epist* 2.1.60-1). Even if Horace is exaggerating here, he could hardly have said this if revivals of early Latin drama were non-existent or even rare. He himself certainly knew his Terence. He quotes closely, for example, from *Eunuchus* at *Serm* 2.3.262ff and refers to Menedemus of the *Hauton timorumenos* at *Serm* 1.2.19ff. Horace would have been no exception among the educated classes of Italy, who were probably introduced to the dramatist in their schooldays. If interest in the early figures of Latin literature declined in the first century of the Empire, Terence soon regained his position in the school curriculum. The surviving commentary of Donatus (fl AD 350) and the references within it to earlier grammarians (eg Aemilius Asper and Probus) make that clear enough.[2]

Because of his popularity many copies of Terence's works must have been in circulation in antiquity. Yet what survives from that period amounts to the codex Bembinus (ca AD 400, lacking most of

Andria and the end of *Adelphoe*) and three small fragments. Besides these, however, there is a daunting number of MSS of Terence which date from the medieval and Renaissance periods. It is on the evidence of these MSS as well as of the Donatus commentary and of the quotations of Terence which appear in the writers of antiquity that the attempt to establish what Terence actually wrote must begin.

In a recent article Giuseppe Billanovich rebuked classicists engaged in studying the tradition of Terence for having concerned themselves too exclusively with the history of the text in remote antiquity instead of having made more use of the material by means of which the transmission of Terence into the Carolingian period might be illuminated.[3] This book reflects the classicists' obsession in that the first three chapters deal with topics relating to the Terence text in antiquity. How far back do our surviving MSS take us? What is the date of the lost MS from which descend all the medieval MSS (in technical terms, their hyparchetype, now usually designated Σ)? Does the possibility of dating the original ancient miniatures which accompanied the text in some MSS provide a date for the hyparchetype of the surviving γ MSS and thus a *terminus ante quem* for Σ? What light does the Donatus commentary shed on the Terence text in circulation in the fourth century? No justification, however, is needed for dealing with these questions. In 1924 Günther Jachmann published a stimulating and influential study on the history of the Terence text in antiquity. Much of what he said was sound, not all was accepted. One of his conclusions which did win acceptance, however, and which is important for the chronology of the tradition in antiquity – that the original miniatures were created to accompany a γ text – will be re-examined here.

The second half of the book will focus primarily on MSS of the medieval period. Here the point which underlies Billanovich's criticism will be borne out. Detailed consideration of some MSS which have long been known but have never, apparently, been closely studied will cast light on the details of how the text of Terence survived into the Carolingian period and on the relationships of the MSS in the two major groups of medieval MSS. Some of these deserve a place in an editor's critical apparatus alongside those which are already there.

I am most grateful to the Canada Council and to its offspring, the Social Sciences and Humanities Research Council of Canada, for the award of research grants over more than a decade. These made it possible for me to visit libraries in Europe and to purchase microfilms of MSS. I owe thanks to several persons: to Professor H.D. Jocelyn and to Professor M.D. Reeve, who read early drafts of chapters and offered helpful suggestions and criticisms; to M. Y.-F. Riou, who supplied me with information about a MS in the Bibliothèque Nationale (lat 2109); to Mrs Mary Lee, who typed with care and patience a difficult manuscript; and to my copy editor at the University of Toronto Press, Miss Joan Bulger, whose concern for the convenience of readers greatly improved the presentation of the material.

The plates have been taken from L.W. Jones and C.R. Morey *The miniatures of the manuscripts of Terence prior to the thirteenth century* (Princeton 1931). For permission to reproduce the illustrations I am grateful to Princeton University Press and to the following libraries: the Bibliothèque Nationale, Paris; the Bodleian Library, Oxford; the Biblioteca Ambrosiana, Milan; and the Biblioteca Apostolica Vaticana.

I am deeply indebted to the Canadian Federation for the Humanities. A generous subvention from its Aid to Publications Programme made this book possible.

JNG
Toronto, 1986

ABBREVIATIONS

AB	*Art Bulletin*
AJA	*American Journal of Archaeology*
AJP	*American Journal of Philology*
BICS	*Bulletin of the Institute of Classical Studies*
CLA	*Codices latini antiquiores*
CP	*Classical Philology*
CQ	*Classical Quarterly*
CR	*Classical Review*
CW	*Classical World*
GGA	*Göttingische Gelehrte Anzeigen*
GL	*Grammatici latini*
HSCP	*Harvard Studies in Classical Philology*
IMU	*Italia medioevale e umanistica*
JAW	*Jahresbericht über die Fortschritte der klassischen Altertumswissenschaft*
LHS	Leumann, Hofmann, and Szantyr *Lateinische Grammatik*
MH	*Museum Helveticum*
NGG	*Nachrichten von der Gesellschaft der Wissenschaften zu Göttingen*
OCT	Oxford Classical Text
PhilAnz	*Philologischer Anzeiger*
PhilWoch	*Philologische Wochenschrift*
RE	Pauly and Wissowa *Real-Encyclopädie der classischen Altertumswissensc*
RFIC	*Rivista di filologia e d'istruzione classica*
RhM	*Rheinisches Museum*
RHT	*Revue d'histoire des textes*
SBAW	*Sitzungsberichte der Bayerischen Akademie der Wissenschaften*
SIFC	*Studi italiani di filologia classica*
TAPA	*Transactions of the American Philological Association*

TLL *Thesaurus linguae latinae*
WSt *Wiener Studien*

Four frequently cited works will be referred to by the authors' names alone:

Jachmann G. Jachmann *Die Geschichte des Terenztextes im Altertum* Basel 1924

Jones and Morey L.W. Jones and C.R. Morey *The miniatures of the manuscripts of Terence prior to the thirteenth century* 2 vols Princeton 1931

Kauer-Lindsay R. Kauer, W.M. Lindsay, and O. Skutsch *P. Terentius Afer. Comoediae* Oxford 1958

Pasquali G. Pasquali *Storia della tradizione e critica del testo* 2nd ed Florence 1952

Studies in the Textual Tradition of Terence

1

Conspectus of the Tradition in Antiquity

Many of the corruptions that still persist in modern editions of Terence's comedies will not be removed by a study of the history of the textual tradition. The quality of the text had already deteriorated – more so than is generally believed, in my opinion – before the archetypal stage. Errors that have persisted into modern editions will be removed more by a critical reading of the text than by the discovery of new readings in hitherto neglected MSS. Those who can benefit most from the abundance of Terence MSS which have survived are probably medievalists and Renaissance scholars, particularly those who are concerned with the history of scholarship and education. One example is provided by the commentaries on Terence which date from the Carolingian and post-Carolingian periods. If those MSS which contain such commentaries can be dated and their place of origin established, the authors of these works may be identified and connections between different centres may be traced. Such studies, however, will benefit from a fuller picture than we now have of the relationships among the Terence MSS, including those which contain only the text of Terence. An exhaustive study of such commentaries is currently being conducted, and already the way in which the results of investigations undertaken for different reasons confirm and complement each other is evident.[1]

A more systematic study of the Terence MSS is also essential for editors and textual critics working on the text of the comedies. Such a study, even if it brings to light few new good readings, should clarify which MSS ought to be considered for a critical edition and how particular MSS, especially those which contain a number of apparently good readings, should be evaluated. Up till now there has been really only one detailed attempt to construct a stemma – and this for only one sub-branch of the tradition.[2] It has proven difficult therefore to evaluate new MSS which have come to light. While most of the MSS which have been used by editors in the past will rightly continue to be adduced as witnesses to the text, without more rigorous examination of the MSS the choice of witnesses will be to some extent an arbitrary one, dependent in part on the choice made in earlier editions, in part on the intuition (sometimes sound, sometimes not) of editors.[3]

This study deals with only some of the problems in the textual tradition of Terence. Chapters 2 and 3 will examine what the miniatures in some of the MSS of Terence and the commentary of Donatus can tell us about the chronology and history of the text in antiquity. Succeeding chapters will be devoted to a study of the two major branches of the medieval MSS. Little will be said about the plethora of fifteenth-century MSS. These are important for the influence that they (or some of them) had on the early printed editions of Terence, but those which I have examined are of little value to the topics which are my concern.

The exact number of MSS which contain all or part of the text of Terence has not been established, but there appear to be over six hundred.[4] Of these, however, only four date from antiquity and three of these are small fragments of the text. The fourth is of course the famous codex Bembinus (Vatican, Vat lat 3226), dated to the fourth/fifth centuries of our era, traditionally designated as A. Its provenance is Italy.[5] All the other MSS date from the medieval or Renaissance period and are often called the Calliopian MSS, because of the subscription which is found in several of the earlier MSS in the form *Calliopius recensui(t)* or *feliciter Calliopio bono scholastico*. Nothing is known of this individual or of his role in the tradition.[6]

Dozens of common errors show that all the Calliopian MSS descend from a common ancestor, designated Σ. Listed below are a few of these errors (against the correct readings of A) which reveal that the medieval MSS have a common source. The words bracketed are erroneous additions to the text and are absent from A:

existumavit esse, sic existumet [sciat praesumat] (*Eun* 5)
bene [pol] fecisti. hodie itura ... quo? quid, hunc non vides? (*Eun* 63)
peiorem partem. quid opust verbis? dum haec [re]puto (*Eun* 632)

aut haec cum illis sunt habenda aut illa cum his [a]mittenda sunt (*Haut* 325)
age, age inventas reddam. o lepidum [caput]! aufer te hinc. iam opust. iam feres (*Ph* 559)
Demipho, te appello. nam [me] cum hoc ipso distaedet loqui (*Ph* 1011)
mea causa causam [hanc] accipite et date silentium (*Hec* 55)
scio te non [esse] usum antehac amicitia mea (*Ad* 250)

The Bembinus codex cannot be descended from Σ, since it has the correct reading in these and many other places where Σ had an error. But is too has interpolations where Σ, on the evidence of the Calliopian MSS, had the correct text:

in convivium illam? miles [in]tendere: inde ad iurgium (*Eun* 626)
quod scis nescis neque de [istoc] eunucho neque de vitio virginis (*Eun* 722)
adeon te esse incogitantem atque inpudentem, Phaedria, [sine modo] (*Ph* 499)
non potero ferre hoc [diutius], Parmeno: perii miser (*Hec* 133)
audisti ex aliquo fortasse qui vidisse eum [se] diceret (*Hec* 550)

These two lists could be enlarged considerably to include further examples of interpolation and other kinds of corruption.[7]

If it is clear that neither A nor Σ is descended from the other, the large number of errors (approaching one hundred) common to both shows that A and Σ are descended from the same archetype (Φ). Again, a few examples of interpolation will suffice:[8]

'accerse ut delectet hic nos.' illa [exclamat] 'minime gentium' (*Eun* 625)
etiam [nunc] non credis indignis nos esse inrisas modis (*Eun* 710)
nullum invenire prologum po[tui]sset novos (*Ph* 14)
neque cum huius modi umquam [tibi] usus venit ut conflictares malo (*Ph* 505)
nam id [omnibus] innatumst. at pol iam aderit se quoque etiam quom oderit (*Hec* 543)
non mirum fecit uxor [mea] si hoc aegre tulit (*Hec* 709)
compressu gravida factast (mensis [hic] decumus est) (*Ad* 475)

It is not easy to establish the date of Φ with any precision. The archetype must of course predate the Bembinus but by how much can be only an approximation. Although the rate of corruption in the descent of a text is not constant and many scribal errors are possible in a single copying, the large number of errors in Φ suggests that it is well removed in time from the first circulation of the plays of Terence, while the extent of corruption in the Bembinus, when compared with Φ, suggests that Φ came into existence well before the approximate date of A, AD 400 (so Jachmann 87). Jachmann in fact concluded that Φ was a descendant of an edition done ca AD 200. For him the *terminus post quem* for Φ is the lifetime of M. Valerius Probus, who was responsible, he believed, for an edition of Terence which was the source of the surviving tradition. But Jachmann thought that Φ contained too many errors for it to have been the unsullied work of Probus. Such an edition of Probus is hypothetical but it is not unlikely that an edition of sorts is the fount of our MSS.[9] There must have been hundreds of copies of Terence in the ancient world, if for no reason other than that he was studied in the schools. It would not be surprising, therefore, if the surviving MSS could be traced back to several hyparchetypes which, however corrupt they may have been individually, shared relatively few errors. That all our MSS (with the exception of one of the fragments from antiquity) must go back to an archetype which contained a large number of errors and which must have arisen centuries after the death of Terence can hardly be coincidence. The unitary nature of the tradition suggests that Φ is a corrupt version of an earlier edition which became the standard text of Terence, even though other coexisting versions did not entirely disappear. Probus may have been responsible for such an edition; it may have been someone else.[10] An important point to note here is that the scene divisions and scene headings in the Bembinus and the Calliopian MSS are in close agreement. Jachmann (ch 2) shows convincingly that the position of the scene divisions and the content of the headings often have little or nothing to do with the theatrical concerns of staging but must have been devised for a reading public. Moreover, since the choice of where to make a new scene was to a great extent an arbitrary one (on some occasions there is no scene division where we might expect one and the converse is also true), the agreement between the Bembinus and the Calliopians in this respect is a strong indication that these MSS go back to a particular edition of the plays.

If we admit the existence of such an edition, Φ would not have been its sole descendant. We know that there were MSS in antiquity which were not derived from Φ because of correct readings attested by ancient grammarians and in particular by Donatus, where A and

…onatus commentary we learn, for
…), *protinam* at *Ph* 190 (also attested
…he MSS, *tennitur* at *Ph* 330 and 331
…*n ius enimvero* AΣ), *nihili* at *Ad* 167
…inst *est iam* or *etiam*. The Donatus
…erences to MSS which differed from
…ne of these may have been inde-
… One of the three fragments from
…ontains the beginnings or ends of
…shares an error with Σ at 489 (in-
…gainst Σ at *An* 581 (*audin* against
…us is not a witness for the section
…to place Π[a] in the tradition. There
…not spring from Φ. We are more
…)xy 2401), as it contains *An* 602-68
and a section of the same play (924-79a) where comparison with the Bembinus is possible.[12] At 928 Π[b] offers the correct reading *cito* against *cito tibi* in AΣ. Furthermore it (barely) preserves the beginning of the alternative and spurious ending of the *Andria* which is not found in the Bembinus or in the early Carolingian MSS and next surfaces in a German MS of the eleventh century (Oxford, Bodl Auct F 6 27).[13] The fragment appears therefore to be independent of Φ. This cannot be said of the third fragment, St Gall 912 (Sa), which preserves a few lines of the *Hauton timorumenos*.[14] At 857 it reads *igitur sum* with Σ (A has *sum igitur*, correctly), but at 878 Sa is correct with the Bembinus, where the Calliopians offer the interpolated *nam*. Sa looks as if it goes back to some point in the tradition between Φ and Σ. Besides Π[b] other MSS which were independent of Φ *may* have survived into Carolingian times, or, if not the MSS themselves, certainly readings from that branch of the tradition. The latter contingency will explain why only E and F have preserved (in their margins) the correct reading at *Ph* 689; it is also unnecessary to postulate the survival of a complete MS independent of Φ to explain the re-emergence of the spurious ending of the *Andria* (this could have been added in late antiquity or in the very early medieval period to a MS descending from Φ). The question of whether such a MS was the source, directly or indirectly, of some of the good readings found in p (Paris, BN lat 10304, s x) will be discussed in chapter 4.

But what of the date of Φ? Jachmann placed it in the early third century; Pasquali (361) was inclined to set it in the second half of the same century. Three major kinds of information can help to establish at least an approximate date for Φ and to flesh out the rather bare skeleton of a stemma of the early stages of the tradition. These are: (1) graphical errors of Φ, A, and of Σ; (2) metrical errors in Φ; (3) citations of the text of Terence by ancient writers.

It is unfortunate that few of the errors shared by the Bembinus and Σ appear to have arisen from the confusion of similarly written letters. Those which I have found, however, are the following:

I/E

Eun 710	credes] credis
Haut 143	exercirent] exercerent
Haut 515	Cliniai] Cliniae
Haut 529	ni sciam] nesciam
Ad 710	iniicit] iniecit

I/T

Eun 117	uti] ut
Haut 461	habuit] habui
Hec 735	obsiet] obstet

E/T

Haut 444	commetare] commeare

This is not an impressive list, either in quantity or quality. Modernizing tendencies may account for some of these errors (eg *Eun* 117, *Haut* 515) and similarity of pronunciation of I and E may explain others.[15] All that one can conclude is that on the evidence, such as it is, an antecedent of Φ written in rustic capitals, the style of writing in which E, I, and T can be readily confused, is a possibility. The postulation of such a MS, however, does not provide much assistance in establishing a precise date for Φ, since rustic capitals were used from a very early date as a book hand, as is shown by the recently discovered Gallus papyrus, dated to the late first century BC.

The large number of metrical errors common to the Bembinus and Σ is more helpful. It is extremely unlikely that unmetrical iambic senarii, the most common verse form in Plautus and Terence, such as the following would have been tolerated before the second century AD at the earliest:

docere, educare, ita ut si esset filia (*Eun* 117)
egon id timeo? quid te ergo aliud sollicitat? cedo (*Eun* 162)
non convenit, qui illum ad laborem inpulerim (*Haut* 165)
monere me hunc vicinum Phaniam (*Haut* 169)
ut facile scires desiderio id fieri tuo (*Haut* 307)
amicum esse quam Antiphoni. hominem ad forum (*Ph* 598)
dic mi, Philotis, ubi te oblectasti tam diu (*Hec* 84)
ere, etiam nunc tu hic stas? et quidem te exspecto. quid est? (*Hec* 430)

Although Cicero himself quotes *Ad* 60 in an unmetrical form (*venit ad me saepe clamitans 'quid agis, Micio'*), in which form the verse has also been transmitted in the MSS, and some verses may have been unmetrical at a fairly early stage of the tradition, the majority of the irregularities would have become established readings in the text at a much later date.

From the indirect tradition the most important evidence appears in Charisius (268,19 Barwick), in a section where the grammarian has been drawing on Julius Romanus, a writer of the first half of the third century. Charisius (ie Julius Romanus) cites the views of Arruntius Celsus on *Ph* 643. Most editors of Terence have accepted the conjecture of Palmerius and printed the passage as follows:

> CH. cedo quid postulat?
> GE. quid? nimium quantum. CH. ⟨quantum?⟩ dic. GE. si quis daret (643)
> talentum magnum ...

In the MSS of Terence, however, the line is transmitted as:

> GE. quid? nimium; quantum licuit. CH. dic. GE.si quis daret
>
> libuit Σ   CH.] DE. Σ

Charisius reads:

> 'nimium quantum' Terentius in Phormione; ubi Celsus 'pro "nimium," ut "immane quantum," "incredibile quantum," licet quidam sic legant,' inquit 'ut legant ut "nimium" servus dicat, "quantum" vero senex; sed †sequentia intelleguntur†.'[16]

It is clear that Celsus could not have had the reading of either the Bembinus (*quantum licuit*) or Σ (*quantum libuit*) in his MSS, since his interpretation (that *quantum* goes with *nimium*) is incompatible with those readings: *licuit* and *libuit* would be left on their own and would be incomprehensible. Jachmann (79-80) concluded that Arruntius Celsus provides a *terminus post quem* for the interpolation of *libuit/licuit* and thus for the existence of Φ.[17] Pasquali (361) was more doubtful: 'è sempre possibile che al tempo di Arrunzio l'edizione Φ esistesse già (e che esistesse quindi l'integrazione *libuit*), ma non fosse ancora la sola in uso.' This, I think, carries scepticism too far. There is no indication that the opponents whom Celsus was criticizing read *licuit/libuit* any more than he did, and it is reasonable to believe that the disagreements between the rival interpretations lay in the assigning of parts and not in any significant lexical variant. Thus not only Celsus but also the targets of his criticism did not read *licuit/libuit*. Some of those he was criticizing may have lived much earlier than his lifetime, but some are likely to have been his contemporaries or near contemporaries. None was apparently acquainted with an 'edition' of Terence in which *Ph* 643 contained the gloss *licuit/libuit*. Jachmann's inference, that Φ postdates Celsus, seems to me to be a reasonable though not a certain one. Arruntius is usually dated to the late second century. Φ therefore is no earlier than the third.

Between Φ and the edition, if it was done by Probus, at least one intermediate stage should be postulated – a MS in rustic capitals in the copying of which the common errors in A and Σ cited above (p 8) were made. Theoretically Φ could be a direct copy of this edition, but the odds against this are high when one considers the number of Terence MSS which must have been in circulation. At some stage the *periochae*, the brief verse summaries of the plot ascribed to Sulpicius Apollinaris (second century AD), were added. As there are no errors common to A and Σ in the text of the *periochae*, we cannot know for certain whether these plot summaries were already present in the intermediate stage. They could have been added to Φ from a different branch of the tradition. If the edition was not the work of Probus and did not come into existence until the second century, the *periochae* may have been part of it. Even so, it is still unlikely that Φ is an immediate copy of such an edition.

What of the stage or stages between Φ and the Bembinus and between Φ and Σ? There is little solid evidence which allows us to reconstruct the details of how the Bembinus descends from Φ. The Bembinus contains scholia, some of which (those on *Ph* 1-59) derive from the original Donatus commentary. But these were added to the MS in the second half of the sixth century. We cannot therefore postulate an antecedent of A with the Donatus notes.[18] It is necessary to fall back on general considerations about the nature of the Terence text in the Bembinus and about the kinds of errors we find in it.

Since the Bembinus has such a large number of interpolations, graphical errors, and corruptions which did not appear in Φ, several intermediaries between Φ and A should be postulated. The scribe of the Bembinus itself has enough sins on his conscience without the sins of predecessors being added to them. Examples of scribal carelessness abound in the MS. A few may suffice:

Eun 794 coram amatorem] CORAMAMAMATOREM
Haut 76 ad te attinent] ATTINENT

Haut 130 ancillae] ANCCILLAE
Haut 189 amicae se erga] AMICAEERGA
Ph 894 magnas] MAGNAGNAS
Hec 615 facere nisi redducere] FACERENISIRENISIREDDVCERE
Ad 316 statuerem] STVEREM
Ad 436 ille ad me attinet] ILLEADMEAT
Ad 600 eius esse] EIVSSE

All these examples can be readily explained. Usually the scribe's eye has jumped from one letter to the same letter nearby. This has resulted in dittography and omissions. For reconstructing antecedents of the Bembinus codex graphical errors which have been caused by the misreading of letters are important. But here care is needed. Some errors will have been prompted by daydreaming on the part of the scribe and will defy any rational explanation. It is only when we find a number of cases where the same letters have been confused that we can suppose these letters to have been similarly formed, and even then the possibility of phonetic similarity has to be excluded. Little weight can be placed on isolated examples of the confusion of particular letters. Franz Brunhölzl, for example, has pointed to errors at *Hec* 302 (*perpulit* for *perculit*) and at *Haut* 1053 (*perpendere* for *pertendere*) as instances which indicate an antecedent in majuscule cursive.[19] (In fact, Brunhölzl was suggesting, somewhat strangely, a prearchetypal MS in majuscule cursive, but this is impossible to demonstrate unless the Bembinus and Σ show common errors which are explicable in terms of majuscule cursive.) In both of these instances, however, one suspects that the first letter of the initial syllable (p) may have prompted the corruption of c to p at *Hec* 302 and of t to p at *Haut* 1053 (cf *cocia* for *copia* at *Eun* 21).[20]

Some of the errors or orthographic irregularities rest on similarity in pronunciation. We find interchangeability of b/v and e/ae: so *labatum* for *lavatum* (*Eun* 592); *putavit* for *putabit* (*Haut* 485); *hereret* for *haereret* (*Ad* 403); *laepidis* for *lepidis* (*Eun* 652). The same is true for the alternation between m/nc which frequently occurs before a velar: so *Haut* 10, *Ph* 458, *Hec* 205, *Hec* 763. When such readings are put aside, the most frequent aberrations to be found concern the confusion of I/E/T:

I/E

Eun 174	iusseris] IVSSERES	*Haut* 92	meritum] MERETVM
Eun 913	promoves] PROMOVIS	*Haut* 647	scilicet] SCILECET
Eun 973	fieri] FIRI	*Haut* 1021	itidem] ETIDEM

Ph 119	ei pater] EPATER	*Ad* 375	hercle inepta] HERCLENEPTA
Ph 385	taces] TACIS	*Ad* 458	dixeris] DEXTRIS
Hec 555	consuesset] CONSVISSET	*Ad* 570	hodie] HODE
Hec 771	deierat] DIERAT	*Ad* 829	die] DE
Ad 108	sineres] SENERES		
Ad 239	vide] VEDE		

Most of these errors have produced readings which are nonsensical or, at least, irregular in their orthography. Many more errors could be added which have been caused by the confusion of I and E.[21]

E/T		I/T	
Eun 708	et east] ETAST	*Haut* 223	stimulant] SIMVLANT
Eun 932	meretricum] MERERICVM	*Haut* 584	actumst hic] ACTVMSIHIC
Haut 467	facere] FACERET	*Haut* 673	desubito] DESVBIO
Haut 569	esset] ESSE	*Haut* 943	mirari tes-] MIRARIES-
Ph 1055	plaudite] PLAVDIT	*Haut* 968	receptes] RECIPIES
Hec 223	abs te] ABSE	*Ph* 150	delatam] DELAIAM
Hec 292	tuum] EVVM	*Ph* 346	coitiost] COTIOST
Hec 384	confugit te atque] CONFVGITATQVE	*Ph* 960	auditura sit] AVDITVRAST
Ad 399	volt esse] VOLESSE	*Ph* 988	ventrem] VENIREM
Ad 458	dixeris] DEXTRIS	*Hec* 268	vi] VT
		Ad 412	est istorum] ESISTORVM
		Ad 417	facito] FACIO
		Ad 584	et] EI
		Ad 601	aut si ita] AVT ITA

It is clear from these lists of errors that the Bembinus must have had an antecedent in rustic capitals, probably the MS from which it was copied. Other errors in the Bembinus may also be explained as misreadings of rustic capitals. The OCT reports the reading of the Bembinus at *Eun* 765 as *istic* (corrected to *istis* by the second hand). No trace of correction can be seen and it is clear enough that the reading is *istis*. This instance shows, however, how similar C and S can be in rustic capitals, as there is not much difference between the final S of *istis* and the initial C of the next word *Chremes*. Confusion of C and S is probably reflected at *Haut* 134 where we find *eiecis* for *eieci* (by dittography of EC, read as IS), at *Haut* 149 (*his* for *hic*), at *Ad* 845 (*is videro* for *istuc videro*); cf also *ingerere* for *inserere* at *Haut* 564 for confusion of G and S. Consistent too with an exemplar in rustic capitals are the errors at *Eun* 1056 (*feceris* for *effeceris*) and *Haut* 777 (*fasse* for *fortasse*). Some errors could have been made when square capitals were being copied: the confusion of B/R (*Eun* 732 *verum* for *verbum; Haut* 727 *renuntiabit* for *renuntiarit; Haut* 976 *parabis* for *pararis*), of P/R (*Hec* 652 *ratrem* for *patrem; Ad* 4 *eripit* for *erit*), and of M/N/IN (*Eun* 368 *cum eam in-* for *cum ea in-; Eun* 477 *palaestram* for *palaestra in; Eun* 788 *nox* for *mox; Hec* 353 *salvam* for *salvan; Hec* 78 *audim* for *audin*). Similar mistakes could have occurred, however, in the copying of rustic capitals and there is no need to postulate an antecedent in square capitals.

What of Brunhölzl's contention that some errors in the Bembinus betray the existence of an earlier MS written in majuscule cursive? There is no evidence to indicate that such a MS was an antecedent of Φ, but the possibility of an intermediary MS between Φ and A in this style of writing is worth considering. The errors to which Brunhölzl paid most attention were those which could have arisen from confusion of C/P/T, of A/R, or of B/D. Apart from the one example of the confusion of P and T cited by Brunhölzl (*perpendere* for *pertendere* at *Haut* 1053) there are possibly two others: *tem tulit* for *tempus tulit* at *Hec* 594 and *aput te tat* for *aput te potat* at *Ad* 799. But neither convincingly shows that P and C must have been similar in form to account for the error. In the former the scribe's eye might have jumped from V in *tempus* to the V in *tulit* before he wrote the second syllable of the word. In the latter the presence of T in *aput* and *te* may have prompted the scribe to jump to the second syllable of *potat* which began with that letter and sound. At first sight there is more evidence for the similarity of C and T:

Eun 521	ecqua] ETQVA	*Hec* 182	e conspectu] ETCONSPECTV
Eun 523	ecquis] ETQVIS	*Hec* 334	auctus] AVTVS
Eun 651	cum] TVM	*Hec* 804	ecquem] ETQV.EM
Haut 677	at] AC	*Ad* 235	tum] CVM
Ph 281	functus] FVNTVS	*Ad* 750	cantites] CANTICES

But it is not necessary to postulate that C and T were similarly written to account for most of these. Pronunciation of the forms *functus* and *auctus* may have prompted the errors at *Ph* 281 and *Hec* 334 respectively; the semantic context may have led the scribe to write *ac* for *at* at *Haut* 677; at *Hec* 182 the scribe's eye may have jumped to the preceding line (in the Bembinus *ET* stands immediately below *IT* of

IGITVR), while *tum* for *cum* at *Eun* 651 could have been caused by the proximity of *tuis* (following *donis*, as *cum* follows *dignus*). The surrounding velars or association with *canticum* may be the reason for *cantices* at *Ad* 750. We are left with *cum* for *tum* at *Ad* 235 and three errors of *ecquis* (or its variants). But oscillation between *ecquis* and *etquis* is extremely common in early MSS and by no means indicates that C and T were written in similar fashion.[22]

To the two instances of the confusion of C and P mentioned above (*perpulit* for *perculit* at *Hec* 302 and *cocia* for *copia* at *Eun* 21) another two may be added: *pavet* for *cavet* at *Ad* 70 and *reicere* for *recipere* at *Hec per* 9.The latter may have arisen from the transposition of C and I, leading to the omission of P. It should be said, however, that C and P could be readily confused in rustic capitals. One needs only to look at the Bembinus itself to see this. For the confusion of B and D I have found three examples: *Eun* 161 *abductast* for *advectast*(?); *Hec* 783 *abest* for *adest*; *Haut* 165 *ablaborem* for *adlaborem*. In the first two, however, the context could have prompted the error (note *abrepta* in *Eun* 156; at *Hec* 783 *adest* follows the imperative *exquire*).[23] Brunhölzl has cited *Haut* 701 (*mentiris* for *mentiaris*) as an example which shows that A and R were confused. The only other instance seems to be *caeca* for *graeca* at *Haut* 4.

In summary, then, when the wavering eye and the wandering mind of the Bembinus scribe are remembered, the number of errors which *may* be explained in terms of similarly formed letters in the capital cursive script is insignificant. There is insufficient evidence to postulate a MS written in such a script (or in a script containing elements of the capital cursive) between Φ and the Bembinus. If such an intermediary existed, it would have provided a rough *terminus ante quem* for Φ, the date of which would have to be the third century at the latest, the last century in which the capital cursive was used.

If we turn to considering the stages between Φ and Σ, there is no evidence to suggest that an antecedent of Σ was written in capital cursive. Graphical errors in Σ are few in number. Corruptions in Σ most often take the form of intrusive glosses, omissions of words, distortion of word order, 'regularization' of tenses and cases. Care has to be taken therefore in looking for errors in Σ which have been caused by the misreading of similarly formed letters. The following four examples, however, may be of such a nature: *Eun* 662 *possit*] *posset*; 690 *rediges*] *redigis*; *Hec* 573 *posset*] *possit*; *Hec* 619 *aberit*] *abierit*. Each of these errors, if graphical, is based on the confusion of I and E. This suggests an antecedent of Σ written in rustic capitals. Nothing in Σ itself or in its descendants points to the existence of a MS in capital cursives within the Calliopian tradition. Again, therefore, there is no help for establishing the date of Φ. Both Jachmann and Pasquali have placed Φ in the third century. That, I think, is as near as one can get on the evidence which we have.

Another question about the history of the transmission of the text in antiquity relates to the date of Σ. J.D. Craig examined the quotations of Terence as they appear in the grammarians of antiquity and concluded that Σ was not in existence until late antiquity, perhaps the fifth century.[24] The Bembinus, he believed, is the representative, though not a very good one, of the Terence text which was in circulation in the ancient period. Now the evidence of the grammarians has to be treated with care. Often they quoted from memory and were therefore prone to inaccuracy, particularly with respect to those parts of a passage which were not specifically related to the word or expression which they were illustrating. But even on the specific points to which the grammarians are referring there can be room for doubt. A store of passages to illuminate or exemplify some grammatical point must have been built up over the centuries in the grammatical tradition. The grammarians will have used many of the examples of their predecessors and one cannot conclude that different readings were not in MSS contemporary with the grammarians. Moreover, the text of the grammarians, like that of any author, was subject to inadvertent corruption, and one cannot discount the additional possibility that later scribes and readers deliberately changed quotations to bring them into accord with the author's text as known to them. Craig was well aware of the difficulties in using the evidence of the grammarians and indeed was overzealous in explaining away the evidence of Calliopian readings in their works. Partly because of this, his view of the 'standard' text of Terence in antiquity and his late dating of Σ has not gained wide acceptance.[25]

A much earlier date for Σ was proposed by Jachmann (115-16). He placed Σ in the later third century but his reasons were far from satisfactory. The Calliopians fall into two major groups, the γ and the δ branches. Jachmann argued that the γ archetype must be assigned to a date earlier than that of the Bembinus since the γ MSS have retained more scene divisions than the ancient MS. The γ archetype must therefore have been in existence in the fourth century at the latest. Accordingly, Σ must have been even earlier. But the assumption of a constant rate of attrition of scene divisions is unacceptable and the chronological framework constructed on it collapses, as Pas-

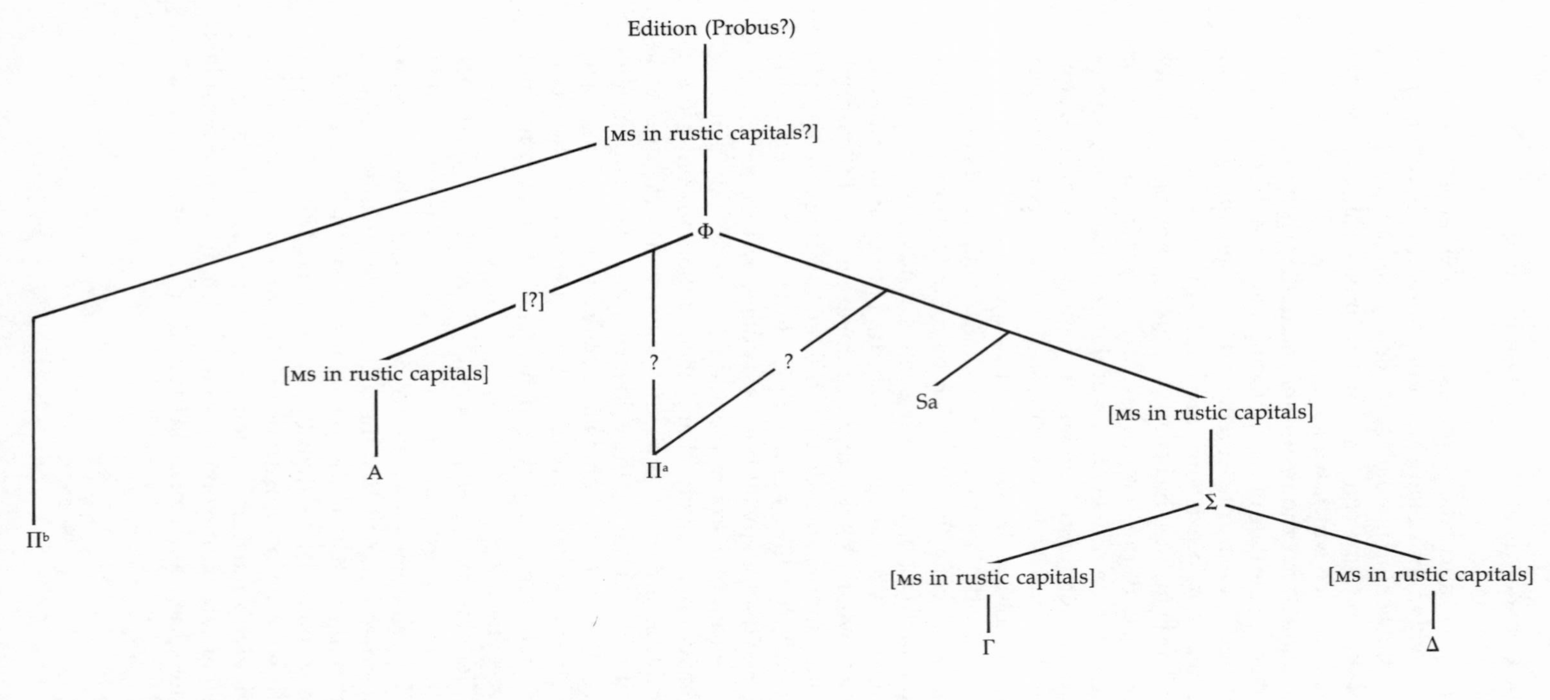
Edition (Probus?)
[MS in rustic capitals?]
Φ
[?]
[MS in rustic capitals]
A
?
?
Πᵃ
Sa
[MS in rustic capitals]
Σ
[MS in rustic capitals]
Γ
[MS in rustic capitals]
Δ
Πᵇ

FIGURE 1

quali (363-4) pointed out. While Jachmann's reasoning on this point is suspect, another aspect of his study which has chronological implications for the Calliopian tradition did win the support of Pasquali and others. This is his claim that the miniatures which are found in several of the γ MSS of the Calliopians were *created* to accompany a γ text. If this claim is correct, the date of the original illustrations will provide a date for the existence of a γ MS and thus a *terminus ante quem* for Σ.[26]. This topic will be the subject of the next chapter. For the moment all that needs to be said is that the consensus of opinion among art historians places the original miniatures in the late fourth or early fifth century. If Jachmann's view of the relationship between the miniatures and the γ text is accepted, the Calliopian archetype must be placed in the fourth century at the latest.

It has been pointed out above that the few graphical errors in Σ indicate a possible antecedent of Σ written in rustic capitals. There are few certain graphical errors which we can use to reconstruct Γ and Δ. For the former can be cited *Hec* 61 (*possit* for *posset*), *Ph* 880 (*dare* for *dari*), *Ph* 528 (*decepit* for *decipit*), and *Haut* 685 (*commodi* for *commode*); for Δ *An* 950 (*Pamphili* for *Pamphile*), *Eun* 1083 (*mirumne* for *mirumni*), *Ph* 742 (*appellasses* for *appellassis*), *Ph* 780 (*solvis* for *solves*). There is not much evidence here, but what there is indicates antecedents for Γ and Δ in rustic capitals. One of these antecedents may have been Σ itself, though it is more likely that there was at least one intermediary MS between Σ and Γ and between Σ and Δ. In all probability, since Σ had an antecedent and descendants in rustic capitals, Σ itself was written in this style of writing. This offers little help for dating the Calliopian archetype. Jachmann's hypothesis about the relationship between the miniatures and the γ text seems to be a crucial one for establishing the chronology of the Calliopian tradition.

The stemma of the early tradition which has emerged from this chapter is shown in figure 1.

2

The Miniatures and the Date of Σ

In the first chapter Φ, the archetype of all surviving Terence MSS (with the probable exception of Π^b), has been placed in the third century; any greater precision seemed impossible. Jachmann decided for the first half of the century, Pasquali for the second. The archetype of all the medieval or Calliopian MSS (Σ) must of course be later than Φ, but by how much?

As has been seen, Craig's view is that Σ did not come into existence until late antiquity, perhaps the fifth century, while Jachmann favoured the third.[1] The dating of Σ will not alter significantly an editor's approach to the text, since often he will still have to evaluate the reading of the Bembinus against that of Σ, both being independent witnesses, simply on the merits of each case. Light may be cast, however, on an important period for the history of the transmission of classical texts. Σ has suffered from much interpolation and other kinds of corruption. There is, for example, a large number of unmetrical lines.[2] Its date, therefore, will provide a picture of the quality and nature of the transmission at that period and will indicate the level of linguistic and metrical expertise in that era. Paul Wessner indeed pointed out the implausibility of Jachmann's dating of Σ in light of what we can assume about the metrical competence of the ancient grammarians. It is only in the fifth century at the earliest (Rufinus of Antioch) and in the sixth (Priscian) that there is a need to affirm that the plays of Terence were written in verse.[3] This criticism of Wessner's was a sound one but was an oblique way of refusing to accept Jachmann's arguments for his chronology. In this chapter an attempt will be made to face squarely the details of Jachmann's case, to show its weaknesses and to bring forward other evidence which points to a quite different conclusion.

First, the reasons for the division of the medieval MSS into two major groups should be clarified. This division is based primarily on conjunctive and disjunctive errors in the text but the different order of plays in the two groups of MSS has in practice been a factor. The γ order has been seen as *An – Eun – Haut – Ad – Hec – Ph,* the δ order as *An – Ad – Eun – Ph – Haut – Hec* (the so-called alphabetic order, if *Phormio* is thought of as *Formio*). The order of the plays, however, is not decisive, since MSS which present the plays in the γ order have been shown to derive at least in part from the same source as the δ MSS.[4] Another distinguishing feature is that illustrations appear in a number of γ MSS, while no member of the δ group contains miniatures which are descended from the source of those in the γ MSS.[5] Attention has also been drawn to the fact that the use of Greek letters as *notae personae* is found in two of the leading δ MSS (D and p), as well as in the Bembinus, but not in any of the early γ MSS. But such an algebraic system is found in a Vienna MS (Nationalbibl lat 85, s xi) in a section of its text which appears to go back to a γ source.[6]

This chapter will focus on the illustrations which appear in the γ branch, since Jachmann proved to his own satisfaction and to others' that the original miniatures from which the Carolingian miniatures are descended were created for a γ text.[7] The date of these originals will, therefore, provide a date for the existence of an illustrated γ MS and a *terminus ante quem* for Σ.

There are more than a dozen illustrated γ MSS whose dates range from the ninth century to the twelfth century. With very few exceptions the grouping of the figures in the illustrations of these MSS is identical, while the postures and gestures of the individual figures are also very similar. There can be no doubt, therefore, that all the illustrations in these γ MSS descend from the same cycle of miniatures.[8] From the view that the original miniatures were created in antiquity there has been no serious dissent. Dispute has centred rather on which period of antiquity witnessed their birth. Friedrich Leo thought that the original illustrations might have come into existence as early as the second half of the first century BC,[9] and in this opinion he was supported by Carl Robert.[10] At the other extreme K. Engelhardt[11] assigned the original cycle to the late fifth or early sixth centuries of our era, and R. Kauer agreed with him.[12] Almost every century between these limits has won some support. K.E. Weston[13] thought that the miniatures had come into being some time before Quintilian, while E. Bethe argued for the second or third century.[14] The fourth century was favoured by G. Rodenwaldt;[15] the early fifth century found adherents in A.W. Byvanck[16] and Jones and Morey,[17] the latter in the most detailed study of the illustrated MSS. Faced with such an array of conflicting opinions, the non-specialist in art history is in the position of a juror who is forced to evaluate on the one hand conflicting expert testimony in the art field and on the other arguments which he is more capable of appraising. Leo's dating springs to a great extent from his belief that the illustrations are based on actual observation of stage productions. Against this view Jachmann, expanding the arguments of Engelhardt, summoned as evidence many examples where the stage action had been misrepresented or misunderstood by the artist. Mute characters are often omitted from the illustrations of scenes in which they appear, as are characters who speak elsewhere but not in a particular scene where their presence, however, is certain. The artist has not drawn, for example, the maidservants who accompany Bacchis on her entrance at *Haut* 381 (cf 245), the slaves at *Hec* 415 (cf 359), Sannio at *Ad* 254, Demipho and Chremes at *Ph* 591, and Dorias at *Eun* 629. Jachmann (21-2) also refers to erroneous representation of the action at *Eun* 923, where Parmeno and Pythias are drawn as if they are engaged in dialogue, although they do not speak to each other until the next scene. At *Ad* 364 the miniature shows Syrus leaving the house and Dromo inside, when in fact Dromo has returned with Syrus from the forum and is sent inside at 376.[18] Because of these examples Jachmann believed that the artist designed the miniatures on the basis of a reading of the text and not a viewing of stage productions of Terence.

It is not impossible, however, to adduce a hypothesis which is a compromise between the views of Leo and Jachmann. One might suppose that the artist had not actually witnessed productions of all or most or even any of Terence's plays but had conceived the illustrations in light of other stage productions which he had seen. We could then accept the artist's misinterpretation of the text without denying that the miniatures reflect current stage practices. The same compromise is possible with respect to another of Jachmann's arguments. He has shown convincingly that the illustrations are based upon the scene divisions and scene headings which must have existed in Φ.[19] Such a hypothesis explains the high degree of coincidence between the order of figures in the miniatures and the order of names in the scene headings in non-illustrated MSS, the latter being based primarily on the sequence in which the characters speak in a scene.[20] It also explains the omission from the miniatures of most of the characters mentioned above, since the names of these characters are also lacking in the scene headings.[21] This connection between the scene headings and the miniatures still does not, however, negate the possibility of the artist's having based his illustrations on actual stage productions, though not necessarily those of Terence's plays. It is possible, therefore, to accept some of Jachmann's findings without denying that there are reference to the contemporary theatre in the miniaturist's work. Nevertheless one might argue against the view of Leo and Bethe that the artist could have drawn inspiration for his miniatures from much earlier art monuments which themselves reflect stage productions of the period in which they were created. Mosaics and paintings which have survived from Pompeii are obvious examples of such sources. Such a hypothesis would explain the impression of theatrical authenticity made by the illustrations but would preclude the conclusion that the artist was depicting the stage conditions of his time. Arguments then can be brought on both sides. A major difficulty is our lack of knowledge about productions of plays in the Christian era. Even for the first century AD we have little specific information about drama in Rome. But the theatre still flourished there and throughout the Empire. Even if mime was by far the most popular kind of production, it does not seem unlikely that there were some revivals of republican comedies.[22]

The consensus of opinion among art historians now appears to favour a late fourth-century or early fifth-century date for the creation of the original illustrations from which those in the medieval MSS were derived. The date is important, whether or not they reflect contemporary stage conditions, because of Jachmann's contention, supported by others, that these miniatures were created for a γ text.[23] If we accept ca AD 400 as an approximate date for the original miniatures, and if we accept Jachmann's view about the relationship between them and the γ text, we must conclude that there was in existence at this date an illustrated γ MS. Thereby a *terminus ante quem* is provided for Σ. If the fourth/fifth-century date for the original miniatures proves to be wrong and if further examination points to an earlier period, then the date for the existence of the γ text is also pushed back and with it the date of Σ. The intimate connection between the miniatures and the γ text which Jachmann identified is, therefore, of crucial importance for establishing the date of Σ. His argument demands scrutiny.[24]

The evidence that the miniatures were created for a γ text

In favour of this relationship between the illustrations and the γ text Jachmann adduced two pieces of evidence, the miniatures at *Haut* 381 and *Eun* 1031. In the latter (plate 1) the figures are drawn in the order (from left to right) Chaerea – Parmeno – Thraso – Gnatho. This order should reflect the sequence in which these characters speak in the scene. But Thraso is the third speaker in only three of the leading γ MSS, all of them illustrated, C (Vatican, Vat lat 3868), P (Paris, BN lat 7899), and F (Milan, Ambros H 75 inf). These three MSS give the words at 1037 (*audin tu, hic quid ait?*) to Thraso. All the other MSS used by editors assign these words to Gnatho, making him the third speaker after Chaerea and Parmeno. At first sight then this illustration seems to be related only to the γ branch of the tradition. However, in their scene headings at 1031 the Bembinus and the δ MSS name the characters in the same order as they appear in the illustrations.[25] Thus the miniatures at *Eun* 1031 reflect the order of names in Σ and Φ, and there is no evidence that the illustrations are connected to the γ text alone. Jachmann himself realized that the evidence provided by the miniatures at *Eun* 1031 is inconclusive.

The illustration at *Haut* 381 (plate 2) is more important. Here five characters are drawn. Bacchis is on the extreme left. Next to her are Antiphila and Clinia, who are embracing each other, and on the right are the figures of Clitipho and Syrus. The problem posed by this miniature lies in the fact that Clitipho leaves the stage at *Haut* 380, at the end of the preceding scene, and is at no time present on stage in II.4 (381-409). He should not then have been included in the miniature which stands immediately before line 381. Two questions arise. Why does Clitipho appear in the miniature, and how does his appearance indicate that this miniature was created for a γ text? According to Jachmann the answers to both of these questions are provided by the evidence of a single Terence MS – Valenciennes, bibl publ 448 (420), designated v in Kauer-Lindsay. This MS, which belongs to the γ class but which is not illustrated, gives lines 400b-1 to Clitipho: *Syre, vix suffero: / hocin me miserum non licere meo modo ingenium frui.*[26] Jachmann (104) concluded that v alone preserves what was in the γ archetype against the other γ MSS, all of which give these words to Clinia, and that, accordingly, this error, unique to Γ, demonstrates that the miniatures were originally conceived for a γ text.[27] Some objections to this come to mind. First of all, it is unlikely that v alone has preserved what was in Γ; it is more likely that the similarity in the names of the two young men prompted a momentary lapse on the part of the scribe. Secondly, Jachmann does not mention the fact that in v CLIT has been changed to CLIN at 400 and that the corrector may have been the first hand.[28] A third objection concerns the action portrayed in the miniature. If indeed the illustrator had used a text in which 400b-1 were given to Clitipho, he would most probably have depicted the action suggested by the text at this point, since it would then be possible to illustrate one moment of the scene when all the characters in the scene were involved. It is indisputable, however, that the figures of Antiphila and Clinia reflect the stage business of 407-8: (*teneone te, / Antiphila, maxume animo exspectatam meo?*), whereas the figure of Clitipho seems appropriate to 400b-1 and the figure of Syrus could possibly be linked with 402. The miniature portrays two different parts of the scene. This is by no means a unique example of the representation of non-simultaneous stage action.[29] What is unusual about the miniature at *Haut* 381 concerns the order in which the two parts of the scene are depicted. Normally, the earlier stage action appears on the left and the later action on the right side of the illustration. Here the order is reversed, unless the figures of Clitipho and Syrus are taken to refer to 409, where Syrus says *ite intro; nam vos iamdudum exspectat senex*, immediately before all the characters leave the stage. But one might have expected Syrus to be pointing towards the door, if this were so.

These considerations and objections cast some doubt on the conclusions which Jachmann drew from the miniature at *Haut* 381 concerning the link between the cycle of illustrations and the γ text. In fact, I believe that this miniature shows that the original illustrations were *not* originally conceived for a γ text – the very opposite of Jachmann's conclusion. If Jachmann's explanation for the presence of Clitipho in the miniature is rejected, what other solution can be offered? First of all, it has to be noticed that the figures of Clitipho and Syrus suit perfectly the stage action at 375-80:

> SY. sed quam cito sunt consecutae mulieres!
> CLIT. ubi sunt? quor retines? SY. iam nunc haec non est tua.
> CLIT. scio, apud patrem; at nunc interim. SY. nihilo magis.
> CLIT. sine. SY. non sinam inquam. CLIT. quaeso paullisper. SY. veto.
> CLIT. saltem salutem ... SY. abeas, si sapias. CLIT. eo.
> quid istic? SY. manebit. CLIT. hominem felicem! SY. ambula.

Here Clitipho tries to approach Bacchis and Antiphila as they are entering, but is restrained by the slave (*quor retines?* 376; cf *sine. SY. non sinam,* 378). One may compare the miniature at *Ad* 776 where Syrus is holding onto Demea's cloak to prevent him from entering the house. This clearly depicts the stage action of 780-1: *mitte me ... non manum abstines?* spoken by Demea. I conclude, therefore, that in the miniature at *Haut* 381 the stage action of 406-8 is shown on the left (Bacchis, Antiphila, Clinia) and the stage action of 376-8 is shown on the right (Clitipho and Syrus). The question which then arises is why the figures of Clitipho and Syrus appear in a miniature which is supposed to illustrate some aspect of the stage action of 381-409. It must be concluded that the surviving miniature is conflated, combining aspects of two illustrations, one of which originally stood at 381 and contained the figures of Bacchis, Antiphila, and Clinia as they now appear at 381, the other of which stood at some point before 376 and contained Clitipho and Syrus as they are now drawn at 381.[30] This conflated miniature must have once stood, one assumes, before any of the action which it depicts. Possibly there was a scene division immediately before 375, prompted by the announcement of the women in that line.[31] It could have been here that the conflated miniature appeared. I suggest that the conflation was caused by the inadvertent failure of a scribe to leave a space for a miniature at 381.[32] The copying artist then combined the three figures of Bacchis, Antiphila, and Clinia from the miniature at 381 in his exemplar with the figures of Clitipho and Syrus, which were present in the miniature at 375. The resulting miniature at 375 then at least depicted action which followed it, even though the conflation as a whole still misrepresented the stage action at the end of the scene, when Clitipho was no longer on stage.

But how then was this conflated miniature moved from 375 to its present position, immediately before 381? The most likely explanation of this change of position of the conflated miniature is that it occurred when the miniatures were being copied from one branch of the tradition into a different one, that is, into the γ branch. The miniatures were originally created for a text which had scene divisions at 375 and 381. In the course of transmission the two miniatures were conflated into one that stood at 375 (in the manner described above). This text had, therefore, a miniature at 375 and no scene division at 381. The miniatures were then transferred into a text which had no scene division at 375 but which did have a scene division at 381. The scribe of this latter text followed the scene division of his exemplar and left space for a miniature at 381 but did not leave space for a miniature at 375. When the artist came to this section of the text, he copied the miniature at 375 in his exemplar into the space left by the scribe at 381. My conclusion then about the miniature at *Haut* 381 is that, rather than supporting Jachmann's thesis about the connection between the illustrations and the γ text, it points to a non-γ source for them. It may be claimed, it is true, that all of the stages in this reconstruction could have occurred within the γ tradition. This could be admitted up to the point where the existence of a conflated miniature at 375 has been postulated. It is the final stage, however – the change in the miniature's position from 375 to 381 – that is very unlikely to have occurred within the γ tradition. There is no parallel within the tradition for such a positional change of a miniature.

Evidence that the miniatures were not created for a γ text

Neither the miniature at *Eun* 1031 nor the one at *Haut* 381 shows in any way that the whole cycle of miniatures was created to accompany a γ text. One of the reasons, however, for the attractiveness of Jachmann's explanation of the relationship between the illustrations and the γ text is that there is apparently no opposing evidence. A second is probably that his thesis provides a highly desirable chronological keystone for the dating of Γ and thus of Σ, once the date of the original miniatures can be established. It has been suggested above, however, that the miniature at *Haut* 381 does in fact offer counter-evidence. But the reconstruction of the history of that miniature is not certain and in the absence of any other evidence the verdict about the source of the miniatures might be more safely summed up as *non liquet*. Further evidence, however, does exist.

The miniature at Ad 364

Jachmann (16ff) adduces the miniature at *Ad* 364 to show, quite rightly, that the illustrator misunderstood the stage action in this scene and was therefore basing his miniature on his reading of the text and not on observation of an actual production of the play. In this illustration (plate 3) Syrus is drawn as if he is leaving the house, issuing instructions to Dromo, who is inside, engaged in cleaning fish. The action clearly depicts the text of 376-8. Here Syrus tells Dromo to clean the rest of the fish, but not to fillet the eel until he returns:

> piscis ceteros purga, Dromo;
> gongrum istum maxumum in aqua sinito ludere

tantisper; ubi ego rediero, exossabitur.

It is certain, however, that Dromo must have accompanied Syrus from the forum and that he is sent inside along with Stephanio (cf 380) at the very time when these orders are given. More important than the illustrator's mistake is the reason for it.[33] In the text of 378 as printed above the reading *ubi ego rediero* ('when I return') of the Bembinus has been preferred to *ubi ego venero* ('when I come') of the Calliopian MSS (*revenero* in G). The reading of the Bembinus is the more difficult and to be preferred to that of the Calliopian MSS, which looks like an explanatory gloss for a word which might have posed problems for readers. The verb *rediero* here means 'come home.'[34] If lines 376-8 were read in isolation, however, a reader would naturally suppose from *rediero* that Syrus was saying these words when he was leaving the house. The artist thought that Dromo was in the house, already occupied in his culinary tasks; he must, therefore, have read *rediero* in his text. The reading of the Calliopian MSS, however, clearly points to *venero* and not *rediero* in Σ and, therefore, in Γ. This miniature thus provides good evidence against Jachmann's belief that the miniatures were created for a γ text. In fact it shows that the illustrations must have been drawn initially for a non-Calliopian MS.

The miniatures at Haut 874 and 954

I have found no other single miniature which is as helpful as that at *Ad* 364 for throwing light on this question. Indeed it is fortunate that even one illustration has been found which depicts a section of the text where there happens to be a significant textual conflict among the MSS.[35] There is, however, another problem posed by some miniatures which is also relevant to the subject of this enquiry.

Rarely do the major illustrated MSS differ with respect to the position and the content of the miniatures which they contain. One of the exceptions to this close similarity occurs at *Haut* 874 (V.1) and 954 (V.2). The situation is shown in table 1. In the Vatican MS (C) there is a miniature at both places. In the first (plate 4) Menedemus and Chremes appear; in the second (plate 5) there are four figures in the order (left to right) Clitipho – Menedemus – Chremes – Syrus. This arrangement is what one would expect from the evidence of the Bembinus and of most other non-illustrated MSS, which mark scene divisions at 874 and again at 954, when Menedemus, who has gone inside at 948-9 to speak to Clitipho, returns to the stage, accompanied

TABLE 1

	C	P	F
Haut 874	Miniature (2 figures: Menedemus – Chremes)	Miniature (4 figures: Menedemus – Chremes – Clitipho – Syrus)	Same as in P
Haut 954	Miniature (4 figures: Clitipho – Menedemus – Chremes – Syrus)	Scene division (heading only; no space left for miniature)	Scene division (no heading, but blank space left for miniature)

by the young man and Syrus.[36] In C the order of figures in the miniatures is regular in that it is in harmony with the order of speaking in both scenes. In both P and F, however, there is only one miniature, at 874 (plate 6), and no miniature is found at 954. The miniatures at 874 in P and F are very similar and must derive from the same source or one must derive from the other. This illustration contains four figures in the order Menedemus – Chremes – Clitipho – Syrus. This order of figures agrees with the order of speaking in the section of the text 874 to 1002. Neither P nor F has a miniature at 954 but P certainly marks a new scene at this point, since there is a scene heading with the names Menedemus, Clitipho, Chremes, and Syrus. This scene heading has been written in the manner found in non-illustrated MSS, and no space left has been left for an illustration between the scenes. In F there is no scene heading but some lines have been left blank at the foot of the page after 954a and the form of the initial letter of *itane*, the word with which the new page begins, indicates that the scribe felt that a new scene began at this point. It can be said, therefore, that the three MSS C, P, and F observe scene division at 874 and 954, but that P and F are unusual in that they lack an illustration at 954. Since P does have a scene heading at 954, the miniature with four figures at 874 illustrates a scene (874-954a) in which only two characters appear. F has avoided this irregularity by not providing a scene heading at 954.

When the miniature in PF at 874 (I shall from now on speak of what are actually two illustrations as one) is compared with that in C at 954, it will be readily observed that the four figures are the same but that the first and third figures have changed positions. The first figure in PF (Menedemus) corresponds exactly to Chremes, the third figure in C, while Clitipho stands in third position in PF but in first position in C. The second and fourth figures in both miniatures are drawn in exactly the same fashion, but in PF the second figure is named Chremes, while in C it represents Menedemus. Syrus occupies the same position in both illustrations and is drawn in the same way.

Before we can see how these particular illustrations pertain to the relationship between the original cycle of miniature and the γ archetype, it is necessary first to explain how the discrepancy between C and PF came about and in this way to reconstruct what appeared in the illustrated γ archetype. Indeed this problem has been discussed up to now solely within the framework of the γ tradition. Jones and Morey believe (2.58) that in 'the ultimate archetype' (ie Γ) the four-figure miniature which properly belongs to v.2 appeared by error at 874, as it does now in PF, thus illustrating the first two scenes of Act v (874-1002): 'The mistake was corrected by C, which moved the miniature to its proper place ... To illustrate v.1 C repeated the illustration for IV.8. In the transfer C took occasion also to change the figures of Clitipho and Menedemus and the labels of the two *senes* [ie Chremes and Menedemus] to the normal order.' What Jones and Morey seem to imply, though the meaning of their words is not clear, is that an antecedent of Γ had a miniature at 954 which was the same as the one which now appears in C at this point, and that in Γ this miniature had erroneously been moved to 874 with the order of figures changed. At any rate the miniature in PF at 874 could not have originally been designed to stand at 954 in its present arrangement, since Menedemus and Chremes do not address each other in v.2. Jones and Morey also seem to accept (2.200-1) that the miniatures originated with a MS descending from Σ. The implication is that this had a γ-like text, though it may not have contained all the errors which were present in Γ.

Jachmann (138-48) had earlier stated his views on the disagreement between C and PF at *Haut* 874 and 954 with greater clarity and forcefulness. He thought that C faithfully preserves the miniatures in the form and position in which they were created for the first illustrated γ MS.[37] The variation in PF arose from the desire to suppress a scene division, and thus a miniature, at 954. This was achieved by dropping the miniature at 874 and by replacing it with the miniature which stood at 954 and which then had to serve two scenes. The figures in the miniature had, however, to be rearranged to bring them into harmony with the order of speaking. The repositioning of the mini-

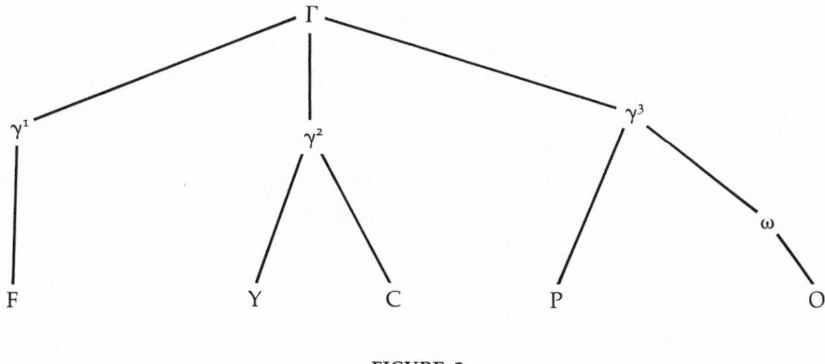

FIGURE 2

ature and the rearrangement of the figures resulted in what now appears in P and F.

Some criticisms may be levelled against Jachmann's reconstruction. The first is the lack of economy in the procedure adopted by whoever was responsible for the four-figure miniature that appears in PF at 874. If one wanted to combine the two miniatures at 874 and 954, the simplest and most obvious procedure would have been to take the figures of Clitipho and Syrus from the miniature at 954 (the same in form and arrangement, according to Jachmann, as the one which now stands there in C) and to add them to the two figures of Menedemus and Chremes at 874. By Jachmann's explanation we must accept that the miniaturist responsible for what appears in PF chose not to retain any of the three groupings in his two models (one pair of figures in 874, which he removed, and two pairs in 954, which he rearranged), but to create two new groupings out of them. It is not impossible that this might have happened. What makes it less likely, however, is consideration of the stemma of the γ MSS, as far as it can be reconstructed with some degree of certainty. The most detailed attempt to establish such a stemma was made by R.H. Webb in 1911.[38] The results of his study may be illustrated by the stemma in figure 2.[39] This stemma is reasonably sound, though some modification and expansion are necessary. It will be shown, for example, that γ^2 and γ^3 do not descend independently from Γ but from a common intermediary.[40] But no such modification will remove the problem which the relationship of C, P, and F poses for Jachmann's reconstruction of how the discrepancy between C and PF arose. Either these three MSS are descended from Γ independently of each other or C and P go back to Γ by way of a common intermediary but still independently of F. How then is the common error in P and F with respect to the miniature at *Haut* 874 to be explained? The uneconomical nature of the error makes it unlikely that it occurred independently in each MS. We must conclude, therefore, that either P and F have preserved the situation in Γ and that C, accordingly, has drawn its miniatures from some lost source which was related to Γ, but which was free from this error, or that C has preserved what was in Γ and that the common error of P and F is to be explained by horizontal influence. I know of no other evidence, however, of any comparable horizontal contact between any two of these three MSS in the case of the miniatures. It is, therefore, more likely that P and F preserve what was in Γ, as Jones and Morey believe. This view becomes almost certain when one examines Y (Paris, BN lat 7900), the MS most closely related to C, and finds that a blank space has been left for an illustration at 874 and that there is only a heading with no blank space at 954. Y therefore may be placed alongside P and F against C, although in its text, as the stemma shows, Y stands often with C against P.

There are other grounds for rejecting Jachmann's explanation than these stemmatic considerations. These lie in the relationship between the figures of the miniatures and the action which they are supposed to illustrate. Jachmann virtually ignores this aspect of the problem. He does point out that the gesture of Chremes in PF at 874 (Menedemus in C at 954) is very uncommon. He does so, however, only to show that the miniature at 874 in PF and at 954 in C can in no way be independent of each other. Indeed he expressly states (147) that there is no need in the context of his discussion to investigate what the gesture signifies. I believe, however, it is in such an investigation that confirmation of what has just been suggested can be found.

This figure (Chremes at 874 in PF, Menedemus at 954 in C) has been drawn with the right hand raised to the face. In C and P the hand is slightly clenched and rests on the right cheek just below the eye. In F the hand is not clenched and is raised somewhat higher than in C and P. The question that we must now pose is whether this gesture suits Chremes in V.1 (as in PF) or Menedemus in V.2 (as in C).

It is in the first scene of Act V that Chremes discovers at last that he and not Menedemus (as he had supposed) has been the dupe of the intrigues which he himself set in motion. He has believed that Bacchis, a courtesan and a lady of expensive tastes, is the lover of Menedemus' son. In V.1 Menedemus tells of what has happened in his house between Bacchis and Clitipho, the son of Chremes. A couch had been taken into a room at the back of the house, Bacchis had followed Clitipho into the room, and the door had then been shut (902-9). Chremes now realizes that Bacchis is his own son's lover and thinks that he is ruined (902-9):

ME. est mihi ultimis conclave in aedibus quoddam retro:
huc est intro latus lectus, vestimentis stratus est.
CH. quid postquam hoc est factum? ME. dictum factum huc abiit Clitipho.
CH. solus? ME. solus. CH. timeo. ME. Bacchis consecutast ilico.
CH. sola? ME. sola. CH. perii. ME. ubi abiere intro, operuere ostium.
  CH. hem?
Clinia haec fieri videbat? ME. quidni? mecum una simul.
CH. fili est amica Bacchis; Menedeme, occidi!
ME. quam ob rem? CH. decem dierum vix mi est familia.

The two figures of Menedemus and Chremes in the miniature at 874 in PF capture effectively the dramatic moment of this disclosure that Chremes' son is the courtesan's lover. Menedemus is clearly addressing his neighbour, and the gesture of Chremes suits his consternation and dismay. One may wonder, however, whether it is purely coincidental that the gesture of Chremes can be interpreted so naturally by a modern viewer. Did the gesture have the same significance for the original miniaturist of the Terence MSS? Its infrequency in the miniatures makes it possible to examine all the other occurrences of it in some detail.

The miniature that is most helpful for elucidating the gesture's significance appears at *Hec* 243 (plate 7). In this illustration the relevant figure is Sostrata. She appears on the right-hand side of the illustration, the two old men Phidippus and Laches occupying the left side. There can be no doubt that the artist chose to illustrate the final part of the scene. The previous scene (II.1; 198-242) consists of a dialogue between Laches and Sostrata in which Laches blames his wife for the estrangement between their son and Philumena. Their conversation does not come to any definite conclusion and is interrupted by the entrance of Phidippus, the father of Philumena, at 243. Sostrata is ignored until near the end of the scene (270-1):

PH. aliud fortasse aliis viti est: ego sum animo leni natus:
non possum advorsari meis. LA. em Sostrata. SO. heu me miseram!

Laches then turns back to Phidippus and the two men go off to the forum at 273, where a new scene is marked. Line 271 is the only part of the scene where Laches shows any awareness of the presence of Sostrata and the only part where Sostrata speaks. That the artist chose to illustrate 271 is shown by the fact that Laches is drawn looking towards Sostrata. The gesture of Sostrata must therefore illustrate the words *heu me miseram*, just as the manner in which Chremes is drawn at *Haut* 874 in PF reflects the words and emotion of *perii* ... *ei mihi* ... *occidi* (906-8).

The miniature at *Haut* 242 (plate 8) is also relevant. Here, on the left, are two slaves, Syrus and Dromo, facing each other; on the right are the two young men, Clinia and Clitipho. Like the slaves, they are facing each other but Clinia is drawn with his upper body and head turned away from Clitipho. It is Clinia who makes a gesture similar to that of Chremes. At first sight the miniature looks as if it depicts two separate parts of the scene. As has been mentioned, this occasionally happens. Whenever possible, however, the miniaturist attempted to illustrate one particular section of the text where all the characters in the scene are involved in the action. Since in this scene Dromo leaves at 250, the first nine lines of the scene (242-50) were the obvious section for the miniaturist to illustrate:

> SY. ain tu? DR. sic est. SY. verum interea, dum sermones caedimus,
> illae sunt relictae. CLIT. mulier tibi adest. audin, Clinia?
> CLIN. ego vero audio nunc demum et video et valeo, Clitipho.
> DR. minime mirum: adeo inpeditae sunt: ancillarum gregem
> ducunt secum. CLIN. perii! unde illi sunt ancillae? CLIT. men rogas?
> SY. non oportuit relictas: portant quid rerum! CLIN. ei mihi!
> SY. aurum vestem; et vesperascit et non noverunt viam.
> factum a nobis stultest. abi dum tu, Dromo, illis obviam.
> propera: quid stas?

The two young men are already on stage when Syrus and Dromo enter at 242. Dromo leaves at 250 and Syrus does not see Clinia and Clitipho until 256. The young men, however, overhear the conversation of the slaves as they enter. Syrus notices at 242-3 that the women they are supposed to be escorting have been left behind. 'That's not surprising,' replies Dromo, 'they are so laden. They are bringing a gang of slavegirls with them.' Syrus repeats this information later: *portant quid rerum!* (247). The reaction of Clinia to the remarks of the two slaves is interesting: *perii! unde illi sunt ancillae?* (246); *ei mihi!* (247); *vae misero mi, quanta de spe decidi!* (250). Clitipho is puzzled and asks what is upsetting him (251). Clinia explains the reason for his anguish in 252-3 and 257-8. When he left Antiphila, she had only one servant. In his absence she has become wealthy. Clinia thinks she must have been unfaithful to him and taken other lovers to accumulate her wealth. Clinia's exclamations are similar to those of Chremes at *Haut* 906-8.

In the miniature at *Ad* 299 (plate 9) three figures are drawn. On the right are Sostrata and Canthara. They are looking at each other but both appear to be pointing towards Geta, the figure on the left, who is depicted in a fashion similar to Chremes at *Haut* 874. Geta has entered at 299 and his words are overheard by the two women, already on stage. The miniature probably reflects the action at 308-10:

> SO. non intellego
> satius quae loquitur. CA. propius obsecro accedamus, Sostrata. GE. ah
> me miserum, vix sum compos animi, ita ardeo iracundia.

Here again the gesture under consideration is linked with anguish (note *ah / me miserum* in 309-10), though on this occasion the anguish has more than a tinge of anger. Geta believes (erroneously) that Aeschinus has abandoned the young girl of the household in favour of the slave girl whom he has abducted from her owner.

These three examples are cited by Jachmann (147) to show the rarity of Chremes' gesture at *Haut* 874 in P and F. Jachmann also refers to the drawing of Geta at *Ph* 534 as an example of the same gesture; Geta, however, says nothing similar to *perii* or *me miserum* in the scene. In fact, the figure of Geta at *Ph* 534 is not drawn in the same manner as Chremes. The slave's hand is not raised as high, being lifted to the mouth rather than to the side of the face. The difference is clearer in F (plate 10) where Geta's chin is resting on his hand. Such a gesture suits the action of that part of the scene (553-5) where Geta is trying to think of a plan:

> AN. vide siquid opis potes adferre huic. GE. 'siquid'? quid? AN. quaero obsecro,
> nequid plus minusve faxit quod nos pigeat, Geta.
> GE. quaero. – salvos est, ut opinor.

The figure of Geta is therefore irrelevant to this enquiry.

There are three other miniatures which contain figures making this gesture or a slight variation of it: *Ad* 209, *Eun* 817, and *Eun* 943. These may be discussed more briefly. In the first (plate 11) Sannio is reacting to Syrus' disclosure that he knows Sannio is about to leave Athens and is therefore in no position to contemplate a court case. It will be difficult therefore for him to recover the girl whom Syrus' master has abducted. When Sannio realizes this, he exclaims *nusquam pedem! perii hercle!* (227). At *Eun* 817 the relevant figure is Thais, but she is not drawn the same way in C and P as she is in F. In C and P her clenched hand is raised no higher than the collar bone. In F, however, the clenched fist rests on the brow or upper cheek (plate 12). That F more accurately reflects the original miniature is shown, I think, by the presence in the scene of words similar to those found in other scenes. At 827-8 Thais exclaims: *hem? misera occidi, infelix!* when she is told by Pythias that the 'eunuch' was Chaerea, the brother of Thais' lover, and that he has ravished Pamphila, the young girl of Athenian birth who is in her charge. In the miniature at *Eun* 943 (plate 13) Parmeno's hand is raised much higher than in the other examples of the gesture, resting on the top of his head. This gesture may be distinct from the others, yet here again a dramatic moment of the scene concerns a disclosure and a reaction of consternation. In this scene Pythias plays a trick on Parmeno. She tells him that the girl whom Chaerea has raped is an Athenian citizen and that Chaerea has been apprehended by the young girl's brother. The miniature may well portray the action of 964-7:

> PY. vide, Parmeno,
> quid agas, ne neque illi prosis et tu pereas; nam hoc putant
> quidquid factumst ex te esse ortum. PA. quid igitur faciam miser?
> quidve incipiam?

Examination of the examples of this gesture vindicates the initial interpretation of the miniature in PF at *Haut* 874. The two figures of Menedemus and Chremes illustrate the moment when Chremes learns the truth (904-10). This suggests, therefore, that these two figures were originally created for v.1 and not for v.2, where the same figures occur in C, Chremes becoming Menedemus. Is it possible, however, to find a moment in v.2 where the gesture is appropriate to Menedemus? The figures of Clitipho and Menedemus in this miniature must depict the first part of the scene where they converse (954-60), since Menedemus falls silent after 960 and may leave the stage at this point. Thus the only words which the figure of Menedemus can illustrate are those at 957-9:

scio tibi esse hoc gravius multo ac durius
quoi fit; verum ego haud minus aegre patior, id qui nescio
nec rationem capio, nisi quod tibi bene ex animo volo.

These words hardly warrant the manner in which Menedemus has been drawn. In fact, it is Clitipho who is the more upset of the two, and it would not have been unexpected if he had been drawn in the same way as Menedemus: cf *quid ego tantum sceleris admisi miser?* (956). As it stands, the miniature prompts the viewer to wonder what Clitipho is telling Menedemus to provoke this reaction. The figures of Clitipho and Menedemus at 954 in C do not then agree with any part of the action in v.2, while the figures of Menedemus and Chremes at 874 in P and F suit perfectly the action of 904-10. Jachmann is, therefore, wrong in stating that C has retained the original miniatures of the illustrated archetype and Jones and Morey are equally wrong in thinking that the four-figure miniature at 874 in P and F originally and correctly stood at 954.

The conclusion that Menedemus and Chremes of the miniature in PF originally appeared at 874 to illustrate v.1 is not new. Earlier than Jachmann or Jones and Morey, Kauer had stated this to be the case, although he assumed rather than argued the point.[41] His complete reconstruction of the history of the problem is quite complex. He postulates three stages. Initially there were three miniatures which illustrated v.1 and v.2. These stood at 874, 954, and 980 (where there is a scene division in D, G, and p), and contained the figures as described below:

874 Menedemus – Chremes (the same figures as at 874 in P and F)
954 Clitipho – Menedemus – Chremes – Syrus (now completely lost)
980 Clitipho – Syrus (now the two right-hand figures at 874 in P and F)

Kauer suggested that a scribe who was copying from an exemplar which contained these three miniatures deliberately left no space for the miniature at 980, because, Kauer alleged, he knew of some MSS which did not have a scene division at this point. When the artist came to 980 there was no space in which to copy the miniature that occurred at this point in the exemplar. He could not add the figures of Clitipho and Syrus to the miniature at 954 since there was no room for them there. He therefore added them to the miniature at 874 where there was space to accommodate them along with Menedemus and

Chremes. Accordingly, the second stage of Kauer's reconstruction is reached:

874 Menedemus – Chremes – Clitipho – Syrus (as at 874 in P and F)
954 Clitipho – Menedemus – Chremes – Syrus

Subsequently an artist omitted the illustration at 954, thinking it superfluous to draw another miniature containing four figures which also appeared in the preceding illustration at 874. The merit of this final stage of Kauer's reconstruction is that it attempts to explain the scene division which must have been marked in the immediate archetype of C, P, and F. Since Kauer places the responsibility for the loss of the miniature at 954 in the hands of the artist, there must still have remained at this point the space left by the scribe for the illustration. In P (or an antecedent) a scene heading of the traditional kind was added between 954a and 954b and the empty space which had been left unfilled was removed. In F the space has survived. An artist of C or a predecessor improvised and filled the two spaces at 874 and 954. Just exactly how this artist innovated will be looked at below (p 39).

Despite the importance of this final point Kauer's reconstruction does not stand up to close scrutiny. We are asked to believe that, when an artist found no space for the figures of Clitipho and Syrus at 980, he added them to the miniature at 874, although it must have been obvious both from the text and the presence of the miniature at 954 that these two characters did not appear on stage in v.1 (874-954a). More plausibly the artist would have seen that Clitipho and Syrus appeared in the miniature at 954 and realized that the miniature at 980 in his exemplar could be dropped without any difficulty. This weakness in Kauer's explanation of the first error leading to his second stage makes discussion of the remainder of the reconstruction almost superfluous. But even the final part of the reconstruction is not persuasive. Would an artist, faced with space for an illustration at 954 in his MS, have chosen to leave it blank, simply because the same four figures appeared at 874? Even if we were to accept Kauer's theory up to this point, it seems more likely that the miniature at 954 was omitted by mistake and that the artist for some reason jumped from the illustration at 874 to that at 1003.

I conclude, as did Kauer, that the figures of Menedemus and Chremes at 874 in PF were originally drawn to illustrate v.1. I also conclude that the four-figure miniature at 874 in PF was the only illustration for 874-1002 in the immediate illustrated γ archetype of CPF. It remains to consider whether the figures of Clitipho and Syrus in the same miniature were *originally* drawn to depict the action of the scene beginning at 980. They must of course relate to this section of the text, as they now stand, since this is the only part of the text after 874 where these two characters are in conversation with each other. Neither of the figures is drawn as distinctively as that of Chremes at 874 in P and F. Syrus could equally well have appeared in a miniature at 954, where, as in C at 954, he would presumably have been in conversation with Chremes (cf 972-7), or at 980, in a dialogue with Clitipho. The way in which the latter figure is drawn, however, does not suit his words to Menedemus at 954-60 or his reaction to Chremes at 968-71. The gesture suggests an admonitory tone which is absent from his dialogues with both the old men. It is true that such a tone is not much in evidence in the scene that begins at 980 either. At 982, however, Clitipho says rather sternly to Syrus: *inrides in re tanta neque me consilio quicquam adiuvas?* These words match the manner in which the young man is drawn. The two figures of Clitipho and Syrus were therefore originally drawn to illustrate the action at 982-3.

Let us summarize the position. The figures of Menedemus and Chremes at 874 in PF depict the stage action at 906-8, and the figures of Clitipho and Syrus in the same miniature reflect the stage action at 982-3. The presence of both pairs in the same miniature can be explained by only two hypotheses. The first of these is that there never were miniatures at 954 and 980. When the illustrations were first conceived, the artist had to draw one picture for 874-1002. He decided to depict the first part of this 'scene' with the figures of Menedemus and Chremes and the second part with Clitipho and Syrus. In this way he succeeded in including all the characters in one illustration. The second hypothesis is that in the original illustrated MS there were miniatures at 874, 954, and 980, as Kauer has suggested, and that in a later MS the figures of Clitipho and Syrus were added to the miniature at 874 from 980 *at the same time as the miniature and the scene division at 954 (and 980) were dropped.* It is inconceivable that the miniature and scene division at 954 should have been retained once the miniature at 980 was amalgamated with the miniature at 874, just as it is inconceivable that a scene division would be kept at 980 when the figures of Clitipho and Syrus were moved from there to before 874. The conflation of the miniatures at 874 and 980 must have occurred simultaneously with the loss of the scene division at 980 and the loss of the miniature and scene division at 954. Both of these hypotheses are in discord with what we must postulate in the immediate γ archetype of CPF where there was the four-figure miniature at 874 (as in PF) *and* a scene division and blank space left before 954b. If indeed the miniatures were originally conceived for a γ MS, an ancestor of the archetype of CPF, how is this difficulty to be resolved?

One possibility is to suppose that the scene division at 954 was indeed lost in an early illustrated γ MS but was reintroduced into a descendant (possibly the archetype of CPF), being drawn from a MS in a different branch of the tradition. There is, however, little evidence to indicate influence of this kind in the γ tradition. Moreover, it is hard to believe that a scribe would be inclined to introduce a scene division without an illustration into a MS where illustrations were in fact the indicators of scene division. When this possibility is rejected, the problem seems insoluble. Indeed it is insoluble as long as we assume that the illustrations were created for a γ MS. If, however, the illustrations were conceived for a different branch of the tradition and transferred from there into the γ tradition, a solution to the difficulty presents itself.

The problem here is similar to that which is posed by the miniature at *Haut* 381, discussed above. The illustration there contains five figures, although only four characters appear in the scene. Here at *Haut* 874 we find a miniature with four characters, although only two appear in the scene, marked off as it is by a scene division at 954, where Clitipho and Syrus enter for the first time in the act. As in the case of the miniature at *Haut* 381, I suggest that the anomaly was created in the process of adding illustrations to a γ text from a MS which belonged to a different branch of the tradition. When the scribe was copying the γ text to which the miniatures were to be added, he had to be careful to leave blank spaces at the appropriate points. In nine cases out of ten the position of the miniatures would probably have coincided with the scene division in the scribe's exemplar, a γ text. For the most part then the procedure followed by the scribe would have been to leave a space at the scene division in his γ text. What I suggest happened in Act v of *Hauton timorumenos* is this. The scribe left a space for a miniature at scene 1 (874) and then automatically left a similar space at 954, since the γ text from which he was copying had a scene heading there. In the illustrated MS, however, there was no scene division, ie no miniature, at this point. When the artist added the illustrations to the text he copied the four-figure miniature from the illustrated MS at 874. This was the same as that which now appears in P and F. He was then confronted with a space at 954 for which he had no miniature in the illustrated MS. He could not improvise because the figures of Clitipho and Syrus were already in the miniature at 874. If he drew an illustration of his own at 954, he would create a discrepancy between the miniature for scene 1 (874-954a), containing four figures, and the text of that scene, in which only the two old men appeared. What he did was to leave the space blank, anticipating that it would be removed when the MS was copied. This, however, did not happen and the blank space fared differently in C, P, and F. In P, as we have indicated, a traditional scene heading was added and the space was removed. The scribe of F left a space but he seems to have attempted to camouflage the problem. He left only five ruled lines blank after 954a at the foot of the page before beginning 954b at the top of the next. Since normally eleven or twelve lines were left for a miniature, he left just enough space for an illustration if one could be found, since the five lines and the bottom margin are equivalent to about ten lines in all. At the same time the five blank lines would not seem too odd since not infrequently a few lines are left blank at the foot of a page when a scene ends shortly before the end of a page and there is not enough room for a miniature.[42] The scribe of C also left space for an illustration after 954a but the artist of this MS has provided two illustrations. He took the miniature that stood in his exemplar at 874 and moved it to 954, exchanging the positions of Menedemus and Clitipho and switching the name of the two old men. He then added a miniature of his own creation at 874. It has been suggested that he modelled this miniature on the one that appears at *Haut* 841.[43] It seems more likely to me that he chose the illustration at *Haut* 749 as a model (see plate 14).

Conclusion

The threads of the argument can now be brought together. It has been shown that none of the evidence which Jachmann adduced to prove that the illustrations were created for the γ text stands up to scrutiny. Moreover, the miniature at *Ad* 364 demonstrates clearly that the illustrations were created for a non-Calliopian MS, one which read *rediero* and not *venero*, which much have been the reading of Σ and therefore of Γ. In addition, the problems posed by the miniature at *Haut* 381 and the discrepancy between C and PF with respect to the miniatures and scene divisions at *Haut* 874 and 954 are best explained if the cycle of illustrations was *not* conceived for a γ text but was added to a γ MS from a different part of the tradition. The original illustrated MS may be designated Ψ. This is most unlikely to have been either an ancestor or a descendant of the Bembinus. The latter is ruled out by the presence of miniatures at scene divisions which have been lost in that MS (eg *Eun* 943, 1049; *Ph* 441; *Ad* 364, 958). The absence from the miniatures of characters who are named in the scene headings of the Bembinus but who were presumably not named in the non-illustrated MS from which Ψ is descended makes the former improbable.

Whether Ψ was derived from Φ or belonged to a now lost branch of the tradition is impossible to determine with certainty. As has been noted,[44] on two occasions (*Ad* 776 and *Haut* 1045) the illustrations follow the actual order of the speakers where both the Bembinus and D have an abnormal order in their headings. At first sight this may suggest that Ψ is independent of Φ. At *Ad* 776 (plate 15) the illustration shows Dromo on the left. He speaks only the first line of the scene from the doorway of the house (*heus Syre, rogat te Ctesipho ut redeas*) and then presumably returns into the house when he is told to by Syrus (*abi*). Syrus, the second speaker, is drawn second, trying to restrain Demea from entering the house, the door of which is shown on the extreme right of the picture instead of on the left beside Dromo, as one would expect. This reflects the words of Demea at 780-1: *mitte me ... non manum abstines, mastigia?* Two separate parts of the scene are therefore shown. In the Bembinus and D the order of names in the heading is Dromo – Demea – Syrus. The 'correctness' of the order of figures in the illustration may be accidental, arising from the artist's consideration of the stage action. Dromo has to be shown on stage, while the most dramatic point of the scene is the attempt by Syrus to prevent Demea entering the house. The flow of the picture is better if the door to the house is placed on the right. But when this is done, Demea is naturally drawn nearest it. (Another factor may have been the position of Syrus and Demea in the preceding scene, where Syrus is on the left and Demea is on the right.) At *Haut* 1045 (plate 16) the order of names in A and D is Menedemus – Chremes – Clitipho – Sostrata, although there can be no doubt that Sostrata is the third speaker and Clitipho the fourth. The figures in the illustration are drawn in the order of speaking. These facts suggest that A and D reflect an abnormal order of names in the heading in Φ and that the

MS to which the miniatures were added (the exemplar of Ψ) was free of this error, and was not therefore descended from Φ. If the illustrations were created for a MS which had the abnormal order, there was no strong reason for the artist to depart from it. The major feature of the scene is the showdown between Chremes and Clitipho. These two figures could easily have been drawn as the central ones flanked by Menedemus on the left and Sostrata on the right. This illustration, however, is not strong enough evidence to exclude the descent of Ψ from Φ. Against this miniature we must place the one at *Ad* 265, where the order of figures agrees in error with the Bembinus, and the one at *Ad* 466, where the order agrees in error with D.

The scene division in Ψ appears to have been very similar to that of Φ. We find that the Bembinus, the δ MSS, and the γ MSS occasionally have a scene division which has been lost in the others but these are very few in number. The Bembinus alone has scene divisions at *Hec* 816 and *Ph* 884, but in both cases the loss of a scene division in other branches of the tradition would not be surprising. Each scene consists of a monologue by a character who remains on stage alone. In such circumstances a scene division is often not marked in any branch of the tradition.[45] The δ MSS alone mark scene divisions at *An* 965 and at *Haut* 980 (though the scene should perhaps begin at 978 where the metre changes). Scene divisions unique to the γ MSS occur at *Eun* 943 and 1049 and *Ad* 958 (excluding the scene division at *Haut* 593, observed only in F). Thus the distribution of scene divisions in the γ MSS is not significantly different from that in the Bembinus and the δ class of MSS. It is possible, of course, that some unusual scene divisions in Ψ were suppressed when the illustrations were taken over into the γ text. In the attempt to explain the miniature of *Haut* 381 it has been argued that Ψ had a scene division at *Haut* 375. There are other indications in the illustrations of an unusual division in Ψ and these will be discussed in the appendix to this chapter. But such aberrations from the Bembinus and the δ MSS do not necessarily indicate that Ψ is not descended from Φ. An artist using a text which was derived from Φ may on occasion have felt that one scene was better broken into two parts in order to indicate the progression of action.

The source of the miniatures in the first illustrated γ MS could not have been Ψ itself but a descendant of this MS, designated Ψ′. This additional step is required by the reconstruction of the prehistory of the five-figure illustration at *Haut* 381. It has been argued that this

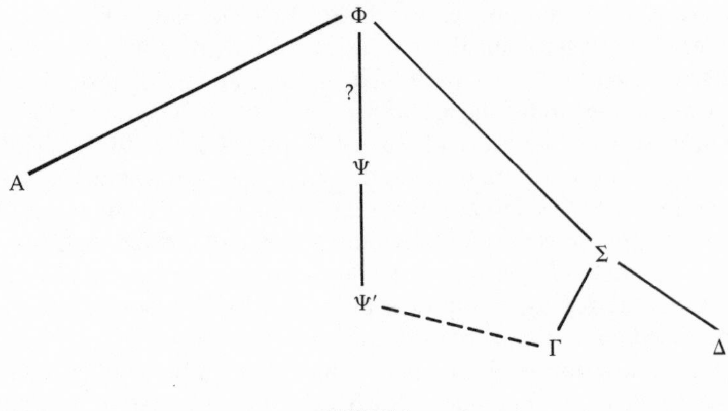

FIGURE 3

miniature was a conflation of two miniatures and that this conflation occurred before the illustrations were added to a γ text.[46] The stemma may be represented as in figure 3.

What are the chronological implications of this stemma for the history of the Calliopian branch of the tradition? The date assigned to the miniatures from which those in the illustrated γ MSS are derived must be the date not of Γ or a descendant but of Ψ. This date can serve only as a *terminus post quem* for the first *illustrated* γ MS. This date does not preclude the existence at that date or even at an earlier date of the γ text. Other evidence, however, to be discussed in the next chapter, suggests that the γ text emerged later rather than earlier than AD 400, if that indeed is the correct period to which the original miniatures are to be assigned. It may be regrettable that this chronological keystone for the history of the Terence text in antiquity has been removed but it is important that the connection between the illustrations and the γ text be severed. The date of the original miniatures is not certain; if an earlier date were to be assigned to them, acceptance of Jachmann's view of their relationship with the γ text would push Γ even further back into antiquity to a date which even some of his adherents would find difficult to accept.

Appendix: The scene division in Ψ

In their position and in the order of figures the miniatures agree with the scene divisions and scene headings in the Bembinus and the δ

MSS to such a degree that they must have been created for a MS which was descended either from Φ or from the 'edition' which was an ancestor of Φ. There are some indications, however, that there were more differences between this MS (Ψ) and AΔ in the distribution of scene divisions than between the first illustrated γ MS and AΔ. Some of the eccentricities of Ψ were lost, I believe, when the miniatures were added to a γ text. It has been suggested above, for example, that there was a scene division at *Haut* 375 as well as at 381 in Ψ, and that there was no scene division at *Haut* 954 in Ψ' (and possibly none at this point in Ψ either).

A scene division at *Haut* 375, where Bacchis and Antiphila apparently make their entrance, would certainly be unusual, since new scenes are normally marked at the point when a new character first speaks and not when his or her entrance is announced. There is another miniature, however, which shows that a scene division at *Haut* 375 was not an unique example of Ψ's eccentricity in this respect.

In the γ MSS *Eun* v.4 (923-70) is divided into two scenes, 923-42 and 943-70.[47] In the first scene Parmeno delivers a monologue (923-40) and then Pythias, who leaves the stage at 922 and re-enters at some point during the monologue, begins speaking at 941 with a two-line aside. She threatens to punish Parmeno for what he has said and done:

> ego pol te pro istis dictis et factis, scelus,
> ulciscar, ut ne inpune in nos inluseris.

In the illustrated MSS there is a miniature before 943, where the metre changes and Pythias begins playing her trick on Parmeno. (She pretends that his master Chaerea has been bound up and is about to suffer the fate of one who has raped an Athenian citizen.) The miniature at 943 (plate 13) portrays Parmeno's alarmed reaction to this news.

The miniature for 923-42 (plate 17) seems to misrepresent the stage action of this scene since the two characters are apparently engaging in dialogue when in fact Parmeno does not become aware of Pythias' presence until 943 in the next scene. That the artist has erred is certainly the initial impression and it is not surprising that Jachmann adduced this miniature (among others) as evidence that the miniatures were not based on the artist's experience of theatrical productions of the plays. Closer examination, however, prompts second thoughts. The first point relates to the figure of Pythias. There is little doubt that she is drawn as if she were about to leave the stage. Her striding gait makes that evident.[48] Now Pythias does not leave the stage between 942 and 943, but is it possible that the artist thought that she did? It is not inconceivable that he did so, since there was a scene division at 943 and the same two characters who appeared in 923-42 were the sole characters in 943-70.[49] The exit of one of them would then be the cause of a scene division between 942 and 943. For reasons which I hope will become clear I do not think that the illustrator was guilty of this error. For one thing it is doubtful whether the manner in which Pythias is drawn suits the vigorous tone of her words at 941-2 (quoted above). The outstretched arm usually signifies simply that a character is referring to another.

The second point is whether or not the two characters are actually engaged in dialogue. Taken by itself the figure of Parmeno is not untypical of how the speaker of a monologue is drawn, and if the scene consisted only of 923-40 and the miniature of Parmeno alone, nothing unusual would be present (cf the figure of Syrus at *Haut* IV.2, plate 18). Because there are two figures in the miniature, each of whom is speaking, it does not necessarily follow that they are speaking to each other. A good example of how appearances may deceive occurs at *Ad* III.2 (299; see plate 9). The initial assumption of the viewer is that Geta is talking to the two women, Sostrata and Canthara, or at least to the latter who is looking towards him. But the miniature reflects the text of 308-10 (see above p 33) where the two women speak to each other and Geta is not yet aware of their presence on stage. In the case of the miniature at *Eun* 923, therefore, one cannot say with certainty 'Das erste Bild ... zeigt Parmeno und Pythias in lebhaftem Gespräch' (Jachmann 21).

The difficulties caused by the miniature at 923 are resolved if the figure of Pythias is taken to represent, not 941-2, but 921-2:

> ibo intro de cognitione ut certum sciam:
> post exibo atque hunc perterrebo.

Indeed, the way in which she is drawn suits these two lines perfectly. She announces her exit at 921 and refers to Parmeno in 922.[50] But if the figure illustrates 921-2, the miniature containing the figure must have appeared at some point before these lines. Now at 917 Pythias sends Chremes and Sophrona inside. At 918 she sees Parmeno approaching:

virum bonum eccum Parmenonem incedere
video.

Thus there is an exit at 917 and a scene division between 917 and 918 would not be in any way intolerable, although more often than not in these circumstances no scene division is marked.[51] It would be possible to have one scene division between 917 and 918 and another between 922 and 923. I suggest, however, that there was only one scene division in Ψ and that it occurred between 917 and 918. The miniature which now illustrates 923-42 originally illustrated 918-42. The illustrator chose to depict the moment when Pythias is about to exit and Parmeno is about to speak. The apparent discrepancy between the miniature at 923 and the action of 923-40 arose because the γ text which the scribe was copying and to which the illustrations of Ψ′ were to be added had no scene division at 918 but did have one, like the Bembinus and the δ MSS, at 923. The scribe left space for a miniature at 923 instead of at 918 as in Ψ′. The artist of the γ MS then copied the miniature at 918 in Ψ′ at this point. Admittedly, the figures must have been drawn in the wrong order in Ψ′ but this is the only reconstruction which will satisfactorily explain the manner in which Pythias is drawn.[52]

The scene division at 918 in Ψ could, as has been said above, have been prompted by the exits of Chremes and Sophrona at 917. Another reason, however, may have been the announcement of the arrival of Parmeno. If this were so, we would have a parallel for the postulated scene division at *Haut* 375, the point where no one exits but where Bacchis and Antiphila are announced.

Two further examples of Ψ's innovation in scene division occur at *Hec* III.4 (415; see plate 19) and *Hec* V.4 (841; see plate 20). The miniatures at both these places are unusual in that one character is drawn twice in each. At *Hec* III.4 Pamphilus and Sosia face each other on the left side of the illustration, engaged in dialogue. On the right-hand side Pamphilus addresses Parmeno, who is about to leave (cf 443). At *Hec* V.4 Pamphilus and Parmeno are on the left, while Pamphilus is drawn again on the right, conversing with Bacchis. The structure of the two scenes is similar. At the beginning of each scene there are three speaking characters on stage. The first part of the scene is taken up with a dialogue between two of them while the third is silent, the second consists of a dialogue between the third and one of the other two. In *Hec* III.4 Sosia, who converses with

Parmeno first, leaves the stage at 429 before Parmeno addresses the waiting Pamphilus. At *Hec* v.4 Parmeno actually remains on stage in the second half of the scene when Pamphilus and Bacchis converse but is silent through most of their dialogue.

In late classical and biblical texts it is not unusual to find illustrations which contain the same character drawn twice or more. Two or three parts of a narrative are often combined in one miniature. In illustration no. XXXIV of the Ilias Ambrosiana there are two scenes, each containing the figures of Dolon, Odysseus, and Diomedes.[53] Such double or triple scenes may be conflations of illustrations which were once separate, appearing at frequent points within the columns of text on papyrus rolls.[54] The history of such illustrations, however, is not relevant here. The point is that the artist responsible for the Terentian miniatures would have precedents for designing the illustrations at *Hec* III.4 and v.4 in the way in which they now appear. Yet such a design would be foreign to the principles underlying the Terentian illustrations, namely that one miniature was to be drawn for each scene and that the characters in each scene were to be drawn only once. The anomaly of these two illustrations is best explained if the original artist decided to break each of these scenes into two parts and conceived an illustration for each part. There was therefore a scene division at *Hec* 430 (immediately after the exit of Sosia) and at *Hec* 854 (when Pamphilus sees Bacchis). The surviving miniatures at *Hec* III.4 and v.4 are therefore conflations. The conflation occurred either in Ψ′ or, what is more probable, when the illustrations were taken from Ψ′ and added to a γ text.

Finally it remains to discuss the miniature which appears in F alone at *Haut* 593 (plate 21). Is this illustration the invention of the artist of F (or a predecessor) or has F alone preserved an illustration of Γ which has been lost in the other illustrated MSS? The text of this section (588-93) is as follows:

> SY. abi sane istac, istorsum, quovis. CH. recte dicit, censeo.
> CL. di te eradicent, Syre, qui me hinc †extrudis†!
> SY. at tu pol tibi istas posthac comprimito manus! –
> censen vero? quid illum porro credas facturum, Chreme,
> nisi eum, quantum tibi opis di dant, servas castigas mones?
> CH. ego istuc curabo ...

Clitipho's exit-line is 589 and Syrus directs line 590 at the departing young man. He then turns to Chremes at 591. A scene division between 592 and 593 is impossible, and if the illustration is authentic, it must have appeared betweem 590 and 591 where the scene division would mark the actual point of Clitipho's departure. It was then moved so that it would not interrupt Syrus' lines at 590-2.

For those who deny that the miniature goes back to Γ the most difficult question to answer is why would a scribe have left space for an illustration if he did not find a scene division and an illustration in his exemplar or if the artist had not marked that a space was to be left. And in the second case why would an artist have wanted to have a scene division here if he did not have an illustration with which to fill the space? Among the major illustrated MSS (C, P, and F) there is only one instance of an invented miniature, that at *Haut* 874 in C, and this was invented in order to fill the two spaces at 874 and 954 when only one illustration was at the artist's disposal (see above p 39). The situation therefore was quite different from what we find at *Haut* 593.

One objection to the authenticity of this miniature which has been raised is that *both* figures gesticulate with the left arm or hand alone.[55] While not infrequently characters use both arms or hands (eg *An* I.5, III.2, III.5, IV.3, *Eun* I.2, III.3, IV.1), there is no other miniature where a character uses only the left arm or hand (cf Quint 11.3.114: *manus sinistra numquam sola gestum recte facit*). Jones and Morey (2.208) suggest, however, that the composition was reversed when the illustration was copied, so that originally the gestures would have been made with the right arm and hand. The surviving miniature is therefore a mirror image of an earlier one. I know of no other example of such reversing in the Terentian miniatures but the misplacement of the scene division may have prompted the artist to reverse the figures in this instance. When the scene begins at 593, Chremes speaks first and he appears on the left side of the illustration, as is normal. But if the model for the miniature originally stood at 591, Syrus would normally be on the left and Chremes on the right. If the figures in the existing miniature are reversed, we would have an illustration which would be beyond reproach if it stood between 590 and 591. In summary the proposed history of the miniature is: (1) a miniature originally stood before 591 with Syrus on the left and Chremes on the right, both gesturing with the right arm and hand; (2) a scribe changed the position of the scene division to before 593; (3) an artist reversed the figures of Syrus and Chremes to bring them into agreement with the order of speaking (or because of the position of the two characters in the preceding illustration where Chremes is on the left and Syrus on the right?).

I am inclined to agree with Jachmann that the miniature is authentic. I am less inclined to agree with him that there was a scene division at *Haut* 591 in Φ. Its appearance in Ψ may have been an innovation of the artist responsible for the creation of the miniatures and need not reflect a scene division in the edition from which Φ and the antecedent of Ψ derive.

1 *Eunuchus* 1031 (P): Jones and Morey no. 310

2 *Hauton timorumenos* 381 (C): no. 362

3 *Adelphoe* 364 (P): no. 500

4 *Hauton timorumenos* 874 (C): no 427

5 *Hauton timorumenos* 954 (C): no. 431

6 *Hauton timorumenos* 874 (P): no. 426

7 *Hecyra* 243 (P): no 603

8 *Hauton timorumenos* 242 (P): no. 355

9 *Adelphoe* 299 (C): no. 491

10 *Phormio* 534 (F): no. 735

11 *Adelphoe* 209 (C): no. 471

12 *Eunuchus* 817 (F): no. 267

13 *Eunuchus* 943 (P): no. 286

14 *Hauton timorumenos* 749 (C): no. 407

15 *Adelphoe* 776 (P): no. 548

16 *Hauton timorumenos* 1045 (P): no. 443

17 *Eunuchus* 923 (P): no. 281

18 *Hauton timorumenos* 668 (P): no. 391

19 *Hecyra* 415 (P): no. 628

20 *Hecyra* 841 (P): no. 673

21 *Hauton timorumenos* 593 (F): no. 385

3

The Commentary of Donatus

The writings of the famous grammarian Aelius Donatus, who flourished in the middle of the fourth century, include a commentary on the plays of Terence. The work survives in about forty or so MSS, though none of these contains a commentary on *Hauton timorumenos*, which, one assumes, must have been lost by an accident of transmission. In its present form the commentary consists primarily of a collection of notes (scholia) which are introduced by a few words drawn from the text of Terence. The format then is similar to that of many modern commentaries in which the notes appear in a separate section after the complete text. In the case of the Donatus commentary, however, we have only the notes and not the specific text for which the notes were written. Nevertheless the content of some of the notes and of the lemmata (the extracts from the Terence text to which the notes are attached) allows us to learn something about the text which Donatus used. It should be possible, therefore, to determine to what extent Donatus' text of Terence resembled that of the Calliopian branch of the tradition. If the commentary is based on a text which contains a significant number of erroneous readings of that branch, then in all probability the date of the commentary (mid- to late fourth century?) provides us with a *terminus ante quem* for the date of Σ or at least a date when some readings which we now think of as Calliopian were in currency. If no Calliopian readings or very few are indicated by the commentary, either Donatus did not have access to a MS with the Calliopian text or the Calliopian text had not come into existence by the time of Donatus. Unfortunately, the situation is more complex than this account suggests. The commentary which has been transmitted to us is not the work as Donatus originally composed it but a late compilation of scholia which were in the original commentary and of later non-Donatus notes. Before the surviving commentary can be of assistance in determining the date of Σ, it is necessary to establish when this compilation took place.

The date of the compilation of the extant commentary

There is no unanimity about how the work assumed its present shape, but the hypothesis presented by Franz Umpfenbach[1] and supported by Paul Wessner[2] is the most probable. Many of the notes of the original commentary were written in the margins of Terentian MSS at the appropriate places. As time passed, other scholia of diverse origins were added to these notes. The surviving commentary came into being when someone undertook to reverse the process and to present the marginal scholia in the Terence MSS as a continuous commentary. That this compiler used at least two versions or two MSS is shown by the transmission of the text which comments on *Phormio* II.3 (348-440). After a misplaced note on 350 the MSS offer a series of scholia on 355-440 which is followed by a second series on 352-440. From this arrangement it appears that weariness (or boredom?) overtook the compiler at this point and he neglected to carry out what was normally the second part of the operation – the integration of the two versions with respect to verse order after they had been copied separately.

Although our concern here is with the date rather than the method of compilation, nevertheless what befell the original commentary and the nature of the surviving work do give some help in establishing a chronology, since some time has to be allowed for the breaking up of the Donatus commentary and for the addition of alien notes to the margins of the Terence MSS. If Donatus wrote the commentary in the middle of the fourth century, the fifth century would be the very earliest possible date for the surviving work. In fact, because of similarities between scholia which appear in the Bembinus, particularly at *Ph* 1-59 (scholia dated to the sixth century), and those which occur in the surviving Donatus commentary it has been suggested that the latter must have been the source for the Bembinus scholiast. In other words the date of the Bembinus scholia provides a *terminus ante quem* for the surviving *commentum Terenti*, the Latin name by which the commentary is now known. This was the conclusion of H. Usener[3] and Remigio Sabbadini[4] and was supported by Wessner in the introduction to his edition of the Donatus commentary (xlv). This view was challenged in 1912 by Einar Löfstedt.[5] He concedes that there are identical or almost identical scholia common to the Bembinus and the extant Donatus. He points out, however, with justification, that the differences are more important than the similarities, since those scholia which are common to both may have been drawn independently from the original commentary of Donatus. Löfstedt focuses his attention on a number of scholia in the Bembinus where the content is fuller and more logically arranged than in the corresponding scholia in our Donatus. Two of his examples will suffice to demonstrate this. At *Ph* 48 (on *ubi erit puero natalis dies*) we read in the Bembinus:[6]

> 'natalis' non pure ponendum est. nam et ⟨h⟩ora natalis dicitur et dies ut hic. apud ⟨H⟩oratium 'pars violentior natalis ⟨h⟩orae.' V⟨e⟩rg⟨ilius⟩ rusticitati serviens 'meus est natalis Iolla.'

In the surviving commentary of Donatus there appears a scholion with similar content:

> cum adiectione temporis cuiuslibet natalis melius dicitur, ut 'natalis ⟨hora⟩' et 'natale astrum.' sed Vergilius serviens personae rusticae 'meus est natalis' inquit 'Iolla' nec addidit 'dies.'

Löfstedt (48) very plausibly suggests that the Bembinus scholion was drawn from a fuller version of the Donatus commentary than that which we now possess since the Horatian citation is missing from it, although both *natalis hora* and *natale astrum* in the surviving Donatus commentary may be linked with the Horatian poem cited in the Bembinus: *pars violentior natalis horae ... utrumque nostrum incredibili modo consentit astrum* (*Odes* 2.17.18ff).

The second example relates to the scholia which explain the etymology of the name 'Phormio.' In the Bembinus the scholion is written at the foot of fol 54^{r} and is attached by a reference sign to *Graeci* in line 26. It reads as follows:[7]

> formon (*φόρμος*, *φορμίον*) dicitur gr⟨a⟩ece saccum(-us) sparteum(-us). ab hoc parasito nomen est, vel ex [...] capacitate. unde Formio correpta prima syllaba apud Apollodorum e[st. non a 'for]mula' ut quidem putant. ergo inde parasitus vilissimae condicionis hom[o dictus est.] si enim a 'formula' esset nomen comoediae, protra⟨h⟩eremus primam syll[abam, si a 'formi]one,' corripere debemus. vidis(-es) ergo *φορ*M*ιο*N*ε*M (*φορμιωνεμ*) dici, non *φαρ*M*ιο*NN*ε*M (*φωρμιωνεμ*), a ['formione'] compositum. *φω*PM*ο*N (*φόρμον*) enim non *φα*PM*ον* (*φωρμον*) Gr⟨a⟩eci scribunt. et 'forma' cum [dicimus, sylla]bam producimus, non corripimus.

The two scholia in Donatus at *Ph* 26 (though separated by a scholion on verse 27) read thus:

> formion tegiculum dicunt Graeci, a quo insternitur pavimentum. unde Φορμίων correpta prima syllaba apud Apollodorum est – non ergo a formula ut quidam putant – et inde parasitus, vilissimae condicionis homo, nomen accepit.

> si a formula esset nomen comoediae, produceremus primam syllabam, si a phormione, corripere debemus.

Here then there are two different explanations of *φόρμος/φορμίον* – *saccus sparteus* in the Bembinus and *tegiculum* in Donatus on *Ph* 26. The one espoused by the Bembinus scholiast, however, is also supported in the surviving Donatus commentary in 1.1 of the notes on the *praefatio* of the play:

> nulla dubitatio est ... errare eos qui in hac Phormionem parasitum putant a formula litis quam intenderit nominatum, cum Graeca lingua fiscus sparteus et stramen nauticum sic dicatur: a cuius rei vel capacitate vel vilitate etiam ab Apollodoro parasitus Phormionis nomine nuncupatur.

Löfstedt (51) concludes that in the original commentary the note on *Ph* 26 was not constituted as it now is and that it mentioned the explanation supported in the *praefatio*. With these and other examples he shows that the Bembinus scholia at *Ph* 1-59 are not drawn from the surviving Donatus commentary and that therefore the date of the scholia, the sixth century, cannot be regarded as a *terminus ante quem* for the composition of the commentary which we now possess. In the last sentence of his article Löfstedt goes even further and suggests that the compilation of the surviving commentary took place after the sixth century. This *terminus post quem* does not necessarily follow from the evidence he puts forward. There may have been several versions of Donatus in currency, including the one which we now possess, and the Bembinus scholia may have been culled from one that differed from our version. Yet when this has been said, the sixth century should probably be accepted as the most likely *terminus post quem* until or unless evidence to refute it can be found.

Löfstedt believed that the notes on *Ph* 1-59 had been taken from a fuller redaction of the original Donatus commentary than that which has survived. The word 'redaction' suggests that the source of these scholia was a continuous text of Donatus separated from the text of

Terence. Recently J.E.G. Zetzel has re-examined the Bembinus scholia on this section of the text and has shown that these were not added directly to the Bembinus from a Donatus commentary but derive from another manuscript of Terence to which had been added scholia, culled ultimately, though not necessarily without alteration, from a Donatus commentary.[8] Since these Bembinus scholia differ from those in the surviving commentary, we now have evidence for at least four Terence MSS containing extracts from the original commentary – the two MSS which were the basis for the surviving commentary, the Bembinus, and the MS which was the source for the Donatus scholia in the Bembinus. It is improbable that there were not more. These must have existed even when the complete original Donatus commentary was still known and accessible. The famous grammarian Priscian (fl 500) probably knew this full commentary. Twice he refers to *An* 536 (*ausculta pauca: et quid ego te velim et tu quod quaeris scies*) in support of the reading *pauca* against *paucis*. Only p[1] offers the former against *paucis* of the rest of the Calliopian MSS (the Bembinus is not a witness for this section of *Andria*). First he says: *nec enim aliter stat iambus qui est quaternarius, quod etiam Donati commentum approbat* (*GL* 3.281,12 Keil). His later comment (at *GL* 3.320,10) reads: *sic enim habent antiqui codices teste Donato commentatore eius*. Now in the surviving Donatus all that we find on these variants is the statement *et 'paucis' et 'pauca' legitur*. While Priscian's second comment may be an expanded inference from the information about the existence of the variants in Donatus, his first comment clearly points to some discussion in Donatus in which preference was given to *pauca*.[9] The original Donatus scholion would have been similar in form to that on *An* 1 (see below p 84). It is always possible that Priscian drew his information from a marginal note on *An* 536 in a Terence MS, but the most likely explanation is that the complete original commentary was his source. That abridged versions of this commentary existed as continuous texts, separated from the text of Terence, I very much doubt. It is difficult to see where anyone would start in deciding what to omit or what to include from the very great variety of topics covered in the commentary. Apart from the enormity of the task the reputation of Donatus would probably discourage any attempts at abridgment.

In summary, therefore, there is no evidence to show that the extant Donatus had come into existence by the sixth century. It seems on the whole more likely that it was compiled after that date, as Löfstedt has suggested. But how much later? After Löfstedt's demonstration Wessner abandoned the date of the Bembinus scholia on *Ph* 1-59 as a *terminus ante quem* for the compilation of the extant Donatus.[10] He later published the Donatus extracts which appear among the scholia in the codex Victorianus (D) of Terence and concluded that they are based on the surviving commentary, since none of the over thirty notes is inconsistent with its content.[11] The scholia in D were written about AD 900, contemporary with the text itself. We are therefore provided with another *terminus ante quem,* albeit a much later one. That our Donatus was already in existence in the ninth century could be inferred from a letter written by Lupus of Ferrières to Benedict III (855-8).[12] In this letter (no. 103) Lupus requested MSS of three works: Jerome's commentary on Jeremiah *post sextum librum,* Cicero's *De oratore,* and the twelve books of Quintilian. The reason for his request was that his MSS of these works were defective or thought to be so. Lupus then requested a MS of Donatus: *pari intentione Donati commentum in Terentio flagitamus.* The natural inference is that Lupus had an incomplete MS of Donatus. We can conclude that Lupus had a continuous commentary, separate from the Terentian text. One is further tempted to believe that Lupus thought his MS to be defective because it lacked the commentary on *Hauton timorumenos,* which does not appear in the extant Donatus. The MS, however, may have lacked more than this. Yet the fact that Lupus had a continuous commentary is in itself significant and points to the existence of a Donatus commentary in the middle of the ninth century. Could this possibly have been a direct descendant of the original Donatus or is it a copy of the now extant Donatus? The former possibility is hard to accept but it needs to be examined since W.M. Lindsay firmly believed (*pace* Wessner) that the Donatus extracts in the Victorianus were not based on the extant Donatus, which he thought came into existence later than Lupus. He suggested that the extracts in D came from or were based upon the full commentary of Donatus.[13]

Lindsay placed great weight on two of the scholia in the Victorianus. One of these relates to *An* 839 which in most of the Calliopian MSS is transmitted thus: *at / vero vultu cum ibi me adesse neuter tum praesenserat.* In D, above the final word of the verse, which appears as *praesenseram,* we read *intellexerat, aliter nt s(e)c(un)d(u)m d(onatum).* Lindsay, concluding that Donatus read the plural form of the verb, has printed *praesenserant* in the OCT. In the surviving Donatus, however, there is no scholion or lemma which attests such a reading. At first sight, therefore, Lindsay's conclusion seems plausible. Wessner, however, offered an alternative explanation. He pointed to the form *senserit* which appears in a lemma of the surviving Donatus and suggested that the alternative ending *-nt*, adduced for Donatus in the Victorianus scholion, was in fact a corruption of *rit*. The scholion could therefore have derived ultimately from our text of Donatus and probably did so.

More problematic is the scholion in D at *An* 720:

> verum ex eo nunc misera quem capit
> dolorem! facile hic plus malist quam illic boni.

Above *dolorem* the scholion reads *vel laborem secundum Donatum*. In our Donatus, however, only *dolorem* is attested – in two lemmata as well as in a scholion which reads *dolorem distinxit probus* (*probe* codd) *et post intulit separatim quod sequitur*. Wessner made no real attempt to deal with this scholion which Jachmann, even before Lindsay, thought might have come from a fuller Donatus commentary than that which we now possess.[14] It is admittedly true that this is the only scholion (apart from that on *An* 839 adduced above) which cannot immediately be linked with the surviving Donatus. It is not sufficient, however, to dismiss it, as Wessner does, by raising the question 'How could a scholiast of the ninth/tenth century have used a fuller Donatus commentary?' when that is the very possibility under consideration. The scholion requires an explanation.

Such an explanation must start with an examination of the relationship between the history of the Donatus extracts in D and the history of the Terence text itself in that MS. Were the extracts already present in the MS of which D is a copy? Or have they been added to D directly, either from a Donatus commentary or from another Terence MS? The first piece of evidence is the text of *Eun* 5, as it appears in D. Here D reads *existimat*, although *existimavit* is found in all other MSS, with the exception of p, which offers *existimabit*. Above *existimat* in D there is a scholion which states *pro 'existimavit' secundum donatum*. On turning to the surviving Donatus commentary we find that the MSS offer on this line the comment *'existimat' pro 'existimavit.'* The agreement between D's reading and the Donatus MSS is hardly to be imputed to coincidence, since *existimat* is impossible metrically in the Terentian verse, and since the text of the Donatus scholion is corrupt (Wessner follows Sabbadini and Bentley in emending to *'existimavit' pro 'existimarit'*). How then is the reading of *existimat* in the Terence text of D to be explained? It seems most probable that a lost antecedent of D read *existimavit*, like other Terence MSS, but that this antecedent contained also a scholion which stated, perhaps, *aliter 'existimat' pro 'existimavit' secundum donatum*. The scholion then prompted the scribe of D (or a scribe of an antecedent of D) to replace *existimavit* by *existimat* and to make an appropriate change in the Donatus scholion by omitting *aliter 'existimat'*.[15]

A more complicated example is provided by the reading *praesenseram* at *An* 839 in D against *praesenserat* in the other MSS. It has been suggested above that the reading *praesenserant* which is attested by the Donatus extract is a corruption based on a misreading of *-rit* as *-nt* (so Wessner). To explain the reading *praesenseram* three stages in the Terence text need to be assumed: (1) *praesenserat*; (2) *praesenserant*; (3) *praesenseram*. The second reading has been prompted by the Donatus gloss, the third by the misreading of the final *-nt* as *-m*,[16] a change which was perhaps affected by the scribe's noticing that the Terence text was the same as that which was indicated as a variant in the Donatus gloss. The simplest hypothesis to account for the three stages is to suppose that the Donatus extracts already occurred in two antecedents of D; in other words, the three readings reflect three MSS with Donatus extracts. It is admittedly possible to reconstruct circumstances which require the presence of the extracts at no earlier point in the D tradition than in the exemplar of D; the first two stages, *praesenserat* and *praesenserant*, could have appear in the same MS, a scribe having changed the former to bring the text into accord with the variant attested by Donatus.[17] That the exemplar contained the extracts, however, must be certain.[18]

The divergence between the scholion on *An* 720 in D, which attests that Donatus knew the variant *laborem*, and the surviving Donatus commentary, in which that variant is not found, may be explained if it is remembered that the Donatus scholia were present in probably two antecedents of D and that the scholia in D also record variants from other Terence MSS. At *An* 784, for example, on *aha necdum omnia* we read *aliter 'an haec tu omnia' scilicet 'audisti' secundum Donatum*. The variant reading has nothing to do with Donatus but is the reading of the γ MSS. Only the second part of the scholion may be referred to Donatus where the scholion *'audisti' subauditur* appears. At *An* 720 I suggest that originally (ie in an antecedent of D) the scholion on *dolorem* read *vel laborem* to which was added the words *sed dolorem secundum Donatum*. The variant *laborem* is the reading of the γ MSS; the second part of the scholion summons Donatus as a witness to defend the inherited reading. In the course of transmission, however, the scholion was corrupted, *sed dolorem* being omitted by accident when the scribe's eye jumped from the *-orem* of *laborem* to the *-orem* of *dolorem*. The scholion in D at *An* 720 is therefore in no way incontrovertible evidence for believing, with Lindsay and Jachmann, that the Donatus scholia in D derive from the complete Donatus or from a fuller version of the commentary than that which we now have. Against this one doubtful example there are over thirty which can be linked with the lemmata or scholia that appear in the extant Donatus. Moreover, two of the scholia in D contain textual corruptions which are found in the MSS of the surviving commentary and which are unlikely to have been present as well in the original commentary (*existimat* at *Eun* 5, and *carior* in the lemma of *Eun* 211). Wessner was therefore justified in believing that the scholia in D were drawn ultimately, though not immediately, from the extant commentary. This must have been in existence in the ninth century at the latest, and it is probably a copy of this commentary which Lupus possessed.

It may be possible to push the date of the origin of the commentary somewhat earlier than the ninth century. That an ancestor of our Donatus MSS was written in uncials may be indicated by a feature of the earliest surviving MS with a continuous commentary separate from the text of Terence, A (Paris, BN lat 7920 s xi). In this MS some of the Latin words which appear next to Greek terms, written in capitals, are written in uncial or half uncial letters:

NāΑΞΙΩΜΑ for *nam ἀξίωμα* (*An* 45; 1.55,14 Wessner)
ΑΠΩCΙΩΠCΙC UEL ЄΜΙΨΙC for *ἀποσιώπησις vel ἔλλειψις* (*An* 149; 1.82,7)
N̄ANAREΛKHTAЄ for *nam παρέλκεται* (*An* 591; 1.184,17)
⁊ALIBI (*et alibi*) connecting two passages of Greek (*Ad* 43; 2.16,25).[19]

A plausible explanation of this feature is that the Latin text was at some time written in uncials and that a scribe, ignorant of Greek, was uncertain where the Greek words began or ended. He therefore faithfully copied what was in his exemplar. This practice has been preserved in A, although this MS was not itself copied from a MS in uncials (see below). But this evidence for an uncial antecedent of the extant Donatus is not overwhelming, although Sabbadini, Wessner, and C.H. Beeson accept it. When the scribe of A departed from his usual minuscule form of writing and wrote a few Latin words in uncials in the immediate proximity of Greek words, he may have been preserving a feature in the transmission of the text which went back to *before* the compilation of the surviving commentary. It has been pointed out that notes were taken from the original commentary and added to the margins of Terence MSS. A scribe who did this will have written the notes in minuscule. But when he came to a passage which included Greek, he may well have copied it faithfully in the script of his exemplar because of his ignorance of Greek. The practice of the scribe of A need not indicate that the surviving Donatus commentary was once in uncials; it may preserve the style of writing in the original commentary. Sabbadini, Wessner, and Beeson believe that the extant commentary had come into being before the date of the Bembinus scholia. If that were true, a copy in uncial (or half-uncial) is credible. But once that *terminus ante quem* is removed as a consequence of Löfstedt's examination of the Bembinus scholia at *Ph* 1-59, there is nothing to prevent one from dating the compilation of the Donatus commentary much later, perhaps the end of the eighth century, where a minuscule script is more likely, though a MS in uncials or half-uncials would still be possible.[20]

Some errors shared by the MSS indicate that the archetype was copied from an exemplar in Carolingian minuscules; so, for example, we find confusion of c and t (*cum* for *tum*, 1.18,18; *latentem* for *iacentem*, 1.218,4; *sit ubi* for *sicubi*, 1.299,15;), of a and u (*excipiatur* for *excipiuntur*, 1.71,21; *meam verebar* for *me amare rebar*, 2.295,15), of u and ti (*ubi* for *tibi*, 1.28,21), of *en* and *eti* (*dicens* for *dicetis*, 1.8 17; *enim* for *etiam*, 1.91,6). Note too the reading *ut* for *vel* (the abbreviation for *vel* being read as *ut*) at 1.120,6.

Beeson also argued that the immediate archetype had an ancestor written in insular script, since there are common errors which are likely to have arisen from the misreading of letters which are similar to each other in that script and from the misinterpretation of insular abbreviations. The letters most readily confused in the copying of a MS in insular script are p, r, and n. Beeson cites three instances of the confusion of *voluptas* and *voluntas* but, as he admits, these errors may not be graphical at all, since the words are often closely associated. For the confusion of r and p he adduces *inceptarum* for *incertarum* (1.110,4) and *parum* for *rarum* at (1.288,10). He does not give any examples of errors betraying confusion of r and n, but two possible instances are *agendo usus* for *ager domus* (1.43,1) and *plenum quam* for *plerumque* (1.91,18). More numerous and more convincing than the purely graphical errors are the wrong expansions of abbreviations. Thus we find, for example, errors involving *si/sed/secundum/scilicet*, *quam/quia/quod* and *dicit/dum/do*. There seems sufficient evidence to conclude that at some time parts of the Donatus commentary were written in insular script. But whether we can conclude that there was a continuous commentary written in this script is another question.

One of the sources used by the person responsible for compiling the extant commentary may have been a Terence MS with marginal Donatus scholia written in the insular script. The errors may therefore have been made when these scholia were transcribed from this MS. Beeson may indeed be correct, but there has been in the past too great a tendency to postulate insular antecedents in the tradition of the classical authors.[21].

When all the strands of this argument are drawn together, no exact date for the compilation of the extant commentary emerges. It may have been done in the later half of the eighth century; a date before the seventh century seems improbable. It is useful to have even an approximate date for when the compilation process occurred, since the earlier the date the higher the proportion of authentic Donatus scholia there is likely to be. If the extant commentary did not take its present form until after the sixth century at the earliest, we shall not be surprised to find a fair amount of addition to the original scholia which were transferred from Donatus to the margins of Terentian MSS. Attempts have been made to separate the authentic scholia from the spurious and some progress has been made, particularly by Sabbadini and Leo,[22] but in the final analysis much has to remain subjective. What seems to be agreed is that a considerable proportion of the transmitted commentary goes back to Donatus himself (sometimes in abbreviated or paraphrased form), even though much of the original work may have been lost.

Multiple authorship of the extant commentary

Three groups of scholia will demonstrate the nature of the extant commentary and the problems that it poses. The first relates to *Hec* 581: *teque ante quod me amare rebar, ei rei firmasti fidem.* On this verse we find two scholia, corrupt in some respects in the MSS and printed by Wessner as follows:

> deest 'tam,' ut sit ordo: et quam te me amare rebar, tam firmasti fidem ei rei.

> ordo et sensus hic est: et quod ante rebar, ei ⟨rei⟩ firmasti fidem, neque me fefellit quod ante rebar te me amare; nam ei rei hodie firmasti fidem, id est probationem attulisti.

It is clear that the former is based on the reading *teque ante quam*, the latter on *teque ante quod*, a reading which is found only in P of the major Terentian MSS against *quam* in the others. Both could not be the work of one man unless something which linked them has been lost. The first scholion could sensibly follow the second if it was prefaced by *si 'quam' legitur*. This, however, is pure speculation and one is compelled to postulate different sources for the two scholia. The correct reading must be *quod*, but even the second scholion cannot with certainty be imputed to Donatus.

More complex are the five scholia on *Hec* 313: *fortasse unum aliquod verbum inter eas iram hanc concivisse*. Wessner prints the relevant scholia thus:

1 ⟨FORTASSE VNVM ALIQVOD VERBVM⟩ I. E. I. H. ⟨CONSCIVISSE⟩ sic Plautus 'fortasse te amare suspicarier;' nam veteres infinito modo adiungebant 'fortasse' [conscivisse].

2 CONSCIVERIT commoverit.

3 IRAM HANC CONSCIVERIT legitur et 'conscivisse.'

4 Et 'conscivisse' est rem novam fecisse.

5 CONSCIVERIT decreverit, fecerit.

Quite apart from their relevance to the question in hand, these scholia are not untypical of the commentary as a whole. First of all, the text of the commentary itself suffered corruption in its transmission after it was compiled. Parts of the first lemma have been lost; *suspicarier* has been transmitted as *suspicavere*; *conscivisse* at the end of the first scholion appears to be an interpolation; and the forms in *conci-* and *consci-* have been confused. Secondly, these scholia on *Hec* 313 are interrupted after the second by scholia on verses 310 and 312. Such misplacement, not infrequent in the text, goes back to the redactor.

It is the content of the scholia that is our concern here, however. This *farrago* could not possibly be in the work of one man. The first scholion presupposes the presence of an infinitive in the text, while the second, third, and fifth are based on a finite form of the verb. Moreover, the writer of the second scholion could not have been responsible for the fifth, since *commoverit* must be a gloss on *conciverit* (despite the lemma *consciverit*). The work of at least three individuals can therefore be detected in the scholia which explain *Hec* 313. Indeed, if none of these three was responsible for the third and fourth scholia, the number of scholiasts is further increased.

If we were forced to connect Donatus with one of the scholia, few would deny him authorship of the first. It follows therefore that scholia 2, 3, and 5, and possibly scholion 4, are later accretions to a single scholion drawn from the original commentary. This group of scholia is admittedly an extreme case but it certainly provides help in evaluating the authenticity of scholia in the extant commentary. Scholia similar to the second and fifth, in which a single word of the text has been glossed by one or two synonyms, should be viewed with suspicion. Thus we should not conclude from the scholion at *Ad* 116, where *feram* is explained by *sustinebo, tolerabo,* that Donatus read *feram* in his text. Even without the evidence which the group of scholia at *Hec* 313 provides we would suspect that many scholia of this kind did not originate in Donatus' commentary but were interlinear glosses and the work of sundry individuals. The same may be said for scholia similar to that of the third on *Hec* 313. Variant readings would frequently have been noted in the text of Terence. Since Donatus himself certainly mentioned variants, not all such scholia can be regarded as late additions. They must, however, be treated with circumspection.[23]

The third group (at *Ph* 377) is much less malleable. Here we have two scholia, the first occurring in the initial series of scholia for *Ph* 348-440 (see above p 61) and the other in the second series:

> DESINE imponit silentium Getae, quasi validiora dicturus sit, et sic et supra 'tace' dixit senex.

> OHE IAM DESINE hac voce ostendit plus iusto pro se locutum videri Getam. nam 'ohe' interiectio est satietatem usque ad fastidium designans. Horatius 'donec "ohe" iam ad caelum manibus sublatis dixerit urge' (*Serm* 2.5.96-7).

The text of Terence reads as follows at this point:

> GE. bonorum extortor, legum contortor! DE. Geta.
> PH. responde. GE. quis homost? ehem! DE. tace. GE. absenti tibi
> te indignas seque dignas contumelias
> numquam cessavit dicere hodie. DE. desine. (377)

The Bembinus offers line 377 as printed. The Calliopian MSS, however, omit *hodie* and the δ MSS read *dicere. DE. hoe iam desine*. Scholiasts in

E and F have added *eho* (or *ohe*) *iam* before *desine*. Although the δ reading has had its champions, the Bembinus should be followed. It is probable that *hodie* was omitted by the first hand of Σ, then added as an interlinear gloss, which was corruptly transmitted in the δ class of MSS. Our concern is not which reading is to be preferred at this point but rather what Donatus read in his manuscript(s). The first scholion points to the reading: *hodie. DE. desine,* since it seems to be concerned with the peremptory tone of the bare imperative, as the reference to *tace* in line 375 suggests. The second is obviously based on the reading *ohe iam desine*. Donatus, therefore, did not write both. If Donatus wrote one, which was it? F. Arens[24] believed that there was a clue in the second scholion which was decisive for rejecting the authenticity of its second part *(nam ... urge*). He emphasized the use of the singular *hac voce* and concluded that the first part of the second scholion was composed as a comment on *desine*. Subsequently someone took the scholion to refer to *ohe iam desine,* which was now the reading of the MS, and added a further comment on the significance of *ohe,* giving the Horatian parallel. This argument is not altogether convincing, since the whole of the second scholion could have been written to explain *ohe* alone, and the discrepancy between the three words of the lemma and the singular *hac voce* could have arisen when the compiler of the transmitted commentary extracted *ohe iam desine* from the text instead of *ohe* alone. Despite this objection I am inclined to agree with Arens that Donatus read *desine* and not *ohe iam desine*. Analysis of the two scholia at *Ph* 377 cannot by itself lead to a decision either way; but *ohe iam* seems to be a late reading and this chapter will show that in all likelihood the Calliopian archetype postdated Donatus.

But agreement with Arens about what was in Donatus' text leads one to consider the source of the second part of the second scholion (*nam ... urge*). Here we have a scholion whose content compares favorably with many of the best notes in the commentary. The information it conveys is accurate and it is supported by a parallel from a classical author. If Donatus is denied authorship of this scholion, how many others have to be cast adrift into the murky waters of late antiquity? I suggest that *nam 'ohe' interiectio est satietatem usque ad fastidium designans. Horatius 'donec "ohe" iam ad caelum manibus sublatis dixerit, urge'* is indeed the work of Donatus. It was written, however, for *Haut* 879, where Chremes comes on stage, looking back into his house and telling his wife to stop thanking the gods for the recovery of her daughter. He suggests that she should not judge the gods by her own standards. They do not have to be told the same thing a hundred times before they understand:

ohe iam desine deos, uxor, gratulando obtundere
tuam esse inventam gnatam, nisi illos ex tuo ingenio iudicas
ut nil credas intellegere nisi idem dictumst centiens.

The scholion was added to the note on *Ph* 377, which originally applied to *desine*, in a MS which read *ohe iam desine*. These three words evoked the *Haut* passage.

The implications of multiple authorship

The discussion of these three groups of scholia illustrates how subjective and how difficult decisions about the authenticity of scholia must often be. The problem is a crucial one, since the basic question to which this enquiry is directed is this: 'Was Σ in existence by the time of Donatus?' Because of the way in which the surviving commentary came into existence, we shall not be surprised to find readings of Σ attested in its lemmata and scholia. The lemmata, however, are of little value. When the compiler drew the scholia from the margins of the Terentian MSS, he himself would often have supplied the lemma from the text of the manuscript. Often, indeed, lemmata and the accompanying scholia are not in harmony. Here is but one example. The text of *Eun* 1063-5 reads:

miles, edico tibi,
si te in platea offendero hac post umquam, quod dicas mihi
'alium quaerebam, iter hac habui,' periisti.

The scholion on *Eun* 1064 reads: *aut deest 'non ⟨est⟩,' ut sit: non est quod dicas mihi, id est, nihil est; aut 'quod dicas mihi' pro 'ut dicas mihi,' ut sit 'quod' pro 'ut;' aut 'quod' pro 'quid enim,' ⟨ut sit: quid enim⟩ dicas mihi. certum est autem veteres sic locutos esse.* These words attempt to explain the use of *quod* in 1064. One of the explanations is that *non est* is to be understood. The lemma, however, reads *nihil est quod dicas mihi*. Wessner bracketed *nihil est*, taking it to be an interpolation arising from the scholion itself. It is more likely that the compiler took *nihil est quod dicas*, the reading of the Calliopian MSS, from the text of the Terentian MS, even though the presence of *nihil est* in the lemma was incompatible with the content of the scholion. In some instances, it is true, the original lemma in the Donatus commentary may have been transferred with the scholion onto the margins of the Terence MSS and may have survived when the compiler did his work. Consequently, lemmata in the commentary which contain a reading different from that which the Terentian MSS have transmitted must be considered by an editor. They may reveal a reading that would otherwise have been lost. This topic, however, is outside the scope of this chapter.[25]

What of the scholia themselves? Given that some scholia may be of the sixth century or later, Calliopian readings will inevitably be found in the commentary. Their presence will not necessarily prevent us from concluding that Σ was not in existence when Donatus was writing his commentary, unless their number is overwhelming, and unless many of them are Calliopian errors. Agreement in the scholia with correct Calliopian readings against errors in the Bembinus are of no significance for establishing the Donatus commentary as a *terminus post quem* or *ante quem* for Σ. The Bembinus, like any MS, is not a totally faithful representative of the class to which it belongs. Its scribe has made many trivial errors and there are numerous interpolations. Some of these may be typical of its class but many of them may have been peculiar to that MS. What will be of significance will be the presence of scholia which attest readings that either agree with the Bembinus against what we can postulate for Σ or differ from the Calliopian MSS at points where we do not have the testimony of the Bembinus.

The Terence quotations in the extant commentary

The following lists include as evidence the text of verses of Terence as they are quoted to illustrate a particular point in a different verse. Here again arises the problem about authenticity. Is it possible that all the scholia containing such quotations were the work of Donatus? The answer is no, and one scholion may be adduced as an example. There are several scholia on *Eun* 785-6 (*sane quod tibi nunc vir videatur esse hic, nebulo magnus est: / ne metuas*). The difficulty here concerns the meaning of *quod*, the usage of which is similar to that at *Eun* 1064. The pertinent scholia on 785 are these:

SANE QVOD TIBI NVNC VIR VIDEATVR ESSE HIC 1 figurata locutio et praeterea ὑπερβάτῳ intermixta, nam hic ordo est: sane hic nebulo ⟨est⟩: ne metuas. 2 An hic ordo erit et sensus, ut sit dictum: ne metuas: sane quod

> tibi vir videtur esse hic, nebulo magnus est? ... 5 Et deest 'non est,' ut sit: non est quod tibi nunc vir videatur esse hic: nebulo magnus est. sic et alibi 'si te in platea hac offendero posthac nihil est q. d. m. "alium quaerebam, iter hac habui," periisti,' ut sit: non est quod dicas mihi.

The first point to be noted is that, while the scholia at *Eun* 1064 offer alternative interpretations which include the possibility of understanding *non est*, at *Eun* 785 the fifth scholion abruptly raises this as a new possibility. The first two scholia explain *sane ... est* as one sentence, whereas the final scholion suggests a different syntax, with a break after *hic*. Because of this I suspect that this final scholion is a late addition to the commentary, influenced by the Donatus scholion at 1064. Note, however, that the text of *Eun* 1064 as quoted in this scholion contains *nihil est quod*, although this text makes nonsense of the final part of the scholion: *ut sit: non est quod dicas mihi*. More than one explanation for this discrepancy between the quoted line and the concluding words of the scholion is possible. I think that it is most likely, however, that the post-Donatus scholiast who adduced the Donatus scholion at *Eun* 1064 quoted the verse without *nihil est* and that subsequently the text of the quotation was changed by someone who read *nihil est quod* in his text of Terence.[26]

This reconstruction of events raises another problem. Even if scholia which contain quotations of other parts of the Terentian corpus go back to Donatus, can we be sure that the quotations inform us of the text used by Donatus? One would not readily ascribe to copyists the diligence and conscientiousness that would prompt them deliberately to bring quotations into harmony with their own text. Yet, if what I have said about the final scholion at *Eun* 785 is correct, we have an example of just that occurrence.

Other examples of this are not lacking. At *An* 399 we read:

> VIDE QVO ME INDVCAS 'quo me inducas' in eadem translatione permansit qua sursum dixit 'hac concludar' (*An* 386).

At *An* 386 Pamphilus describes what will happen if he agrees to marry the girl his father wishes him to: *ut ab illa excludar, hoc concludar*. The Donatus scholion on this is corrupt, but it is clear that its author did not read *hac concludar*, as the scholion on *An* 399 suggests. The Donatus MSS offer *mire hanc cum* (*eum* C) *pronomine significat dicens 'ab illa,' illic nec sexum servavit ne uxor esse videatur*. These words suggest the use of an adverb with *concludar*, which thus contrasts with the personal pronoun in *ab illa*. Wessner plausibly prints *mire 'hoc:' amicam pronomine significat dicens 'ab illa,' huic nec sexum servavit*. The reading known to Donatus then was the adverb *hoc* (= *huc*). One might suppose that in the scholion at *An* 399 the text of 386 was cited as *huc concludar* and that corruption has occurred through the confusion of a and u. But since the Calliopian MSS of Terence offer *hac*, it is more likely that the adverb has been deliberately replaced by *hac* by a copyist who wished to bring the text of the scholion into agreement with the text of Terence which he knew. The same may be said for a scholion at *An* 621 where both 386 and 399 are quoted: *ut 'ab illa excludar, hac c.' et 'vide quo me inducas.'* On other occasions, however, mechanical errors in the transmission of the Donatus commentary are the likely cause. At *Hec* 67 the Bembinus reads *nemo illorum quisquam* against *nemo quisquam illorum* of the Calliopian MSS. The phrase is quoted three times in the commentary. Twice (*Ph* 80, *An* 90) the order is *nemo quisquam illorum*; at *Eun* 240 the quotation agrees with the Bembinus. It is probable that the first two passages have independently suffered unconscious corruption, *nemo* and *quisquam* having been brought together, although it is just possible that the copyist has altered the word order from his own recollection or from consultation of the text. In fact, it would not be surprising if a copyist did on occasion consult the Terence text. Sometimes quotations were not copied out in full, only the first letter of some words being used. In such circumstances corruption is very likely and a scribe may have gone to the nearest Terence MS to correct his Donatus text.

When all this has been said, the reader may be surprised when I proceed to include in the lists that follow the evidence of such quotations. I do so because clearly not every quotation was modified in the manner I have described. At *Ad* 550, for example, the scholiast (I assume he is Donatus) explains *etiam taces* as an archaic equivalent of *tace* and quotes *An* 849 (*etiam tu hoc respondes*) as a parallel. Donatus, therefore, must have read *respondes* at *An* 849. All the Calliopian MSS, however, read *responde*. It is clear, therefore, that the quotation at *Ad* 550 has not been corrupted and that it also gives evidence for the text used by Donatus. In the case of most quotations, of course, no such certainty is possible and their usefulness as evidence of the text known to Donatus is limited.

The nature of the text which was the basis for the original commentary

The first of the lists that follow gives those places in the text where there is disagreement between the text attested by Donatus and the Calliopian text where the Bembinus is missing; the second list shows where Donatus agrees with the Bembinus against the Calliopian MSS. Scholia which simply record variant readings, as for example *legitur et 'conscivisse'* at *Hec* 313, are ignored.

Disagreement between Σ and Donatus where the Bembinus is not a witness

	Σ	Donatus
An 70	huic viciniae	huc viciniae / huc viciniam
An 74	primum	primo (*ad An* 274)
An 204	sed dico	edico (*ad An* 495)
An 205	neque tu hoc	neque tu haud
An 226	at ego hinc me ad forum	at ego hinc ad forum
An 235	nunc	num (*etiam gl. II*)
An 331	promereat	mereat
An 344	abeo	habeo
An 346	PA. interii	CH. interii
An 347	CH.	PA.
An 351	hem	em
An 375	No new scene	New scene
An 386	hac	hoc (= huc)
An 489	quis non credat	quis credat
An 521	tu tamen	tu tamen idem
An 670	adgrediemur	adoriemur
An 722	No new scene	New scene
An 728	iusiurandum	iurandum
An 753	praeterea quam	praeter quam (*etiam p*)
An 781	eho obsecro	au obsecro
An 849	responde	respondes (cf *ad Ad* 550)
Ad 937	aufer *om*	aufer

Agreement of the Bembinus and Donatus against Σ

	Σ	Donatus and Bembinus
An 975	secundis rebus	secundis
Eun 230	ego me turpiter ... dabo	egomet turpiter ... dabo (*ad Ph* 23)
Eun 274	animo	animi

	Σ	Donatus and Bembinus
Eun 299	occeperit amare	occeperit
Eun 300	dices	dicet
Eun 302	senem	senium (seneum *A*)
Eun 306	prorsus	prorsum
Eun 326	PA. quid hoc ...	CH. quid hoc ...
Eun 430	GN. *om*	GN.
Eun 582	hae	haec
Eun 632	reputo	puto
Eun 666	potesse	posse (*etiam pv*)
Eun 748	educta est ita	educta ita (*etiam p*)
Eun 810	CH. satis ...	GN. satis ...
Eun 831	iussisti	iusti (*etiam ε*)
Eun 957	id facturum quod	id quod
Eun 998	necesse	necessus
Eun 1064	nihil est quod	quod (see above p 74)
Eun 1083	PH. ... CH.	CH. ... PH.
Haut 290	passus	pexus (*ad Ph* 106)
Haut 748	nescis id quod scis	nescis quod scis (*ad Eun* 722)
Ph 91	illic	illi
Ph 135	persuasit	persuasumst
Ph 141	omitte	amitte
Ph 176	mihi eius sit	mihi sit (*ad Ph* 175)
Ph 363	in opera/-e	opera
Ph 877	audivi	inaudivi
Hec 433	advectus	vectus
Hec 436	dicam	nuntiem (*ad Hec* 437) (*etiam F*)
Hec 542	ego	ego omitted (*ad Hec* 556)
Hec 618	nescias	nescio
Hec 737	siet	sit
Hec 740	tibi me inmerenti	me *om*
Hec 773	exquire licet	exquire
Hec 867	hi	hic
Hec 875	egon	ego
Ad 62	sumptus	sumptum
Ad 77	nescire se / se nescire	nescire
Ad 104	sivit	siit (siid *A*)
Ad 168	at enim	enim (*etiam p*)
Ad 209	conveniam ipsum	conveniam iam ipsum
Ad 324	animum	animam (*etiam p*)

	Σ	Donatus and Bembinus
Ad 356	adfuisse	fuisse (*ad Ad* 789)
Ad 480	servolorum	servorum (*etiam p*)
Ad 522	misere	misere nimis (miser vivos *A*)
Ad 534	fervet	fervit
Ad 636	facito	facite
Ad 800	numquid	numqui
Ad 837	subvertant	subvertat (*etiam p*)
Ad 841	prima luce	primo luci
Ad 912	fratris	fratri

In most of these examples there is no doubt about the text for which the scholion was written. A few, however, deserve some comment.

An 70

interea mulier quaedam abhinc triennium
ex Andro commigravit huc viciniae

huic Σ

Donatus: HVIC VICINIAE 'viciniae' παρέλκον est, ut 'adhuc locorum' (Plaut *Capt* 385).

Although the lemma offers the demonstrative adjective *huic*, the Plautine parallel and the reference to pleonasm (τὸ παρέλκον) show that the author of the scholion must have read *huc viciniae* in his text. The situation, however, is more complicated. Another scholion on the line records the variant *viciniam* for *viciniae*. This gives the reading *huc viciniam*. That Donatus himself knew this variant is indicated by a scholion on *Ph* 368 on *in* (= *isne*) *malam crucem*: *adverbialiter ut 'huc viciniae'* (as printed by Wessner). The last two words, however, are transmitted in the Donatus MSS as *huic viciniae*. The point of the parallel must lie in the case of the noun, and it would not be helpful to cite *huc viciniae* as a parallel. I suspect that *huc viciniam* is the correct emendation (so Sabbadini). One may compare the scholion at *Eun* 536 (on *malam rem hinc ibis?*): *adverbialiter dixit quemadmodum 'domum ibis.' An* 70 is also cited in the Donatus commentary at *Ph* 95 (on *hic viciniae*): *adverbium in loco est, cuius ad locum 'huic viciniae' ('huc viciniae'*

Wessner). This note also appears in the Riccardianus MS (E) at *Ph* 95, but there the reading is *huc viciniam*, which is to be preferred in the Donatus commentary at *Ph* 95.

It is possible to conclude from all this that Donatus knew the readings *huc viciniae* and *huc viciniam* at *An* 70, that he preferred the former, and that he perhaps explained the accusative in a scholion (now lost) which was similar in content to the one at *Ph* 368. For the purposes of this chapter, however, the important point is that the Calliopian reading *huic viciniae* was not apparently known to him.

An 204

DA. bona verba, quaeso! SI. inrides? nil me fallis. sed dico tibi:
ne temere facias.

sed hoc dico *P*[1]; sed dico *cett*

Donatus (*ad An* 495): EDIXI TIBI hic illud reddit 'edico tibi ne temere facias.'

Since Nonius (280) cites *An* 204 as an example of *dicere* meaning *denuntiare*, it is possible that *edico* in the quotation is corrupt, the change being caused by *edixi* in the text and lemma of line 495. I am inclined to think that the scholiast at 495 is drawing attention to the use of the same verb and would print *edico*. If *edico* is correct, *sed* of the Calliopian MSS can be retained (with 'shortening' of the first syllable of the verb after *sed*), but I would omit it (with Dziatzko). The particle does not seem appropriate here after *nil me fallis*. The reading of the Calliopian MSS arose through purely palaeographical circumstances, FALLISEDICO having been copied at some time as FALLISSEDDICO. Thus *edico* and *sed dico* could have been variants existing at a fairly early period in the tradition. Nonius knew the latter. Whether Donatus also knew it we cannot tell, since no note on the form appears at 204.

An 781

DA. iam susurrari audio
civem Atticam esse hanc. CH. hem? DA. 'coactus legibus
eam uxorem ducet.' MY. obsecro, an non civis est? (781)

eho obsecro Σ *praeter p*

Donatus: AV interiectio est conturbatae mulieris.

The scholion seems to be based on a text different from that of the Calliopian MSS. For prosodic reasons, however, neither *au*, attested by the commentary, nor *eho* of all the Calliopian MSS except p is attractive. Kauer-Lindsay printed *au obsecro* with *au* 'shortened' in prosodic hiatus. There is no difficulty with this but the 'shortening' of *obs-* is very doubtful. The alternative is to elide the interjection but there is no other example of the elision of *au* elsewhere in Terence; cf *Eun* 656; *Ph* 754, 803 (in all three cases the same sequence *au obsecro* occurs and *obs-* must be scanned as a heavy syllable); and in particular *Ad* 336 *āu āu*, where the interjection is a heavy syllable on both occasions. A similar objection holds against *eh(o) obsecro*. Given the prosodic difficulties posed by *au* or *eho*, the absence of any interjection in p gains in significance. This MS often alone of the major MSS preserves the correct reading (see pp 107ff) and I would follow it here. The interpolation of the interjections may have been prompted by the context; cf 766 (*eho an non est?*) and 751 (*au*) on which Donatus comments *interiectio est consternatae mulieris*. The possibility cannot be discounted that the scholion at 781 is simply a doublet of the one at 751, that it was misplaced by the redactor of the surviving commentary, and that it therefore provides no evidence that Donatus or anyone else read *au* in 781.

Eun 299-300

PA. ecce autem alterum:
nescioquid de amore loquitur: o infortunatum senem!
hic vero est qui si occeperit,
ludum iocumque dices fuisse illum alterum,
praeut huius rabies quae dabit.

299 occeperit amare Σ (am. occ. *p*)   300 dices Σ: dicet *A*

Donatus: HIC VERO EST utrum senex an Chaerea? sed senex potius. HIC VERO EST senex. QVI S. OCCEP. Chaerea.

Obviously these three scholia cannot be the work of one person. The second is an abridgment of the first, while the third contradicts the first. Umpfenbach and Kauer-Lindsay inferred from the first scholion that it was based on the reading *dicet* in 300. That inference seems correct, but it is also necessary to assume that this same scholiast read *occeperit* in 299 and not *occeperit amare*. The person to whom *hic* refers must be the subject of *occeperit*, and if *amare* was in the text, the subject of *occeperit* could hardly have been taken to be the *senex*. The commentary therefore attests two Bembinus readings, *occeperit* (correct) and *dicet* (wrong).

Ph 135

GE. persuasit homini; factumst ventumst; vincimur.

persuasit Σ: persuasumst *A*

Donatus: PERSVASVM EST (persuaserat *RC*: -sit *OV*) HOMINI hic iam de Antiphone queritur, cui persuasum sit.

Most editors (Kauer and Lindsay are an exception) print *persuasumst*. It is more likely, however, that the active form was replaced by the passive, through the influence of the following *factumst*: *ventumst*, than that the reverse occurred. The use of the active form also stresses Phormio's responsibility for what has happened. With the passive more blame is attached to Antipho (cf *Ad* 360 *persuasit ille inpurus*, where Demea is diverting blame from Ctesipho, his son, to Aeschinus, the subject of *persuasit*), though even with the active Antipho does not escape guiltless. What did Donatus read? The scholion could well be directed at the tone of *homini*, though there are no other scholia which refer to this. Perhaps *Ad* 111 (on *tu homo*), *et 'tu homo' dicens negat illi familiaritatem*, comes nearest. The scholion does not necessarily point to the reading *persuasum est* against *persuasit*. The presence in the scholion of the passive may result from a paraphrase of the text.

Hec 618

PA. credo ea gratia magis concordes, si redducam, fore?
LA. nescio: verum id tua refert nil utrum illaec fecerint (618)

nescio *A*: nescias Σ

Donatus: NESCIAS VERVM ID TVA REFERT hoc verbum ex aliqua parte confirmativum est et consentientis.

Both Umpfenbach and Arens (49) think that the scholion points to *nescio* rather than to *nescias* in the text. I think they are correct. Pamphilus' question is rhetorical, implying a negative response. The form *nescias* ('one doesn't know') denies that the negative implication is necessarily correct, while *nescio* ('I don't know,' ie 'you may be right') is to some extent a confirmation of Pamphilus' belief.

The most obvious conclusion to be drawn from the evidence of this list is that Donatus did not write his commentary with what could reasonably be called a Calliopian MS as his basic text. Can we go further, however, and say that Σ was not yet in existence at the time of Donatus? Arens states (5): 'Donatum non, ut fere solent nostrae aetatis viri docti, complures vel quam plurimos libros manuscriptos via ac ratione contulisse, sed, id quod antiquis grammaticis satis erat, unius libri variis scilicet lectionibus atque scholiis ornati auctoritate nisum esse per se probabile est.' But it seems to me to be far from probable that Donatus relied on only one MS. If one accepts that Donatus wrote his work to be published as a commentary and to be consulted as one read one's manuscript of Terence, he would hardly have picked on one MS, good though its text may have been, and ignored MSS such as Σ or its copies, the Terence text of which may often have been quite different, if these were in circulation. Apart from this general consideration, the commentary contains numerous references to variant readings. Admittedly many of these may be later additions to the dismembered commentary, as has been pointed out with respect to *legitur et 'conscivisse'* at *Hec* 313 (see p 72). Some of these references, however, must have been in the original commentary. Arens (31-2) himself thinks that the following examples can be ascribed to Donatus:

An 1: APPVLIT in secunda lectione 'attulit' fuit, sed 'appulit' magis; nam postea sic 'animum ad uxorem appulit' (*An* 488).
An 8: ANIMADVERTITE legitur et 'attendite,' unde manifestum est et 'attendite' et 'advertite' non esse plenum, nisi addideris 'animum' (cf *ad Eun* 44).
An 40: HAVD M. F. legitur et 'multo,' hoc est damno, reprehendo. quod si est, sic intellegeretur: 'non nollem factum:' nemo enim potest factum infectum reddere.
An 167: QVI MIHI EXORANDVS legitur et 'expurgandus.' si 'expurgandus,' 'cui' lege, non 'qui,' quia et 'cui' per 'q' veteres scripserunt.
Hec 406: O FORTVNA hic fortunam pro bona posuit. VT NVMQVAM PERPETVO ES BONA legitur et 'data,' nam et sic pro 'bona' intellegitur necessario.

To these examples cited by Arens other candidates may be added:

An 599: DICAM EADEM ILLI in aliis 'idem' scriptum est. quod si est, pro 'item' accipiamus.
An 678: SI QVID PRAETER SPEM EVENIT 'evenit' producta magis, quia hoc perpetuo non vult accidere Pamphilo. ergo 'evenit,' non 'eveniet' aut 'evenit' media correpta.
Eun 163: NVM VBI numquid alicubi. aut si 'nuncubi' legimus, erit temporis adverbium, ut sicubi quo in loco, qua in re.
Eun 307: HEM si cum aspiratione, Parmeno, si leniter, Chaerea.
Eun 1022: Et 'edent' et 'edet' legitur. si 'edent,' figuratum est; si 'edet,' rectum.
Ph 761: HAEC SOLA FECIT si 'hic' legerimus, Antiphonem intellegemus; si 'haec,' Sophronam.
Hec 408: IDEM NVNC HVIC legitur 'idem' et 'eidem.' ⟨si 'idem,'⟩ ego; si 'eidem,' hoc est amori.
Hec 670: QVEM IPSE NEGLEXIT si 'ipsa' legeris, clare dictum est; si 'ipse' pater, lentius dictum est.

Donatus probably also discussed variant readings at *An* 403 in the original commentary, although no such discussion occurs in the extant version. In a scholion on *Georgics* 1.96 Servius, commenting on the double negative in *neque nequiquam*, turns to *An* 403 and criticizes those who read *cave ne te tristem sentiat* in this line. The reason for the criticism is that he believed *cave ne* was equivalent to a double negative and therefore to a positive command (= *cura ut*). This would make no sense in the context and what should be read, according to Servius, is *cave te tristem esse sentiat*. Because of this note in the Servian commentary Wessner suggests that a scholion on this topic had existed in the original Donatus commentary. This seems to be extremely plausible. Servius is then simply copying what was in Donatus' commentary or is attacking the view of Donatus at this point.[27]

As the quotation from his dissertation given above (p 84) makes clear, Arens believed that the variants mentioned in the scholia he cited were recorded in the MS for which Donatus wrote the commentary. Leo's view is, in my opinion, much nearer the truth: 'Dass aber der Commentator frühere, auf andern Texte beruhende Commentare *sowie Handschriften mit vielen sonst nicht überlieferten Lesarten* [my italics] benutzt hat, liegt auf der Hand' (325-6). In support of Leo's view the following scholia may be adduced:

An 963: QVID ILLVD GAVDI EST in aliis Davi persona infertur.
An 978: hi versus usque ad illum 'gnatam tibi meam Philumenam uxorem' negantur Terenti esse adeo ut in plurimis exemplaribus bonis non inferantur.
Eun 312 (*de* sive): si persona Parmenonis est, 'sive' abundat. Et pro expletiva coniunctione est modo; in quibusdam omnino non legitur.
Ad 511: hi sex versus in quibusdam non feruntur.
Ad 601: sane hi versus de⟨esse pos⟩sunt quos multa exemplaria non habent 'nam et illi animum iam relevabis' et deinceps.
Ad 706: hic versus in quibusdam non invenitur.

Only if Donatus is denied authorship of all the scholia which refer to variants and to omissions of lines or passages in other manuscripts is it possible to state that Donatus wrote his commentary for one basic MS. Some of these scholia may be post-Donatus, some variants may have been present in his base manuscript, some notes may have been taken by Donatus from earlier commentaries. To believe that everything is derivative or late is to be excessively pessimistic.[28]

The least that one can say is that, if Σ or copies of Σ existed in the time of Donatus, the commentator knew nothing of them. And yet the very nature of many of the Calliopian readings suggests that Σ was created to be a simplified and popular version of Terence. As soon as it came into existence it would likely have had wide distribution. Certainly the ancient MSS accessible to scribes in the early Carolingian period were all descendants of Σ – at least three γ MSS and at least one δ MS.[29] This is not, I think, coincidence. In late antiquity the Calliopian text had become the vulgate. Σ was unknown to Donatus in the fourth century because it had not yet come into being.

The history of the original continuous commentary is relevant to this question of when Σ came into being. Are we to believe that, when scholia were transferred from the commentary onto the margins of Terentian MSS, the scholia were written in MSS which already read, for example, *nunc quid nam* (*An* 235), *hac* (*An* 386), *iusiurandum* (*An* 728), *animo* (*Eun* 274), *senem* (*Eun* 302), *hae* (*Eun* 582), *iussisti* (*Eun* 831), *necesse* (*Eun* 998), *illic* (*Ph* 91)? Is it not more likely that the scholia were transferred to MSS to whose text they were to a great extent suited? Of course some notes may have been added, through carelessness, to a MS whose text made nonsense of their content, but the number of such scholia would hardly, I think, be as large as that of the notes in the list above. The following hypothesis is more probable. The scholia were first copied into MSS whose text the scholia elucidated rather than contradicted. Then the Terence text deteriorated with each copying while the scholia were transmitted more or less intact, though inevitably they too would suffer some degree of corruption and fresh scholia would be added. The scholia would of course be copied *after* the text had been copied, perhaps even by a different scribe. In these circumstances one can see how the scholia fell out of kilter with the text itself and eventually might have accompanied a Calliopian text. The scribe engaged in copying the scholia would do just that, without examining carefully the already copied text. The scholia would have been little affected by the text. It is quite likely, however, that the Terence text was affected by the scholia, when it was copied from an exemplar which contained them. Indeed some of the readings or glosses which were in Σ, though they did not necessarily appear first in Σ, may have been derived from the Donatus scholia.

	Σ	Donatus
An 728	iusiurandum	aut enim deest 'ius' ut sit 'iusiurandum'
Eun 274	animo	'animi' pro 'animo'
Eun 302	senem	plus dixit 'senium' quam 'senem'
Eun 582	noviciae et puellae	λύσις noviciae et puellae
Eun 582	hae	'haec' pluraliter pro 'hae'
Eun 632	reputo	an ἀφαίρεσις pro 'reputo'
Eun 780	servat domum	nam 'servat domum' rectum erat, non 'servat domi,' si 'custodit' intellegeretur
Eun 831	iussisti	συγκοπή metaplasmus pro 'iussisti'
Eun 861	abeam	'abeam' subauditur.
Eun 957	id facturum quod	deest 'facturum.'
Eun 1064	nihil est quod	deest 'non est,' ut sit 'non est quod dicas mihi,' id est 'nihil est'
Ph 91	illic	et nota 'illi' pro 'illic'
Hec 740	inscitum ... me inmerenti	'inscitum' me scilicet
Hec 773	exquire licet	'per me' hoc est me permittente, ut quod per leges tibi non licet 'per me' liceat
Ad 77	se nescire / nescire se	deest 'se'
Ad 912	fratris	FRATRI elegantius quam 'fratris'

Although most of these corruptions could have occurred independently of Donatus, the possible influence of the commentary should not be ignored. This is true in particular of the corruptions at *Eun* 632 and *Hec* 773, where the interpolated forms are not ones which would be expected normally.

The conclusion is that Donatus did not use a Calliopian MS as his basic MS for the simple reason that Σ was not yet in existence. However, the Donatus commentary shares many readings with the Calliopian MSS against the Bembinus. These number over ninety. In some of these cases the reading of the Bembinus is probably unique to that manuscript and not characteristic of the class to which it belongs; eg *maxumas gratias* (*Eun* 397), *sumptos* (*Hec* 225), *causam et manu* (*Ad* 194). Indeed in the vast majority of those ninety examples the Bembinus is in error. Since it is impossible to know whether these errors were peculiar to the Bembinus, the list which follows includes only those examples where the text attested by scholia in the Donatus commentary shares a certain or possible error with the Calliopian MSS. Discussion of some of these agreements and of other possible common errors which I have rejected will follow.

Errors shared by Σ and Donatus against the Bembinus

	Bembinus	Σ and Donatus
An 921	feras	feres
Eun 104	finctum	fictum
Eun 299	occeperit	occeperit amare (*ad Eun* 348)
Eun 426	lepus tute es	lepus tute es et (*ad Eun* 433)
Eun 1022	in te exempla edent	exempla in te edent (*ad An* 651)
Haut 877	quae sunt dicta in stulto	q. s. d. in stultum (*ad Eun* 6)
Ph 120	ille	illene (*ad Ph* 69, 304)
Ph 184	illuc	illud
Ph 236	audio fateor	audio et fateor (*ad Eun* 371)
Ph 482	videre	venire
Ph 681	inde sumam	id sumam (*ad Ph* 786)
Hec 172	horunc (*etiam p*)	horum
Hec 175	se (*etiam D*)	sese
Ad 116	fero	feram
Ad 265	me	men
Ad 378	rediero	venero (*ad An* 418)
Ad 459	neque id satis pie posse	neque me satis pie posse

	Bembinus	Σ and Donatus
Ad 585	ilignis	iligneis
Ad 690	proloqui	dicere

Three of these examples deserve discussion. In two of them (*An* 921 and *Ad* 459) there is uncertainty about what the correct reading is. In the notes on *Ph* 482 the Donatus commentary is not explicit about the reading on which they are based.

An 921

SI. sycophanta. CR. hem? CH. sic, Crito, est hic: mitte. CR. videat qui siet.
si mihi perget quae volt dicere, ea quae non volt audiet.
ego istaec moveo aut curo? non tu tuom malum aequo animo feras?

feras *A*: feres Σ

Donatus: NON TV TVVM M. AE. A. F. 'malum feres:' non filium, sed amorem in filio significat.

Editors are divided in the choice between *feras* and *feres*. The former is the *lectio difficilior* and is probably correct, but the force of the subjunctive is unclear. Shipp describes it as potential and favours printing *non ... feras* as a question. The difficulty disappears if the verse is printed thus: *ego istaec moveo aut curo? non. tu tuom malum aequo animo feras*. The force of the subjunctive is then jussive. For *non* = 'no,' which is frequent in Terence, cf *An* 932, *Ad* 661; see H. Thesleff *Yes and no in Plautus and Terence* (Helsinki 1960) 56; H. Haffter *MH* 10 (1953) 93.

Ph 482

AN. quantum metus est mihi videre huc salvom nunc patruom, Geta.

videre *A*: venire Σ

Donatus: HVC SALVOM NVNC PATRVVM GETA non optat salvum patruum venire secundum Apollodorum, et ostendit non congruere salutem eius cum commodo suo. 2 An non dicit malum esse et incommodum sibi, sed tantum magni terroris plenum adventum patrui?

The presence of *venire* and *adventum* in the scholia suggests that the scholiast read *venire*. The corruption in Σ is an example of the more common form displacing the less common. For *salvum venire/advenire* cf *Haut* 407; *Eun* 976; *Ph* 255, 286, 610; *Hec* 353, *Ad* 80.

Ad 459

GE. si deseris tu, periimus. HE. cave dixeris:
neque faciam neque me satis pie posse arbitror. (459)

me Σ: id *A*

Donatus: SATIS PIE POSSE deest 'facere.' NEQVE ME SATIS PIE POSSE ARBITROR honesta locutio quae significat: quicquid fecerit pro pietatis debito, illius merito parum esse. sensus autem hic est: neque faciam quod nefas est, ut vos deseram, nec hoc ipsum quod facio satis pium est pro tanta necessitudine. Et bene addidit 'satis,' ut ⟨sit⟩: etsi pie, non tamen satis.

Although the scholion does not explicitly attest *me satis pie*, its content seems to exclude *id satis pie posse* of the Bembinus; *me satis pie* was probably the commentator's text. All editors print the reading of the Calliopian MSS. If this is correct, the text of *Ad* 459 would not fall into the category of errors shared by Donatus and the Calliopian MSS. I believe, however, that *me satis pie* is wrong and that the Bembinus probably offers the correct text.

If the tradition had unanimously transmitted *me satis pie*, the line would not provoke suspicion. The Bembinus, however, provides us with *id* against *me* of the Calliopian MSS. If the latter are correct, how is the presence of *id* to be explained? It could hardly have been inserted into the text to complete the construction of *me ... posse*. If, however, the original reading is *id satis pie posse*, one would not be surprised to find *me*, supposedly the subject-accusative of *posse*, added as an explanatory gloss, perhaps accompanied by *facere*. The Calliopian reading came about when the pronoun was incorporated into the text at the expense of *id*.

There is absolutely nothing wrong with the Latinity of the Bembinus reading. What one would understand there would be not *facere* but *fieri*: *id* must be taken as the subject-accusative. The sense of the line is 'I won't desert you and I do not think it would be at all proper to do so' (literally 'for this to be done').[30] A parallel for the change from active to passive is provided by *Eun* 172-3: *quamquam illam cupio abducere atque hac re arbitror / id fieri posse maxume*; in contrast cf Plaut

Asin 514 *neque edepol te accuso neque id me facere fas existumo,* where active is followed by active, though *id* is also present.

Metrical considerations have led editors to favour the Calliopian reading. There is no difficulty in iambic *satis* (cf *satis tuto* at *Eun* 577). What is exceptional is the juxtaposition of two iambic words in the second metron of the line (ie the third and fourth feet).[31] Here it may be explained as a deliberate effect aimed at underlining the solemnity of Hegio's tone. In this scene (and in IV.3) Hegio is characterized not only by what he says, but also by how he says it. There is a profusion of asyndeton (470, 473ff, 479, 481ff, 502), there is antithesis (490, 501ff), anaphora (494ff), rhyme (472ff), and hyperbole (493, 498). Hegio is depicted as the humble citizen who makes the most of being cast into the limelight as the family's protector.

Little work has been done on whether Terence reinforces the tone of a passage by metrical means. It seems to me that he does. Note line 493 (*summa vi defendam hanc atque illum mortuom*), where every foot except the last is a spondee. At 463 (*quem fratri adoptandum dedisti neque boni*) there is no caesura and it is rare for the third foot to be made up of a spondaic word or word-ending. The effect is to give solemnity to the words of Hegio (cf the sententious words of Micio at *Ad* 833 *solum unum hoc vitium adfert senectus hominibus*). Here at 459 the sequence of iambic words (*satis pie*) may highlight the pretentiousness of Hegio.[32]

In some places where the commentary agrees with Σ it is not easy to decide whether the Bembinus offers the correct reading or the wrong one. In the following passages I believe that the Bembinus is wrong (and thus the agreement of Donatus with the Calliopian MSS is of no significance).

Eun 673

paullum si cessassem, Pythias,
domi non offendissem, ita iam ornarat fugam.

ornarat *A*: adornabat *DGLp*[1]: adornat *ηε*: adornarat *cett*

Donatus: ITA IAM ADORNABAT ut supra 'adornant ut lavet' (*Eun* 582).

The reading of Σ was almost certainly *adornarat*. The Calliopian MSS frequently offer an erroneous compound form for the simple (cf *An*

331, *Eun* 632, *Ad* 356), but there are cases where the compound form is correct or preferable (cf *Ph* 148, *Ad* 510). Since *adornare* is not a common verb, the compound may be correct here; cf *Aul* 157, *Cas* 419; and see Fraenkel *Belfagor* 25 (1970) 686.

Eun 766

hoc modo dic, sororem illam tuam esse et te parvam virginem
amisisse, nunc cognosse.

sororem illam tuam esse *A*: sororem esse illam tuam Σ

Donatus: ordine exsequitur; primo utrum personam habeat, 'dic sororem' inquit 'esse illam tuam'

There is little to choose between the different order of words, and one cannot with certainty give preference to one over the other. The Bembinus, however, displays a tendency to alter the word order in the infinitive construction, placing the infinitive in final position; cf *Eun* 703 *me sobriam esse* (unmetrical) for *sobriam esse me*; *Eun* 779 *hoc fieri non posse* for *hoc non posse fieri*; *Eun* 1038 *gaudeo amorem omnem esse* (unmetrical) for *gaudeo esse amorem omnem*; *Hec* 215 *ruri crebro esse soleo* for *ruri esse crebro soleo*. I would here follow the Calliopian MSS and Donatus.

Haut 950

ME. quid agis? CH. mitte: sine me in hac re gerere mihi morem. ME. sino.
itane vis? CH. ita. ME. fiat. CH. ac iam uxorem ut accersat paret.
hic ita ut liberos est aequom dictis confutabitur;
sed Syrum – quid eum? – egone si vivo adeo exornatum dabo

Syrum quidem *A*: Syrum ME. quid eum? CH. Σ

Donatus (*ad Ad* 400): QVID EVM VIDISTIN HODIE 'quid eum' initium interrogationis futurae de persona alicuius. sic in Heautontimorumeno 'sed Syrum – quid eum?'

The last two words of the scholion are transmitted in the Donatus MSS as *quidem* (*quidne* V) *meum*, but the content of the scholion points to the original reading *quid eum*. Most editors of Terence follow the Bembinus. It is certainly impossible for Menedemus to speak the words *quid eum* at 950 (*pace* Kauer-Lindsay, following the Calliopian MSS). Menedemus must leave the stage at some point at 948ff, since he must enter at 954 with Clitipho after informing him of Chremes' intentions. If *quid eum?* is given to Menedemus, one would expect him to wait for the answer to his question and then there would be insufficient time for Menedemus to leave the stage and have enough time offstage in which to tell Clitipho the news. Menedemus must exit at 948. *quid eum?* is the *lectio difficilior* and is to be preferred. In his anger Chremes breaks off after *Syrum* and then asks himself *quid eum?* One may compare the words of Geta in a similar context at *Ad* 315: *tum autem Syrum impulsorem – vah, quibus illum lacerarem modis.* The Calliopian MSS have preserved the correct text but the self-addressed question was misunderstood and assigned to Menedemus. The corruption from *Syrum quid eum* to *Syrum quidem* in the Bembinus is an easy one.

Haut 950 does not therefore provide an example of an error shared by the Calliopian MSS and the Donatus commentary.

Ph 265

DE. unum quom noris, omnis noris. PH. haud itast.

cum noris *A*: cognoris Σ

Donatus: VNVM COGNORIS OMNES NORIS iterum non 'duos' sed 'omnes.' Et varie 'cognoris ... noris.'

Here I am inclined to prefer the reading of the Calliopian MSS. The absence of subordination ('know one, know all') gives a sharper tone to Demipho's words.

Ph 836

PH. vicissim partis tuas acturus est. AN. quas? PH. ut fugitet patrem.
te suas rogavit rursum ut ageres, causam ut pro se diceres. (836)

suas *A*: suam Σ

Donatus: TE SVAM ROGAVIT RVRSVM VT AGERES 'partem' iterum subaudimus. et est ζεῦγμα a superiore.

Although in the Donatus commentary the term 'zeugma' usually means the same word or phrase is to be understood from a preceding clause, it can also refer to a change of number. It is used in this way at *An* 33, where *artibus* is to be understood from the preceding line: *nil istac opus est arte*. In the scholion on *Ph* 836, however, the presence of *iterum* prompts suspicion that the scholion originally read *'partes' iterum subaudimus*, and that *partes* has been corrupted to *partem* because of *suam* in the lemma. Accordingly, *de Donato non liquet* (see apparatus in OCT).

Hec 98

PH. sed quid hoc negotist modo quae narravit mihi
hic intus Bacchis?

quae Σ: quod *A*

Donatus: QVAE NARRAVIT MIHI 'quae' qualia scilicet et quanta ... 'quae' acuendum est ut sit qualia et quanta.

In the context *modo ... Bacchis* is more appropriately taken as a relative clause and not as an exclamation, grammatically independent of the preceding question. If *quae* is read, there is a violent, though not (I think) impossible, example of discord between antecedent and relative pronoun (see LHS 2.431; Lindsay *Syntax of Plautus* 3-4; Allardyce *Syntax of Terence* 5-6). I am inclined to read *quae*, the *lectio difficilior*, and to see *quod* as a 'correction' made to regularize the syntax. See below (p 172) on *Haut* 953.

Ad 649

MI. neque enim diu huc migrarunt. AE. quid tum postea?

migrarunt *A*: commigrarunt Σ

In the scholion on 648 Donatus quotes the first five words of the line thus: *neque enim huc diu commigraverunt*. The scholiast read, therefore, the compound form of the verb (transmitted in the uncontracted form) and apparently a text with a different word order. Corruption may have occurred, of course, in the transmission of the commentary itself. Although it has been noted that the Calliopian MSS have a tendency to replace a simple verb by a compound, I am inclined here to print *commigrarunt*, scanning the second foot, *di*(*u*) *huc com-*, as an anapaest, although only Marouzeau of modern editors has preferred the Calliopian reading. In early Latin *migrare* means 'to go away,' 'to leave:' Plaut *Epid* 342 *ego hinc migrare cesso; Curc* 216 *migrare certumst iam nunc e fano; Trin* 639 *neque mens officio migrat; Amph* 1143 *ego in caelum migro.* The verb *commigrare* is used to describe someone's *coming to* the place where the speaker now is: so, for example, *An* 70 *ex Andro commigravit huc viciniae*; Plaut *Poen* 94 *huc in Calydonem commigravit hau diu*; cf also *Cist* 177, *Trin* 1084, Turpilius 79, 81. In this line, therefore, I assume a scribal error in the Bembinus rather than an interpolation in the Calliopian MSS.

On the composition of this second list no two scholars would agree. When inclusion depends on what is often an arbitrary decision on the correct reading, disagreement is inevitable. At *Hec* 288, for example, the Bembinus reads *ac* against *at* of the Calliopian MSS. The scholia on this verse in Donatus points to *at*. I find it impossible to choose between the readings. Similarly, at *Ad* 509 we find *evadit* in the Bembinus and *evadet* in the Calliopian MSS. The scholion in Donatus attests the latter. Most editors prefer the present tense but since I and E were often confused by the scribe of the Bembinus or by a predecessor (see above p 11), it is equally possible that the future tense is correct. An example which may have a better claim to be included is *Ad* 728. The Bembinus reads *puer natus* against *puer est natus* or *puer natus est* of the Calliopian MSS. Donatus appears to have read *puer natus est*. The different position occupied by *est* in the Calliopian MSS may indicate that it has been interpolated, but again certainty is unattainable.

The inclusion of other examples which have been rejected as common errors of Σ and Donatus or have been overlooked would not substantially alter the picture which emerges from the two lists. Against seventy-six cases of agreement of Donatus with the Bembinus against the Calliopian MSS (or differences from the Calliopian MSS where the Bembinus is lacking) the list of errors shared by Donatus and Σ numbers nineteen. Eight of these rest on quotations in other parts of the commentary and are therefore less than certain. The scholion at *Ad* 116 attesting *feram* is probably not the work of Donatus (see above p 72), while *horum* in the scholion on *Hec* 172 (for *horunc* in the Bembinus and p) may have arisen through the influence of *horum* in the lemma. We are left with a list of nine errors, most of which are trifling: *feres* for *feras* (*An* 921), *fictum* for *finctum* (*Eun* 104), *illud* for *illuc* (*Ph* 184), *sese* for *se* (*Hec* 175), *men* for *me* (*Ad* 265), *iligneis* for *ilignis* (*Ad* 585).

This list of Calliopian errors attested in Donatus does not therefore provide serious counter-evidence to that provided by the first list, from which I have concluded that Donatus did not know Σ or any of its descendants. He did know some readings which also appeared in

Σ, but this does not mean that Σ was in existence in the time of Donatus, since not all of the errors in Σ originated in that MS. Some must have been inherited.

The evidence presented here does not *prove* the non-existence of Σ in the time of Donatus. It is possible that the 'edition' may have been done in one of the provinces in the Empire and that it existed for some time before becoming the most popular text of Terence in late antiquity. But the period to which the subscriptions in the traditions of classical texts point is the late fourth, fifth, and sixth centuries, and most of those named in the subscriptions did their work in Italy.[33] The working hypothesis should be that Σ did not appear until after Donatus, and probably not before the fifth century. Such a view is in harmony with what has been shown in the preceding chapter, that ca AD 400, the date assigned to the originals of the surviving miniatures, cannot be taken as a *terminus ante quem* for Σ.[34]

4

The Δ Branch of the Medieval Manuscripts

The simplest explanation of the large number of errors shared by the γ and δ MSS against the correct reading in the Bembinus is that both groups are descended (through hyparchetypes Γ and Δ respectively) from the common archetype Σ which contained these errors. Theoretically, however, other explanations are possible. Karl Dziatzko, for example, postulated three families of MSS in antiquity.[1] These were: (1) a group to which the Bembinus belonged; (2) a group descending from Σ which represented the Calliopian recension and from which the γ MSS are descended; (3) a family which was quite similar to the Bembinus class and from which the δ MSS are derived. The similarities between the γ and δ groups of MSS arose, Dziatzko believed, through contamination of the δ hyparchetype (Δ) by MSS of the Calliopian recension (ie γ MSS). The advantage of this theory is that it is incapable of being disproved. Every error shared by the γ and δ groups may be imputed to contamination. Such a speculative hypothesis does not readily invite unqualified support. If it were correct, however, we should expect to find at least some significant errors common to Aδ, since the contamination of Δ by a γ MS would hardly be so extensive that all these common errors were obliterated. Without such common errors Dziatzko's reconstruction is purely theoretical and lacks substantiation. In support of his theory about the similarity between the Bembinus class and the δ MSS he cited two examples. One is *Haut* 935 where ADGp read *quod rogo* against *quod volo* of γL, but Dziatzko rightly prints *quod rogo* in his edition, and thus the agreement of ADGp here means nothing. More helpful to his case might have been *Ph* 1028, which he also cited. Here AD[1]L[1] offer *faxo tali sit mactatus atque hic est infortunio* against *faxo tali eum mactatum ...* of the other MSS.

Donatus has an interesting note on this line: *'sum' modo* (Wessner: *summo* codd) *pro eo quod est 'eum:' sic frequenter veteres. Ennius 'omnes corde patrem debent animoque benigno circum sum'* (*Ann* 470-1 Vahlen^2). The Ennius quotation makes it clear that the writer of the Donatus scholion must have read *sum* in his Terentian text. Although few editors have printed *sum mactatum*, one is reluctant to cast aside the very unusual reading, since this rare archaic form for *eum* is unlikely to have been introduced into the text. If *sum mactatum* is correct, however, it would not be surprising to find early variants in the text at this point, either *sit mactatus* (*sum* having been connected with *esse*) or *eum mactatum*. This possible common error shared by the Bembinus and the δ MSS does not, therefore, necessarily indicate contact between the δ class and the branch of the tradition to which the Bembinus belongs. Dziatzko in fact prefers *sit mactatus*, which may be correct.[2] Thus his reconstruction of three classes in antiquity appears to be based primarily on A and the δ MSS sharing what are believed to be correct readings. In essence it springs from his belief in the superiority of the δ MSS over the γ MSS and is an attempt to explain this.

This belief has been shared by many scholars who have worked on the textual tradition of Terence. Dziatzko's theory was anticipated by Ritschl, who linked D and G with the Bembinus.[3] Umpfenbach (*praef* lxviii-ix) thought that the δ archetype, like Γ, descended from Σ but that it (or at least the hyparchetype of D and G, the only two δ MSS used by him) had been corrected from commentators and grammarians such as Donatus, Servius, and Priscian. That such authors were the source of the good readings in the δ MSS was disputed by G. Prinzhorn, who thought that D and G had been corrected from a MS similar in nature to the Bembinus.[4] A different tack was taken by Leo and Jachmann. They believed that the δ MSS represent the prior tradition of Σ and that the δ text suffered, for the worse, a revision in late antiquity from which emerged the γ MSS.[5] 'Uber den Vorrang des δ- vor dem γ-Text kann in Ernst ein Zweifel nicht obwalten': so wrote Jachmann,[6] and his sentiments were echoed by Craig: 'Where Δ and Γ are contrasted, Δ is almost always right,' Craig states, and elsewhere he refers to 'Δ's constant superiority to Γ.'[7] It would be true to say that the superiority of the δ MSS over the γ class has gained the status of received doctrine among most of those who have worked on the history of the text.[8]

An editor is more interested in whether a MS or group of MSS is an independent witness to the text than whether, by and large, it is superior to the others. If the editor has only two MSS to hand, then it will be useful to determine their comparative merits. In cases of

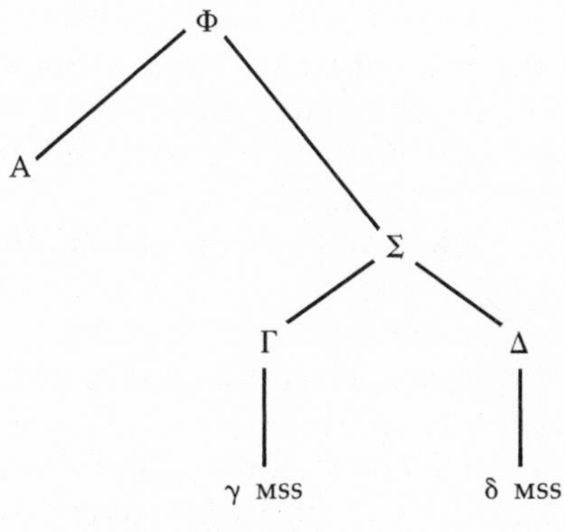

FIGURE 4

doubt he may choose the reading of the better MS, but even then there is no guarantee that what the author wrote has been preferred. The stemma of the Terentian tradition may be represented as in figure 4. What the editor wishes to know is whether the principles of stemmatic theory may be applied in order to establish the reading of Φ. If Γ and Δ are derived from Σ without suffering contamination from each other or from other sources, agreement of one of these hyparchetypes with A against the other will supply that reading, exceptions being made naturally for errors which could have occurred independently in the different branches of the tradition. If it emerges that the δ MSS preserve more frequently than the γ MSS correct readings with A, then we may be justified in saying that the δ branch of the Calliopians is superior to the γ one. For the most part, however, this superiority in itself will not affect the choice of the text to be printed. An exception may occur in those places where the testimony of the Bembinus is missing and we have to choose between the γ and δ readings. But here each instance has to be judged individually, and attention has to be paid to the nature of the errors commonly made in the γ and δ branches as well as to their overall superiority.

The extent to which the readings of Φ can be reconstructed mechanically will be the topic of the final chapter. Before this can be done, however, it is necessary to determine what the readings of Γ and Δ were. It is clear that the medieval tradition of Terence is an open one and that most of the medieval MSS have suffered contamination. This does not mean, however, that Γ and Δ were necessarily contaminated. What it does mean is that it may be difficult to reconstruct with certainty the readings of Γ and Δ from the evidence of the later MSS. In the case of Γ, however, its readings will generally be established by the evidence of CPEF, even though the latter two appear to be more contaminated than C or P. The δ MSS as a group have received less attention and it is to these I now turn.

The δ MSS and the status of p

While the view that the δ MSS are superior to the γ group in the number of good readings which they preserve has won wide acceptance, to different scholars the δ MSS have meant different things. Umpfenbach uses only D (Florence, Laurentianus 38 24) and G (Vatican, Vat lat 1640). D is dated to the early tenth century and has German ancestry.[9] G was written in the eleventh century. A few years after his edition was published, p (Paris, BN lat 10304, s x) and L (Leipzig, I 37, s x) were publicized, in 1873 and 1876 respectively.[10] The evidence of L soon made its way into editions and commentaries, but p was less fortunate. It received only passing mention by Dziatzko in his 1884 edition and was ignored by Tyrrell in the OCT of 1902. The first editors to report extensively the readings of p were Kauer and Lindsay in their OCT of 1926. The quality of this MS fully justifies the belated attention paid to it. There is no doubt that it contains many excellent readings which do not appear in the other major Calliopian MSS, and sometimes its text is correct against all the other witnesses, including the Bembinus. In any attempt to reconstruct the text of Δ the MS is clearly of the utmost importance. Very little is known of its early history. It is dated in the catalogue to the tenth century and was once at Beauvais as a note in the bottom margin of what is now p 232 indicates: *s(an)c(t)i pet(r)i beluacensis*.

How are these excellent unique readings of p to be explained? Lindsay was in no doubt: 'it ... often preserves alone the true δ-reading where DGL have changed it (under the overpowering influence of the multitudinous γ-family) into the γ reading ... It is now and henceforth a sheer waste of time to mention these discussions of the δ text which are previous to the publication of this important member of the δ-family, this Paris MS p. The text of *ces autres* is not the real δ text.'[11] These are strong words, but not everyone has been persuaded. In his Budé edition (1.89) J. Marouzeau admits that quite often p alone presents what seems to be a correct reading. He concludes, however, that these unique readings resemble corrections rather than inherited readings: 'ce manuscrit porte la trace d'une revision savante, heureuse parfois, mais c'est à ce titre qu'il doit être utilisé, donc avec la plus extrême circonspection.'[12]

If Lindsay is correct, we must take full account of p when trying to establish the text of Δ. If Marouzeau is right, then it is probably DGL which substantially preserve what was in Δ, and p which has drawn its good readings from different and alien sources. Neither of these scholars defended in detail his opinion about p. Marouzeau, it is true, pointed out that p also shows readings which appear as glosses in other MSS: *An* 348 *et id scio; Eun* 113 *etiam tum; Eun* 286 *etiam nunc tu*. But the appearance of some corrections and of intrusive glosses in the text of p does not mean that all its good readings have arisen through correction or borrowing. The MS is certainly interpolated to some extent: cf, for example, *An* 504 *tibi forte narrare; An* 516 *promoventur; An* 704 *immo iam hoc; Eun* 192 *sies mihi; Haut* 840 *relictis omnibus rebus*. But the same could be said of the Bembinus. Are we to be equally sceptical about the source of the good readings which appear in A alone and are we to assign them to the work of a 'reviseur savant'? Marouzeau's opinion of p led him to cite its readings only sporadically in the Budé. The same procedure is followed by Martin in his recent edition of *Adelphoe*, while for *Hecyra* T.F Carney primarily follows Marouzeau's text, 'as there were methodological flaws in the construction of the most recent OCT of Terence.' These flaws are identified as 'over-reliance on the "mixed" MSS and on MS p.'[13] Apparently, the status to be accorded to p requires investigation.

No stemma for the four δ MSS has been put forward with the support of detailed evidence. The reason for this will soon become clear to anyone who undertakes the task. The difficulties which arise may be illustrated by the following lists of omissions in *Phormio* and *Adelphoe* shared by two or more of the δ MSS:

Ph 70	me *om DL*	*Ad* 64	ipse *om LpV*
Ph 114	eum *om DGL*	*Ad* 64	-que *om GV*
Ph 182	iam *om DGp*	*Ad* 105	id *om LV*
Ph 340	et (*prius*) *om DLp*	*Ad* 284	tu *om DGp*
Ph 375	ehem *om DGp*	*Ad* 329	hoc *om DGL*
Ph 397	ea *om DGp*	*Ad* 597	te *om DGL*
Ph 419	haud *om DL*	*Ad* 602	iam *om Lp*
Ph 496	tu (*tertium*) *om GLp*	*Ad* 656	quid *om DGL*
Ph 763	hoc *om DL*	*Ad* 682	in me *om Dp*

In both plays there are examples which point to contradictory relationships among the four MSS. *Ph* 70, 419, and 763 give conjunctive errors to DL, but how then can one explain the omissions common to DGp at 182, 375, and 397? Why does L not share in these omissions?

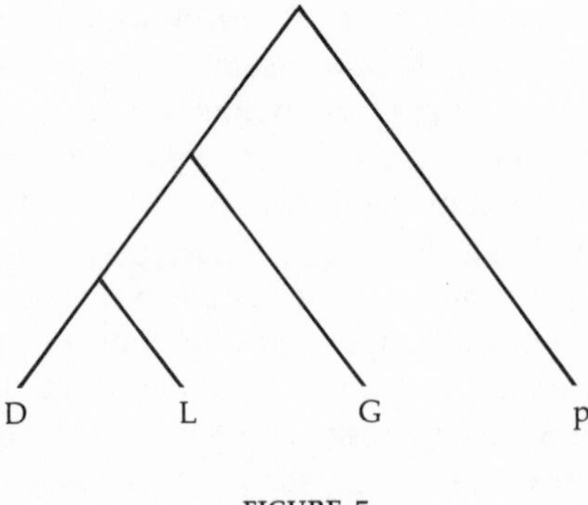

FIGURE 5

Since at other points in this play L exhibits γ readings (*adventus* 154; *intellextin* 198; *insidiis* 229; *reperiam iam* 235; *carcere* 373; *expeto* 378; etc), it is probable that L or an ancestor has been contaminated by a γ source. The examples from *Phormio* can then be translated into the stemma in figure 5. This still leaves *Ph* 496 where D offers *tu*, omitted by GLp. Has D been corrected from some γ source or has L been contaminated by G or p or a related MS? The examples from *Adelphoe* produce similar difficulties. Conjunctive errors at lines 64 and 602 link L and p, but p does not share in the errors of DGL at 329, 597, and 656. What is to be made of the omission of *in me* at 682 in D and p? Did this occur independently in each MS? Such questions are multiplied many times over when a full list of errors shared by two or three of the δ MSS is compiled. There is little doubt that within the δ class there was a considerable amount of mutual borrowing among its branches. It is also true that most if not all of the surviving δ MSS were contaminated by γ MSS. Some examples for L have already been given. For G we may mention *An* 507 *setius puerum deferent huc ante ostium*; *An* 510 omission of *hanc*; *Ad* 312 omission of *ego*; *Ad* 746 *facias*; *Ph* 368 *abi hinc in*. The text of D seems to have suffered least but there are numerous agreements between the γ MSS and D^2.[14] Evidence for the contamination of p by the γ branch will be offered below. All this hardly induces optimism in any attempt to construct a stemma of the δ MSS and to decide whether the good readings of p were inherited from Δ or resulted from the work of one or more *reviseurs*. Some progress, however, can be made on both points.

I shall begin by examining the places in the text where p agrees with the γ MSS against DGL (or against DG in *Haut* and *Hec*).[15] Included are some examples where p agrees with the γ MSS against only

D and L, since G has clearly suffered contamination. The list and statistics that follow are based on the apparatus of the OCT, though I have checked all the readings of p myself. There are in fact some errors in the OCT, and I give first a list of p readings where the apparatus in Kauer-Lindsay is either wrong or misleading:

An 390 certa consilia
An 532 obviam Chremem
An 637 fides est
An 700 hae
An 766 semper has fugi

Eun 654 dederat dono
Eun 904 apage sis p^1
Eun 1041 est *om* p^1

Haut 601 argenti haec

Ph 217 mane mane p^1 (*ante rasuram*)
Ph 850 vapulabis

Hec 237 dimittere

Ad 573 hanc
Ad 590 quicquid quod quidem *om p*
Ad 809 duo olim

When these readings are taken into account, the figures for the agreement of the γ MSS and p against the consensus of the other δ MSS are as follows: *Andria* 24, *Eunuchus* 54, *Hauton timorumenos* 17, *Phormio* 28, *Hecyra* 1, *Adelphoe* 44. This gives a total of 168 cases of agreement.[16] Of these I regard the following 32 as certain or probable errors.

An 647 satis esse] esse satis *DGL*
An 857 veritas] severitas *DGLEv*
An 938 hoc tanto tam repentino bono] tanto hoc tam rep. bono *DGLV*: tanto tam rep. hoc bono *A*
An 947 di bene ament] di ament *AD¹GL*

Eun 427 laute lepide] lepide laute *ADGL*
Eun 498 quom *om γGp*
Eun 758 au *γGp*: ah *ADL*
Eun 764 mane mane] mane *ADGL*
Eun 777 istunc] istut *A*: istum *DGL*
Eun 849 quid me autem *C¹P¹p*: quid mea autem *cett*
Eun 996 inrumpere] rumpere *ADL*
Eun 1042 tum tu frater] tu frater *ADL*
Eun 1074 et *Aγp*(*ante rasuram*): ut *cett* (*om G*)

Haut 217 mihin γ(*praeter E²*)*D²Lp*: mihi *AD¹E¹*
Haut 333 cedo quid *γD²Lp*: quid *AD¹G*
Haut 391 aliquid nobis est *γD²Lp*: aliquid est *AD¹G*
Haut 601 argenti haec *γD²Lp*: haec argenti *AD¹G*
Haut 873 te sciente *γLp*: te scientem *ADG*

Ph 249	molendum mihi esse (*vel* est)] molendum esse *ADGL*
Ph 529	esse sci(e)bat] sc. esse *ADGL*
Ph 588	et ideo istaec] et istaec *ADGL*
Ph 748	exis aut] exis *ADGL*
Ph 858	tu quoque hic aderas $\gamma D^2 L^2 p$: tu quoque aderas *cett*
Ad 209	iam faxo] faxo *ADGL*
Ad 330	nostrum] nostrumne *ADL*: *om G*
Ad 633	fores miser $\gamma D^2 p$: fores *A*: miser *cett*
Ad 635	ut *γpA*: uti *DGL*
Ad 681	o mi pater] mi pater *ADGL*
Ad 716	neque fabrica illic] neque illi(c) fabrica *ADGL*
Ad 904	uxorem quaeso accersis] uxorem accersis *ADGL*
Ad 916	quid ago γ(*praeter* F^1)*Lp*: quid ego *cett*
Ad 937	veniam quaeso filio] veniam filio *DGL*

On the constitution of this list no two editors would agree exactly.[17] Most editors, for example, print *hem? modone id demum sensti* at *An* 882, where *hem* is omitted by C^1P^1p and the Bembinus is not a witness. One may compare, however, *An* 743, where *hem* is an unmetrical addition in DGLEv and appears as a gloss in C but is absent from the text of CPp. I would omit the interjection at *An* 882 as well. It is in *Andria* particularly, where we lack the testimony of the Bembinus, that most doubts arise. An example is at *An* 647 (a trochaic septenarius). In the OCT the verse is printed thus:

PA. falsus es. CH. non tibi sat esse hoc solidum visumst gaudium

but the readings in the MSS are misreported. DGL read *esse satis* (not *sat esse*) and γp read *satis esse*. The papyrus fragment Π^b has now provided the correct *non* for *nonne* of the Calliopians (*-ne* looks like an intrusive gloss), and there is no longer any need to read *falsu's* with earlier editors. If the line begins *falsus es. non tibi*, we can read either *sat esse*, following the word order of γp but changing *satis* to *sat*, or we can print exactly what is in DGL – *esse satis*, the first syllable of *esse* being lightened after *tib*(*i*). I have given preference to the latter, although *sat esse* may possibly be correct. Similar doubts recur at *An* 562, where I prefer *dein* of γp against *dehinc* of DGL, the latter being printed by Kauer-Lindsay. In Terence *dehinc* usually means 'from now on,' ie from the time of speaking: cf *An* 22, 190; *Eun* 14, 296, 872; *Ad* 22. At *An* 562 this meaning would be appropriate if Pamphilus were already married, but what Simo is saying is that *once* Pamphilus is married he will *then* escape from his liaison with Glycerium.[18] I may be wrong on both *An* 647 and 562, but if so, they cancel each other out in the statistics. Some editors would also include in this list of γp errors *Eun* 371 (*deducam*), *Eun* 811 (*iam haec tibi*), *Ad* 189 (*est orta*), *Ad* 302 (omission of *se*), *Ph* 310-11 (*at ego*), and *Ph* 413 (*item*), but in these lines I think that γp have the correct reading, with or without the support of the Bembinus.

What is the significance of this list of errors of γp? Out of the total readings shared by γp (168) against DGL there are 32 errors. The errors constitute, therefore, 19 per cent. Some of the errors could have arisen independently in the γ MSS and in p, through regularization of word order (*Ph* 529), or by the incorporation into the text of glosses which appeared in Σ (*Eun* 1042; *Haut* 333, 391; *Ad* 633, 681) or by modernizing tendencies (*Ad* 635). Many, however, are more likely to have arisen through contamination of p (or an ancestor of p) by a γ MS (for example, *Eun* 498, 758, 777, 1074; *Haut* 217; *Ad* 209, 330). Now if p has been contaminated by a γ MS, some of the correct readings which it shares with the γ MSS may be of the same origin. But it is significant that p shares correct readings with the γ MSS 81 per cent of the total number of agreements between them against the δ MSS. Is it probable that a corrector of the ninth or tenth century, or even of the fifth century, was learned enough to improve the text of his MS to the extent which one needs to suppose if most of the γp readings were introduced into p (or an ancestor) from a γ source and not inherited independently by p and the γ MSS from Σ?

In a recent monograph on the ninth-century MSS of Lucan, a poet who matched Terence in popularity in the middle ages, H.C. Gotoff gives full information on ninth-century corrections in several MSS.[19] An examination of a sample of these will give some indication of the skill of correctors at that period. In Z (Paris, BN lat 10314) Gotoff (111ff) lists 72 readings of Z² in the first two books of *De bello civili*, corrections of casual errors being excluded. Of these only 14 are correct, ie under 20 per cent. The remainder add to rather than diminish the corruptions in Z. The corrector of another MS, A (Ashburnham, Paris, BN lat nouv acq 1626), fares somewhat better.[20] In the first three books of Lucan's poem there are 63 corrections, of which 32 restore the true reading. Here then approximately half of the changes are in fact correction. Some of these, however, are simple corrections of obvious errors: *praecepisse* for *praecipisse* (2.106), *vulnera* for *vulnerae* (2.138), *fulminibus* for *fulluminibus* (2.269), *voverunt* for *vovererunt* (3.127), etc. When these are ignored, the proportion of correct readings drops to about 40 per cent. These figures of 20 per cent and 40 per cent contrast markedly with the 81 per cent achieved by the corrector(s) of p, if the γp readings owe their origin to a γ MS.

Perhaps these two Lucan MSS are exceptions. Statistics for a contaminated MS of Macrobius (T: Escorial Q-I-1) are given by James Willis.[21] In the first fifty pages of the *Saturnalia* this MS (or an antecedent) has been corrected from a different branch of the tradition in 35 places. A false reading has been incorporated into the text in 14 of these instances. Thus the percentage of correct readings is 60 per cent. Overall, therefore, the text has been improved. This corrector still falls considerably short of the achievement of the corrector(s) of p. Willis, however, also refers to a ninth-century MS, the Bambergensis (B), and states (23) that the corrector in B 'has usually made the text better, and ... he has not introduced characteristic errors from another source, as the ancestor of T did.' Although no statistics are given, this statement suggests that the corrector in B approaches or even surpasses the level of achievement in p. But when the corrections in B are examined, it will be found that many of them are corrections of trivial or casual errors of B^1: so, for example, *elegenter* for *elegantur* (p 4, line 5 of Willis' edition); *relinquatur* for *relinguatur* (4,24); *huius* for *hius* (5,27); *instituendam* for *istituendam* (7,15); *auspicandi* for *auspicondi* (10,10); *solita* for *solite* (13,30); *perfecto* for *perfectio* (28,27). When these are discounted, I find that for the first thirty pages of the text in Willis' edition the number of good and bad readings of the corrector is approximately the same. In no way then does the corrector of the Bambergensis match the corrector(s) of p. Indeed if the corrector of B was superior to the corrector of T, the figure of 60 per cent for the latter may be flatteringly high.

It should be kept in mind too that many of the corruptions in the γ and δ MSS of Terence do not betray themselves by their linguistic incomprehensibility. The corruptions have often occurred through interpolation, insignificant omissions, 'regularization' of word order and syntax, and the removal or incorporation of archaisms. The modern scholar can often recognize these errors because he has the knowledge to distinguish between metrical and unmetrical lines. The medieval scribe did not have expertise in the characteristics of Terentian verse. To take but one example, let us suppose that a corrector of the medieval period read *Ph* 588 in his MS as *scio ita esse et istaec mihi res sollicitudini est*, while another MS which he consulted presented this verse with *ideo* between *et* and *istaec*. How would he decide which was correct? Has one MS erred in omitting *ideo* or has the other MS erred in adding it? The answer is that he would not know. The large number of unmetrical lines which must have appeared in Σ (I have counted over seventy examples in *Andria* and *Eunuchus*) shows that this inability to choose stretched back into late antiquity. It is beyond the bounds of credibility therefore that a corrector of p or of one of its antecedents would have had the ability to select good readings from a γ MS as successfully as he would have had to if these readings were not inherited. *Some* contamination from a γ source is certain. If the number of good γp readings emanating from such a MS equalled the number of bad, there would still be over a hundred good γp readings to account for. It might be argued that the source of p's readings was an excellent γ MS which lacked many of the errors now found in the surviving γ MSS. In this way the problem of the very large proportion of good γp readings would be mitigated. But such a solution is no solution at all. Such a MS, when shorn of so many γ errors, would lose the characteristics of the branch to which it is supposed to belong. I therefore reject this hypothesis. It is less attractive than another one, that p inherited most of the good readings which it shares with the γ MSS from Δ and that many errors of DGL were committed at a later stage of the δ tradition – in the hyparchetype of these MSS. This would equally well account for the frequency with which DGL stand in error against p.

The rejection of the hypothesis of a γ MS as the source of most of the good γp readings does, however, lead into a second feature of the text of p. Not only does this MS contain a large number of good γ readings against DGL but it also offers a considerable number of true readings which are not found in any of the major Calliopian MSS. Is it possible that both these sets of readings were drawn from the same source – a MS which perhaps went back ultimately to a stage in the tradition prior to the Calliopian archetype? Or was this MS a member of the class to which the Bembinus belongs? In order to answer these questions I list first of all those good readings which are unique to p among the Calliopians. The reading given first is that of p, the second being the consensus of the others.

An 344	Pamphile: o Pamphile
An 398	aliam: alia
An 536	ausculta pauca: ausculta paucas / paucis
An 661	me ducturum $p\Pi^{b}$: me esse ducturum
An 671	nisi si: nisi
An 753	praeterquam: praetereaquam
An 763	adposisti: adposuisti
An 781	eho *om p*: au *Donatus*
An 813	ei pP^{3}: eius
An 852	dixti pP^{3}: dixtin

An 974	conloquar *pA*: adibo et conloquar
Eun 17	condonabitur *pAE*^{2}: condonabuntur
Eun 98	exclusti: exclusit
Eun 115	audisse: audivisse
Eun 132	esse: esse *om*
Eun 157	dictast *pA*: est dicta
Eun 164	in te claudier *pA*: interclaudier / -cludier
Eun 240	sit *pA*: siet
Eun 255	adventamus *pA*: advenimus / convenimus
Eun 324	quemquam ego esse hominem *pA*: ego quemquam hom. esse / quemquam esse ego hom. / quemquam hom. esse
Eun 347	ilicet *pA*: scilicet
Eun 349	ago equidem *pA*: equidem ago
Eun 389	iubeam *pA*: iubeo
Eun 399	magno *pA*: magnam
Eun 402	vero *pA*: verum
Eun 462	ehem *pA*: hem / em
Eun 511	cum illa *pA*: cum ea
Eun 708	et ea est *pA*: et eam est
Eun 738	eccam ipsam *pA*: eccam ipsam video
Eun 748	educta ita *pA*: educta est ita
Eun 810	idem hoc tu *pA*^{2}: quid nunc tu *A*^{1}: idem tu hoc
Eun 1043	tu *pA*: tu *om*
Haut 127	faciebant *pA*: faciebat
Haut 265	te erga *pAη*: erga te
Haut 365	misere *pA*: miserum
Haut 379	sapias *pA*: sapis
Haut 408	exoptatam: exoptata *ADGLv*: exspectata
Haut 665	in tollendo *pA*: in tollenda
Haut 832	hac me *pA*: me hac nunc / hac nunc
Haut 842	nunc me *pAη*: me nunc / nunc
Haut 1050	egon *pA*: egone
Ph 235	an *pA*: anne
Ph 350	age *pA*: ages
Ph 415	turpe civis *pA*: civis turpe
Ph 561	efferet: feret *A*: et feret
Ph 633	vis *pA*: velis
Ph 727	illas nunc ego *pA*: ego illas nunc / ergo illas nunc ego / ego nunc illas
Ph 952	haec hic *pAv*: hic haec
Hec 106	amabunt: ament *A*: bene ament
Hec 172	horunce: horuncc *A*: horum
Hec 468	modo: omnia / omnia modo
Hec 573	nosci *pA*: noscier
Hec 779	tua se uxor credidisse: tua se ux. se cred. *A*: tua se ux. falso cred.
Hec 865	harunc: harum
Ad 104	siit *p*: siid *A*: sivit
Ad 168	enim *pA*: at enim
Ad 265	ecfert *p*: offert *G*: effert
Ad 270	quo *pA*: quod
Ad 283	tum *pA*: tunc
Ad 477	deserit *pA*: deserat
Ad 480	servorum *pA*: servulorum
Ad 528	mentem *pA*: mente
Ad 809	duo *pA*: duos
Ad 837	subvertat *pA*: subvertant[22]

Again, as in the case of the previous lists, unanimous agreement on the presence of all these examples is unattainable. Some would be excluded by some scholars, while others would be added. At *Eun* 192 p alone offers *istoc* against *isto*, and at *Eun* 725 *occeperat* for *inceperat*. Have these archaisms been introduced into the text by p or have they survived in p alone? Another example is at *Hec* 803. As it is transmitted in the Bembinus and the rest of the Calliopians, the line will not scan (it is a trochaic septenarius) except with hiatus:

accedebam: adulescens, dicdum quáeso és tu Myconius

Editors have read *tun es Myconius* (Goveanus) or *dicdum mi quaeso* (Dziatzko). But p offers *quaeso mihi es*. This is adopted (with *mi* for *mihi*) by Kauer-Lindsay, though with some hesitation. Indeed *mihi* looks suspiciously like an intrusive gloss which fortuitously gives a metrical line, but the position of the pronoun (after *quaeso* rather than after *dicdum*) may indicate that p is correct. The OCT editors show no hesitation, however, at *Ad* 337, where they print *videtur esse* of p against *videtur usquam esse* of the Bembinus and *videtur esse usquam* of the rest of the MSS. Here *esse* is more likely than *usquam* to be the intrusive gloss. In p the gloss has not just been added to the text but has replaced *usquam*. Some of the other p readings favoured in the OCT have been omitted from the list for a different reason – they have been misrecorded. At *Haut* 321 *potis est* is the reading of p[1] (*potis es* after erasure). Similarly at *Haut* 368 it is not certain that *gratissimum* was the reading of p[1] (*gratissima* after erasure). Some of the information is just wrong; *An* 594 *apparentur* (not *-etur*); *An* 751 *dicturan* (not *dictura*); *Ph* 230 *deficies* (not *deficias*); *Ph* 670 *filius* (not *filium*); *Hec* 214 *egone* (not *egon*); *Hec* 524 *sum* (not *sim*). Conversely p reads *duo* at *Ad* 809 and *nunc me* at *Haut* 842 and these examples have been included in the above list.

Whatever modifications it may suffer, the list of good readings unique to p among the Calliopians is an impressive one. Most of them are shared with the Bembinus but some are peculiar to p: *Eun* 98, 115, 132; *Haut* 408; *Hec* 106. In *Andria*, for most of which the testimony of the Bembinus is lacking, this MS is particularly valuable. What is the source of these good readings in p, now that a γ MS has been ruled out for most of them? Some of the readings are attested in Donatus and Eugraphius, though sometimes only by a lemma, or by Priscian: *An* 398, 536, 661, 753; *Eun* 164, 347; *Hec* 106; *Ad* 168, 837. But there are hardly enough occurrences of this nature to suggest that such writers were the source of p's excellence. Where then have these good readings come from?

One obvious possibility is that a MS independent of Σ and perhaps related to the Bembinus has provided most if not all of the readings which are peculiar to p among the Calliopians. Although the Bembinus was probably not an outstanding member of the class to which it belonged – there are too many careless errors and too many interpolations for that to be true – nevertheless we should expect to find some errors common to p and A if indeed p has been influenced by an early MS related, however loosely, to the surviving ancient MS. What follows is a list of the twenty verses where p and A are or may be in common error:

Eun 265 (iambic septenarius)

PA. viden otium et cibus quid facit alienus? GN. sed ego cesso?

faciat *pA*

Eun 378

age eamus intro nunciam: orna me abduc duc quantum potest.
PA. quid agis? iocabar equidem. (378)

ais *pA*

Eun 442

... si quando illa dicet 'Phaedriam
intro mittamus comissatum.' Pamphilam (442)
cantatum provocemus.

tu Pamphilam *pA*

Eun 666 (iambic octonarius)

sed nil potesse; verum miserae non in mentem venerat

posse *pAv*

Haut 357

quapropter haec res ne utiquam neglectust mihi

neglectum est *pA*

Haut 518 (senarius)

CH. quid tu istic? SY. recte equidem; te demiror, Chreme, (518)
tam mane, qui heri tantum biberis.

sed te demiror *pP*[2]: sed te miror *A*

Haut 848

CH. quaeso quid tu hominis es? ME. quid? CH. iamne oblitus es

quid est CH. iamne *pA*

Haut 928

immo abeat multo malo quovis gentium

abeat potius multo quovis *A*: abeat multo quovis *p*

Haut 1006 (iambic octonarius)

oh pergin mulier esse? nullamne ego rem umquam in vita mea

oh *om pA*

Ph 776

ita faciam, ut frater censuit, ut uxorem huc eius adducam

eius huc *pAF*

Ph 840

sed ostium concrepuit abs te. AN. vide quis egreditur. PH. Getast.

qui *pA*

Ph 1019

ea mortem obiit, e medio abiit qui fuit in re hac scrupulus

morte *p*[1]*A*

Hec 164 (senarius)

haec, ita uti liberali esse ingenio decet

ut *pA*

Hec 412

vereor, si clamorem eius hic crebro exaudiat

audiat *pA*

Hec 485

quibus iris pulsus nunc in illam iniquo' sim

siem *pA*

Hec 728

nec pol me multum fallit quin quod suspicor sit quod velit

quid velit *pA*

Hec 787 (iambic septenarius)

BA. ob eam rem vin ergo intro eam? ΓA. i atque exple animum is, coge ut credant

i atque] itaque *A* (i atque *corrector recens*): i itaque atque *p*

Ad 324

animum recipe. GE. prorsus ... SO. quid istuc 'prorsus' ergost? GE. periimus.

animam *pA*

Ad 801

numqui minus
mihi idem ius aequomst esse quod mecumst tibi (801)

quid *pA*: quam D^1F

Ad 877 (trochaic septenarius)

age age, nunciam experiamur contra ecquid ego possiem

experiamur porro contra *pA*

Again the exclusion of some possible examples in this list is explained by errors in the apparatus of the OCT. At *Eun* 1072 p reads *ego rivalem* (not *rivalem ego*) and at *Haut* 1053 it reads *quid istic* (not *quid istuc*). On both occasions therefore p agrees with the other Calliopian MSS and not with the Bembinus. At *Eun* 765 the Bembinus offers *istis* and not *istic* with p, as is stated in Kauer-Lindsay. I have not included in this list *Ad* 309, where the reading of p^1 is reported as *proprius* in the OCT – the same reading that appears in the Bembinus. In p the fifth letter of the word has been erased. It looks to me as if the letter was e and not r.

From this list of possible or certain errors three are of a trivial nature: *Ph* 840, *Hec* 728, and *Ad* 801. Seven others could also have occurred independently. Three of these have resulted from the modernizing of forms or of syntax: *Eun* 265 (subjunctive for indicative); *Eun* 666 (*posse* for *potesse*); and *Hec* 164 (*ut* for *uti*). Conversely, at *Hec* 485 *siem* has replaced *sim*, caused probably by the word's being at the end of the verse where *siem, siet*, etc appear most frequently. The replacement of *neglectu* by *neglectum* at *Haut* 357 is also not surprising. Although *neglectu* is dative, one may compare how the ablative of the supine tends to be replaced by the neuter participle used nominally: see the critical apparatus of the OCT at *Ph* 456, *An* 236, and *Hec* 277. I cannot attach much significance to the corruption of *mortem* to *morte* at *Ph* 1019, since this was caused by the preceding *ea*. At *Eun* 378 *ais* for *agis* is not a surprising error in the context.

Of the remaining ten cases of agreement between A and p three may not be errors at all and could be added to the earlier list of good readings shared by p and the Bembinus. Most editors have preferred the Calliopian reading at *Ph* 776: *ut uxorem eius huc adducam*. The word order in pAF, however (*ut uxorem huc eius adducam*), is the more irregular and may be correct. At *Hec* 412 *audiat* of pA is attractive because of the tendency in the Calliopian tradition for compound words to replace simple verbs. These two examples could be added to the list of good readings of pA. I would retain the third doubtful instance, although most editors would count it as an example of a good reading common to pA. This is *Ad* 324, where I prefer *animum* to *animam* of pA. The latter has been printed by all modern editors and has sometimes been supported with strong words. For Faernus *animam* was a 'certa lectio,' while Turnebus was only slightly less sure: 'fere meam obstrinxerim fidem "animam" legendum esse.' The context shows, however, that Geta is not breathless, like the typical *servus currens*, but in despair at having to break the bad news to Sostrata that Aeschinus has apparently abandoned the household. Especially significant is Geta's exclamation *ei mihi* in 323. It is true that Canthara's question which immediately follows Geta's exclamation – *quid festinas, mi Geta?* – may suggest that Geta is out of breath and that support is thereby given to *animam*. One may also argue, however, that these words led to the change from *animum* to *animam* and that the reverse change is less likely, given the frequency with which breathlessness is a stock feature of the *servus currens*. Moreover, *festinare* can denote mental disturbance (cf Plaut *Cas* 432; *TLL* 6,1 617,72ff). It is worth noting too that the final part of the Donatus scholion on line 323 (a later addition?) reads *'festinas' autem perturbaris et commotus es* and seems to be based on the reading *animum*, although the second scholion on 324 presupposes *animam*. If the pA reading is an error, however, its significance may not be great. The corruption could have occurred independently in the two manuscripts or the two forms, *animum* and *animam*, may have been variants at an early stage in the tradition.

The remaining seven examples will be discussed individually, since they are of more significance than those that have been mentioned.

Eun 422: *tu Pamphilam* gives an unmetrical line and *tu* must be an interpolation. It is not, however, an obvious or expected one. Possibly its presence arose from a purely graphical error. Line 440 ends in *tu Pamphilam* and the scribe's eye may have jumped to this verse. It is more probable, I think, that originally it was a gloss, *Pamphilam cantatum provocemus* being regarded as a direct quotation, balancing the protasis *siquando illa dicet 'Phaedriam / intro mittamus comissatum.'* The pronoun *tu* was added to make this clear and to balance *illa*.

Haut 518: *sed* of pA is required if *miror* of the Bembinus is preferred to *demiror* of all the Calliopians. While the latter often offer a compound for the simple verb (see pp 91-2), they are not always wrong in this respect. At *Ad* 510 *evomam* is required against *vomam* of the Bembinus. Moreover, it would not be untypical of the scribe of the Bembinus to write *temiror* for *tedemiror*: cf *potis* at *Ad* 774 for *potastis* or *potatis; estumes* for *existumes* at *Eun* 758; *insti* for *institi* at *Ph* 604. The decisive point, however, is the presence of *sed* in only A and p. This looks very much like an intrusive gloss. Such interpolations are frequently found in all or some of the Calliopian MSS: cf *Eun* 545, 1089; *An* 11(?), 204(?); *Ad* 264. Connective particles are less commonly interpolated in the Bembinus but examples do occur: so *nam* at *Hec* 161. With Umpfenbach and Kauer[23] I prefer *te demiror* and regard *sed te* in pA as a common error. Most editors have read *sed te miror*.

Haut 848: I apply the same principle to this example as I did to the preceding one. It is more likely that *est* has been interpolated in pA than that *est* has been omitted in the other MSS, though one may contrast the presence (correct) of *esse* in p at *Eun* 132, where it has been lost in the other MSS. At *Haut* 848 editors are divided in their choice.

Haut 928: the omission of *malo* in pA, not recorded for the Bembinus in the OCT, could easily have occurred independently after *multo*. The situation is complicated by the presence of *potius* in the Bembinus (not in p, as Marouzeau states). Some editors have read *potius malo* but it is then more difficult to explain the appearance of *multo* in all

MSS. I prefer *multo malo* with Kauer-Lindsay and Marouzeau. *potius* is then an intrusive gloss, resulting perhaps from the feeling that *immo abeat potius multo* was equivalent to *immo abeat multo malo*. The omission of *malo* in the Bembinus is therefore probably connected with the presence of *potius*. This cannot be the case in p, where I think that *malo* has been lost through a purely graphical error. Since the reading of p does not make sense, it is hardly likely that contact with the Bembinus class has prompted the omission. If p offered *potius multo* with the Bembinus, the common error would have significance.

Haut 1006: the omission of *oh* in pA looks like the best evidence for some contact between p and the Bembinus class. The reading of pA gives a trochaic septenarius after iambics at 1003-5 and before an iambic sequence at 1007-12. Yet the intrusion of a trochaic line in such a sequence is not unknown in Terence. A similar sequence occurs at *An* 175ff:

DA. mirabar hoc si sic abiret et eri semper lenitas
verebar quorsum evaderet.
qui postquam audierat non datum iri filio uxorem suo,
numquam quoiquam nostrum verbum fecit neque id aegre tulit.
SI. at nunc faciet neque, ut opinor, sine tuo magno malo.
DA. id voluit nos sic necopinantes duci falso gaudio

The change from iambics in *An* 175-7 to two trochaics in *An* 178-9 is not motivated by any striking change in tone, as one might explain the change of metre at *Haut* 1006. Other examples of the intrusion of a trochaic line in a series of iambics are not lacking; cf *An* 864, *Eun* 298, *Haut* 187 (and possibly *Eun* 376, though here a change from *dixti* to *dixisti* would give an iambic verse). One may note too how in this scene of *Haut* the metre changes to trochaics at lines 1013-16 and reverts to iambics at 1017-19. There is no reason to reject the reading of pA on metrical grounds. The choice lies between supposing that *oh* has been omitted in pA or added in the other MSS. Since interjections are frequently added in the Calliopian MSS (see above pp 82, 104), pA may well be correct here.

Hec 787: although the sequence *i atque* could readily have led to the corruption *itaque* in several MSS, the reading of p (*i itaque atque*) seems to have resulted from the incorporation into the text of a gloss recording a variant reading. Since the Bembinus offers *itaque* for *i atque* offered by the others, the similarity of p and A looks significant despite the possibility of independent error. Editors differ in how they print the line. Umpfenbach, Dziatzko, and Fleckeisen follow Brix in deleting *atque* and reading *i exple*. Another possibility is to delete *i* and read *ita; atque exple*; for *ita* = yes cf *Ad* 287, 521; *Eun* 697.[24]

Ad 877: the Calliopian text scans and is probably correct. Therefore, *porro* in pA must be an intrusive gloss, motivated perhaps by recollection of *Ad* 631 (*nunc porro, Aeschine, expergiscere*) or *Hec* 778 (*porro hanc nunc experiamur*). K. Sydow conjectured *age nunc experiamur porro contra* (not as reported in the OCT) but this seems to be too far from the paradosis to be convincing.

From the initial list of errors common to p and A six survive which provide the best evidence for some contact between p and the Bembinus tradition. These are *Eun* 442 *tu Pamphilam; Haut* 518 *sed te; Haut* 848 *quid est; Hec* 787 *itaque; Ad* 324 *animam; Ad* 877 *experiamur porro contra*. The paucity of these examples and their nature do not strongly support a belief in close or extensive contact between the p tradition and a MS belonging to the Bembinus class. All six errors have occurred through the intrusion into the text of explanatory glosses or of variants. One would have liked to find a larger number of common errors of a varied kind – omission and peculiar word order – which could not have occurred independently and which were definitely wrong. The interpolated nature of A and of Σ clearly bears witness to the existence of many MSS in late antiquity which were equipped with interlinear and marginal glosses. It may simply be an accident that with one exception (P at *Haut* 518) none of the major Calliopian MSS contains these five glosses which have crept into the text of A and p. Yet the cumulative effect of the errors which are peculiar to p and A cannot be discounted. Some of these may be trivial and more may be thought to have occurred independently, but the fact that p alone of the Calliopian MSS shares this number of errors with the Bembinus points to some contact with a MS belonging to the branch of which the Bembinus is a member.

What would be the nature and extent of such a contact? It has been recognized that p or an ancestor was contaminated by a γ MS. Such a contact explained the errors shared by γp. If it is allowed that approximately 60 per cent of the γ readings taken into the p tradition at this time were correct readings, then against the 32 γp errors it may be assumed that 48 correct γp readings also emanated from this source. Of the total of 168 γp readings this would leave 88 which may have come from the same source as the pA readings. Now the number of good readings unique to p or shared by p and A is 64 (in the list on pp 107ff) and the number of possible errors shared by p and A comes to 20. Some of the errors unique to p will also have come from this contaminating MS. How many is pure guesswork. It is not perhaps unreasonable to calculate them as 20, equal in number to the possible errors shared by p and A. Thus the total number of readings which may have originated in a non-Calliopian MS comes to 192 (88 + 64 + 20 + 20). Of these, 37 were errors (17 shared by p and A and the hypothetical 20 errors unique to p). The result is that 81 per cent of the readings which entered the p tradition from this alien source are correct readings. When the possible influence of the γ tradition was discussed, the conclusion was that no scribe would have been well enough equipped linguistically and metrically to choose good readings approximately four times out of five. Obviously, the less corrupt a MS is, the more probable it is that anyone using it to correct another MS will introduce good readings. One is forced to conclude that if a contaminating source provided a large number of p's good readings, it must have been a MS of very high quality indeed – certainly one that was superior to the Bembinus.

Since only one MS of Terence (apart from a few fragments) has survived from antiquity, we are dependent for much of our knowledge of the state of the text at that period on citations in grammarians and commentators. Here too Donatus can be of assistance. In the third chapter we have looked at wrong Calliopian readings upon which certain scholia in the commentary were based and noted numerous scholia which were written for a text which was different from the Bembinus where it was in error. The authenticity of the scholia which attest these readings is less vital here. If some of the scholia originated some time after Donatus, they simply attest readings which were in existence even later than the Bembinus.

The commentary attests some readings which have been lost in all surviving MSS. Thus in *Adelphoe*, for example, there is evidence for *nihili* (167), *occeperis* (206), *pote* (264), *ellam* (389), *ubi vidi* (618), and *potastis* (774). More frequently, however, there are scholia based on the correct text against errors in the Bembinus. A sample of these is given:

Eun 384 despicatam] despectam *A*: Donatus: HABENT DESPICATAM contemptam ac despectam ... vel certe alterius verbi declinatio ab eo quod est conspicor despicor.

Eun 397 maxumas] maxumas gratias *A*: Donatus: subauditur 'gratias' ab eo quod supra dixit 'magnas vero agere gratias Thais mihi.'

Eun 626 tendere] intendere *A*: Donatus: proprie dixit 'tendere' quod significat pertinacem contentionem. Vergilius 'vasto certamine tendunt.'

Eun 805 scibis] scies *A*: Donatus: SCIBIS et 'scies' et 'scibis' dicitur per productionem tertiae coniugationis.

Eun 821 rem quid] rem aut quid *A*: Donatus: haec ἀσύνδετα instantis dominae vultum habitumque demonstrant.

Examples like these can be given for all the plays where the Bembinus is a witness. These examples confirm what one would suspect – that in the time of Donatus and probably later there were in currency MSS which were free of many of the errors which appear in the Bembinus. The large number of good readings in p could be explained if such a MS were their source.

This, however, is only one explanation of p's high quality. Another is that many of the good p readings were inherited from Δ and that the influence of the non-Calliopian MS was quite slight. This latter hypothesis seems the more attractive one, since to believe that approximately 150 good readings and an unknown number of errors entered the p tradition from a single alien source means accepting, first, that a non-Calliopian MS of high quality was available, and, secondly, that the correcting process was extensive, yet selective – extensive in the number of changes that were made, selective in that many of the errors of Σ and Δ were not removed. This selectivity brings us back to the striking success rate (81 per cent) in the alterations that were made. It is difficult to accept that the corrector changed the text for the better four times out of every five at the same time that he left untouched many errors from which the non-Calliopian MS must have been free.

In summary the investigation has shown that the p tradition has been contaminated from a γ source and a non-Calliopian MS but that the number of readings derived from these sources is fairly insignificant compared with the number of good readings which were inherited by p from Δ. It seems impossible to decide in individual cases where these good readings came from. These conclusions are more in line with Lindsay's evaluation of p than Marouzeau's, though neither of the extreme views of these scholars is altogether correct. What has emerged is that any reading of p which has *prima facie* claims to being correct deserves careful consideration, since its source may be Δ or a non-Calliopian MS. It follows that such readings of p should be recorded as fully as possible in any edition of Terence. The OCT of Kauer-Lindsay ought to be the model in this respect rather than the Budé of Marouzeau.

The non-uniqueness of p and some other δ MSS

One factor which has given superficial plausibility to Marouzeau's view that p's good readings were not inherited from Δ but resulted from horizontal influences was the uniqueness of p's good readings among the Calliopian MSS. Given the very large number of medieval MSS, it seems strange that p alone of these should offer so many readings that are worthy of adoption. It is dangerous, however, to talk of uniqueness in this case, because so many of the Terence MSS have not been fully collated. The rest of this chapter will be devoted to consideration of four MSS which are members of the δ group for at least part of their text. First, it will become clear that p's uniqueness is diminished. Secondly, an attempt will be made to construct a stemma for the δ MSS for *Eunuchus*. It has already been pointed out how difficult, if not impossible, it is to construct a stemma for the four major δ MSS, D, G, L, and p. Naturally, the fewer MSS one works with, the more unrefined is the stemma. For example, two MSS X and Y may be thought to be copies of the same exemplar. Let us suppose that two other MSS are found (W and Z) which are neither ancestors nor descendants of X or Y. W often agrees in error with X against Y, while Z shares errors with Y against X. Hyparchetypes for W and X on the one hand and Z and Y on the other have to be postulated. The relationship between X and Y is therefore shown to be less close than it originally seemed. Similarly, it is hoped that the addition of four MSS to the δ group may help to clarify the relationship between p and DGL.[25]

The purpose of a stemma is to enable an editor to reconstruct mechanically the readings of hyparchetypes and thus of the archetype itself. But this is possible only where a tradition is closed. In traditions like that of the Terence MSS, however, where contamination is widespread, such mechanical procedures are often impossible. Even when it is clear that several MSS are closely related, the exact relationships of these MSS to each other often cannot be precisely established. Thus certainty about the readings of hyparchetypes is not always attainable.

One may well ask why one should take the trouble to attempt a stemma in these circumstances. One reason has already been given: examination of the eight MSS may elucidate the relationship between p and DGL. A second reason is more general; it will be shown that the δ tradition is more complex and has more members than has generally been thought. Thirdly, detailed knowledge of these four additional MSS may make it possible to link other MSS with the δ group. Finally, and again generally, the attempt may demonstrate some ways of grappling with a highly contaminated group of MSS.

The four additional MSS are P^c (Paris, BN lat 7900A, s ix/x), P^b (Paris, BN lat 9345, s xi), N (Leyden, Voss Q 38, s x), and V^b (Vienna, Nationalbibl Pal 85, s xi).[26] These four MSS have the plays in the γ order with the exception of V^b, in which the last three plays must have appeared in the order *Ad – Ph – Hec*, although the MS now breaks off at *Ph* 967. If these MSS present the plays in the γ order against the 'alphabetic' order in DGLp, how does one know that they are related to the δ MSS? Their text presents a mixture of γ and δ readings but such a blend could have arisen if they were descended from Γ and had been contaminated by the δ MSS. The significant feature of these MSS is that for considerable portions of their text they share numerous errors in the verse division with DGL (p is written as prose) against the correct verse division in the γ branch. This is conclusive evidence that these MSS belong to the δ tradition and thus ultimately descend from Δ. The details of the verse division have been given in *TAPA* 105 (1975) 123-53, to which the reader is referred. The evidence for *Eunuchus* appears on pp 129ff of that article.

These four MSS have been contaminated by the adoption into their text of variants found in other MSS. Some of these variants came from MSS in the δ tradition, others came from γ MSS. But they are contaminated in a different way as well. For sections of their text the primary exemplar has changed. N, for example, was copied from a γ exemplar for *Phormio*, *Hecyra*, and *Adelphoe*. The exemplar for most of the text of the other three plays was a δ MS. This is shown by examination of the verse division and by the text itself. The situation, however, is more complicated than that. In one section of *Eunuchus* the exemplar has changed from a δ to a γ MS. I have previously isolated this section as approximately lines 668-839.[27] On further examination of the text I would now move the place of transition from 668 to 605 or thereabouts. A change of exemplars has also occurred in P^b, P^c, and V^b. Most of the text of P^b has been drawn from a δ exemplar but the end of *Phormio* (from 765ff) derives from a γ source. Many common errors in the verse division show that P^c and V^b are drawn from a hyparchetype within the δ tradition for *Andria, Eunuchus, Hauton timorumenos,* and *Adelphoe*. But this hyparchetype itself changed models halfway through *Hauton timorumenos,* abandoning a δ exemplar for a γ one. Moreover, for *Phormio* and *Hecyra* P^c is descended from a γ MS and is related to F and v, as the text and verse division show. Even where the sources of the MSS remain within the δ tradition, the relationships among them may vary in different parts of the corpus. In *Adelphoe* P^b appears to go back to an earlier point of the δ tradition than $DGLP^cV^b$. But in *Eunuchus,* as will be seen, P^b is more closely related to DGL than are P^cV^b. Thus a stemma established for one section of the text will not necessarily be valid for other sections.

Before the stemma for *Eunuchus* is attempted, I give a list of those readings of p which also appear in at least one of $NP^bP^cV^b$. The variations in the affiliation of these MSS should be kept in mind when the lists are examined. I begin by recording the good or possibly good readings of p.

An 344 o *om N*
An 398 aliam *N*
An 661 me ducturum *N*
An 671 nisi si V^b
An 852 dixti NP^b
An 974 conloquar *N*

Eun 98 exclusti P^c: *-sisti* V^b
Eun 115 audisse P^cV^b
Eun 157 dicta est P^c
Eun 164 in te claudier N^2: in me claudier V^b
Eun 240 sit NV^b
Eun 255 adventamus NP^cV^b
Eun 349 ago equidem NV^b
Eun 748 educta ita *N*: ed. illa V^b
Eun 810 idem hoc tu $P^bP^cV^b$
Eun 1043 tu *N*

Haut 842 nunc me NP^b

Ph 235 an V^b
Ph 776 eius huc V^b
Ph 415 turpiter civis V^b
Ph 952 haec hic P^c

Ad 283 tum V^b

To these one may add *An* 854 *audies* ENV^b; *Haut* 81 *est usus homini* EV^b; *Haut* 83 *ei mihi* EηN; *Ph* 108 *in* EV^b; *Eun* 1035 *scis me* NE. As one would suspect, agreement between p and one or more of these MSS is not confined to good readings. Indeed the number of common errors is greater:

An 435 atque V^b
An 436 hoc *om* V^b
An 530 haud dubium id mihi est NV^b

An 553 fabula est *N*
An 605 video ipsum V^{b}
An 616 eho tu *N*
An 679 aut $P^{b}P^{c}$
An 932 tum *om* *N*
An 680 tute melius V^{b}
An 953 iam *om* P^{c}
An 686 te mihi *N*
An 954 magis aliud habet P^{c}
An 698 quam *N*
An 704 immo *N*
An 813 ac *N*
An 885 verum in te *N*
An 910 hic *om* NV^{b}
An 914 subsistat *N*: subsistet $P^{c}V^{b}$
An 928 ibi *om* NV^{b}

Eun 16 cesset V^{b}
Eun 96 quod V^{b}
Eun 104 si *N*
Eun 150 fiat *om* P^{b1}
Eun 260 me esse in tanto honore $NP^{c}V^{b}$
Eun 265 faciat $NP^{c}V^{b}$
Eun 286 tu $NP^{c}V^{b}$
Eun 298 amore hic loquitur *N*
Eun 299 amare occeperit *N*
Eun 309 utilitatem in ea re V^{b}
Eun 363 vis me aliud $NP^{c}V^{b}$
Eun 571 tacitus sis citius $P^{b}P^{c}$
Eun 596 nos *om* P^{c}
Eun 969 si sapis N^{1} (*ante rasuram*)
Eun 970 omnem rem ordine *N*
Eun 986 ille iam quid *EN*
Eun 1008 sum iam *EN*
Eun 1014 patri insuper etiam *EN*
Eun 1071 id non facere *EN*

Haut 108 quid NP^{b}
Haut 176 tibi ego hic adfuturam *N*
Haut 310 illaec NP^{b}
Haut 378 non sino *N*
Haut 388 res est $NP^{b}P^{c}V^{b}$
Haut 505 eo hoc fit NP^{b}
Haut 518 sed te NP^{b}
Haut 758 quis homo est *N*
Haut 759 nescioquid iam *N*
Haut 855 comparent *N*
Haut 968 te *om* P^{c1}

Ph 141 mitte V^{b}
Ph 177 ego *om* V^{b}
Ph 197 potes uno verbo V^{b}
Ph 249 molendum mihi esse in V^{b}
Ph 429 se habent V^{b}
Ph 461 de hac re dederit V^{b}
Ph 553 potes opis V^{b}
Ph 721 idoneum illum V^{b}
Ph 743 te semper V^{b}

Hec 164 ut P^{b}
Hec 547 ei cui P^{b}
Hec 574 de P^{b}
Hec 603 rem incommodam P^{b}
Hec 738 curo P^{b}

Ad 548 sese $P^{c}V^{b}$
Ad 551 ego *om* $P^{c}V^{b}$
Ad 876 gaudio(?) V^{b}
Ad 880 posthec non posteriores feram V^{b}

The uniqueness of p's text is considerably diminished by the evidence of these two lists. Since $NP^{b}P^{c}V^{b}$ must derive from Δ for parts of their text, all these shared readings are hardly to be imputed to contamination. Some of them were probably inherited by $NP^bP^cV^b$ from the same source as p. But what is that source? To find out it is necessary to attempt to construct a stemma.

A stemma of the δ MSS

The *Eunuchus* has been chosen for this attempt to construct a stemma, since all eight MSS are drawn from the same hyparchetype for this play, the exception being only lines 605-839 in N, as mentioned above. N also lacks the text from line 384 (*despicatam*) to line 470 (*exire*), while 848-1021 have been lost in G. The simplest procedure is to list first of all the conjunctive errors and see what emerges. Since there has been some contamination among the MSS, some of these errors may also occur occasionally in another MS. This has been recorded in brackets after the reading. The minus sign has been used to indicate that a MS does not share in a reading.

Errors of DGLNp$P^bP^cV^b$

302 omnes senem perdant
387 factum merito
451 at
490 adsentari huic animum
501 forte huc Chremes
520 se posse a
536 malam in rem
568 occepi
628 potuerit (-*N*)
639 potest (-*NV^b*)
643 illum ego (-*N*)
654 dederat dono (dono *om N*)
663 siet (-*N*)
673 adornabat (-*N*)
688 vetus vietus (-*N*)
694 hoc nunc mihi (-*N*)
727 mihi verba (-*N*)
769 haec animo
770 ipsi opus est patrono
783 iam hoc (-*N*) (tamen hoc *P^b*)
785 videtur (-*N*)
797 eam] illam (-*N*)
813 ubi tu velis (-*N*)
822 misera dicam (-*N*)
836 iube conprendi (-*N*)
837 illi
894 dum is venit
916 isti (-*V^b*)
926 omittam
952 huius
959 facinus facere audet
965 hoc ita putant (-*V^b*)
985 tunc
1005 autem hoc
1010 non potest satis
1021 stultum istum adulescentem (stultum *om V^b*)
1031 vivit hodie (vivit me hodie *G*)
1057 a me praemium (a me et praemium *G*)
1079 noctesque et dies
1088 accede ubi vis (accede Thais ubi vis *P^b*)
1089 ignorabant sed postquam

*Errors of DGLP*ᵇ

1-29 *post v* 30
7 conscribendo
14 frustetur (fraudetur *L*)
30 est (*prius*) *om*
68 expressit (-*G*)
115 audivisse (*N*)
144 eam ego (*P*ᶜ)
239 prae me contempsi (*P*ᶜ)
239 quid agis homo
240 siet (*P*ᶜ)
255 advenimus
260 me esse tanto honore
269 eludere (*P*ᶜ)
300 alterum illum (*P*ᶜ)
349 equidem ago (equidem ego *P*ᶜ)
364 deducant / -antur (-*G*)
434 ista
485 tibi *om*
515 omnia et ipsa
526 natu est
548 auscultare (-*L*)
599 omnes simul
740 effodiantur
743 hic *om*
766 te *om* (*p*)
777 portas
865 contumelia hac (*P*ᶜ)
958 vellem (*N*)
965 ne *om*
1004 ridiculum
1085 recipiamus

Errors of DGL

197 parum (*p*)
277 menses hos
371 ducam
646 a capillo
689 est *om*
711 quod] quid
740 atque
748 te illaque
749 dono tibi
756 apage sis *om*
785 vir nunc (*p*)
786 dare

*Errors of NpP*ᶜ*V*ᵇ

152 nil mihi respondes (*L*)
260 me esse in tanto honore
265 faciat
273 equidem (*L*) (-*P*ᶜ)
286 tu hic (*recte* ?)
332 prorsus (*P*ᵇ)
363 numquid vis me aliud
364 deducam (G)
498 quom *om* (*GP*ᵇ)
510 acc.(*vel* arc.) domum (*P*ᵇ)
593 in lectum (G)
601 aspecto (*P*ᵇ)
747 quid est sic est Chreme (-*P*ᶜ)
996 intro inrumpere

Errors of Np

104 si
210 posses

239 quid ais homo
291 et] quod
298 amore hic loquitur
299 amare occeperit
594 hinc] hic
764 mane mane
970 omnem rem ordine(m)
986 ille iam quid
987 in astum
1008 sum iam
1014 patri insuper etiam
1071 id non facere

Errors of P^cV^b

171 quid istuc
247 est *om*
298 fortunatum
349 quid sit
352 Thaidem et ei
360 vidisse illam
414 magis molestus mihi
440 nominavit
456 nos *om*
468 pulchra
468 dona credo
485 tibi tempus
516 dare sese
574 rogas ut viderem
613 possim porro
643 conqueram
692 rogo
693 annos] ad nos
703 credis satis
729 mens suum satis
746 istius modi
748 ita *om*
755 ad te] atque
781 hic *om*
805 THR. hem *om*
934 videtur nihil
1003 ad nos venit intro
1008 de te ridendo
1040 tota est Thais
1058 si efficio ut mihi hoc postulo
1069 credere ambos
1078 nemost] nemo potest

The evidence of these three lists can be translated into a stemma without any difficulty. The eight MSS are linked by a large number of common errors. They therefore descend from the same hyparchetype, as the stronger evidence of common errors in the verse division indicates. This hyparchetype we shall regard as Δ. The MSS then fall into two groups, each consisting of four MSS: $DGLP^b$ and NpP^cV^b. These groups can be further subdivided into DGL and P^b on the one hand and Np and P^cV^b on the other. The stemma is as shown in figure 6.

Evidence is available, however, which contradicts this stemma. There are instances where P^cV^b agree in error with $DGLP^b$ against the correct reading in Np and other instances where $P^bP^cV^b$ share errors against Np and DGL. Another piece of contradictory evidence is the verse division. In one section of the text (*Eun* 315-50) N has the same errors in the verse division as L and P^b where V^b has the correct division

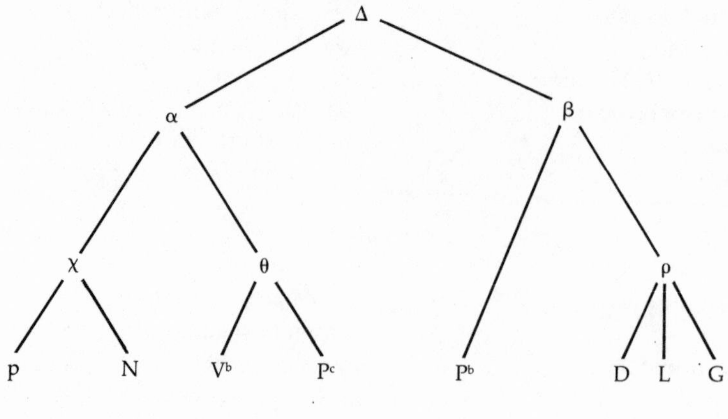

FIGURE 6

and P^c is in independent error. This suggests that N should belong to the DGLP^b branch.

Errors of DGL$P^bP^cV^b$

331 delirare
355 contra dono
377 potes
450 tu iratus
464 dona tibi adsunt
469 exire foras
503 deducito
521 in die (die in *P^b*)
532 insidias mihi
563 nempe ut opinor (*Np^2*)
676 est obsecro homo
731 tu multum pol hilarior quidem
811 haec iam (haec tibi iam *L*)
881 ita] tam (*N*)
883 isto Chaerea (istoc Chaerea *P^b*)
954 rescivit esse factum
966 ortum esse
986 ille quid iam
999 male (e)venturum
1043 tu *om*
1052 hui (*-D*)

Errors of $P^bP^cV^b$

216 au memini
418 quid nisi
454 visa sum modo vocem
650 quid istuc est
689 est haec
722 scias (*N*)
727 vicit me vinum
728 ac
772 sequimini me
786 quid tibi videtur
793 te *om*
826 nos aut quam (*N*)

873 et ex malo
893 ipse hic aderis
929 sumptu sine
967 ah ecce
1060 futuram
1083 nisi
1085 volvo
1093 ego vobis in hoc
1093 eloquentiam (*N*)

These two lists point to a stemma in which an ancestor of P^cV^b is descended from the same hyparchetype as P^b. If this were the case, the errors and correct readings shared by P^cV^b and Np against $DGLP^b$ must have arisen through contamination of the hyparchetype of P^cV^b by the Np tradition. Such conflicting evidence is typical of a contaminated tradition and it is problematical to decide which of the two stemmata is correct. This problem will be laid aside for the moment and the difficulty posed by the verse division with respect to the position of N in the stemma will be discussed first, since some of the features that arise from this problem are relevant to the connection between P^b and P^cV^b.

At *Eun* 315-50 LNP^b have the same errors in the verse division against the correct division in V^b and different errors in P^c. In an earlier publication it has been stated that there is no reason to think that V^b changed exemplars for this section of the text.[28] Consequently, the hyparchetype of P^cV^b also had the correct division in lines 315-50 and therefore went back to an earlier point in the δ tradition than the common ancestor of L, N, or P^b. This obviously contradicts the stemma on p 126 with respect to the position of N. Further investigation, however, shows that this view should be modified.

From line 353 to the end of the play P^c and V^b share a large number of distinctive errors in the verse division. There can be no doubt that they are drawn from the same hyparchetype. Up to 353, however, the division does not provide any evidence to prove that their relationship in the first third of the play is the same as that in the remainder. In V^b the verse division is substantially correct until 353. In P^c too the division is good until 301 where errors begin. It seems, therefore, that for 1-352 only the text itself has to be relied upon and, as has been said, the text of V^b in this section shows no apparent signs of a change in affiliation. Fortunately another MS can be of assistance. This is a MS in The Hague (Koninklijke Bibl 72 J 49, s xiii) which shares many of the distinctive errors of P^cV^b in the verse division in *Eunuchus* as well as elsewhere. In its text for the first third of the play, however, this MS (H) appears to be more closely related to V^b than to P^c.

Agreements of HV^b against P^c

28 quo] qui HV^b
77 quam *om* HV^b
77 quas *om* P^c
123 quoque *om* HV^b
164 claudier] interclaudier P^c
179 ego non] egone HV^b
187 me macerabo biduom] macerabo biduom me HV^b
205 venturum ad] venturum se ad HV^b
222 nimis mihi indulgeo] mihi indulgeo nimis HV^b
227 ineptus magis] ineptus nec magis HV^b
238 noti me] me noti P^c
239 contempsi prae me] prae me contempsi P^c
240 siet] sit HV^b
254 prorsum] prorsus HV^b
268 hic *om* P^c
269 ludere HV^b: eludere P^c
273 quidem] equidem HV^b
287 ad istam] ad istanc HV^b
289 advenire] adventare P^c
300 illum alterum] alterum illum P^c
303 illum flocci] illum non flocci HV^b: non illum flocci P^c
308 te] tute HV^b
309 in ea re utilitatem] utilitatem in ea re HV^b
316 tam] tamen P^c
350 vidi novi] vidi et novi HV^b

Readings of HP^c against V^b

7 easdem scribendo] eas describendo HP^c
41 dictum sit] sit dictum HP^c
69 dabis ultro] dabis ei ultro HP^c
89 quia vero] vero quia HP^c
98 hunc exclusti HP^c: excl. hunc V^b
150 id (*alterum*) *om* HP^c
157 dicta est] est dicta V^b
214 quod] quoad HP^c
316 bona est] est bona HP^c
341 dicit] loquitur HP^c
345 huc cum] cum huc *H*: cum adhuc P^c
349 ago equidem] equidem ego P^c: isthaecquidem ego *H*

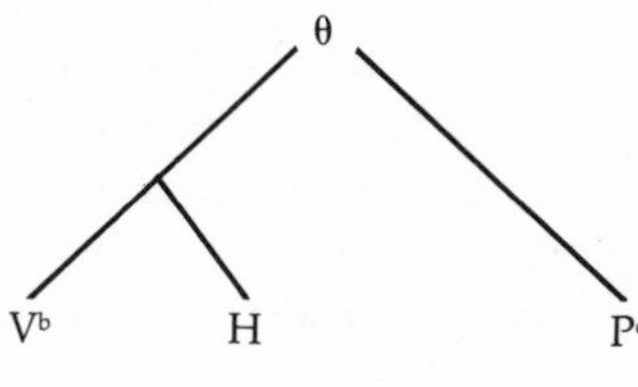

FIGURE 7

While it is not impossible that H is actually more closely related to Pc than to Vb and that the preponderance of HVb readings is to be explained by contamination of H from Vb or a related MS, it is more probable that H and Vb go back to a hyparchetype descended from θ. Additional support for the textual evidence is the presence of two errors in the verse division shared by H and Vb in the early part of the play. In HVb line 281 begins with *tum* where Pc is correct (though it errs in 280 – *Laudo / detineo* – and 282 – *Admittar / ad*). Line 212 ends at *effectum* in HVb and at *minime* in Pc. The evidence of the text and of the line division point to the stemma in figure 7. *At 312-50, however, H and Pc share many errors in the verse division*. These errors presumably also appeared in θ. How then does Vb have the correct verse division in this section of the text? What probably happened was that in an exemplar of Vb the errors in the verse division at 301ff, inherited from θ, were noticed and the correct division was indicated by marks in the text.[29] The scribe of Vb or of an exemplar followed the verse division as indicated by these marks until 353 where the marks either ceased or were no longer observed. My conclusion is that the correct division in Vb for this section against common errors in LNPb was not inherited from Δ but was derived from a secondary source. Thus the errors in verse division which N shares with L and Pb do not mean that N must derive from β or ρ.[30]

Before an explanation for the common errors in PbPcVb and DGLPbPcVb is given, comparison of Vb and Pc will show to what extent one or both of these MSS have suffered contamination. These MSS share a large number of errors in the verse division that are not found in DGLNPb. One would expect them to be very similar in their text. The list of common textual errors (above p 125) is indeed impressive, but comparison of the two MSS with H for the first 350 lines of *Eunuchus* has also shown 37 points of difference. Yet the extent of disagreement between Vb and Pc is not significantly higher in the first third of the play than it is for the rest of the play. In the following list of readings where V^b and P^c differ, readings which appear to be errors peculiar to V^b or to P^c (or to the θ branch if H is included) are not noted, since the purpose of the list is not to determine which of the two MSS makes fewer errors but rather to discover what, if any, affiliations with other groups of MSS are indicated by the text. In this list if a reading is not followed by any manuscript symbols, all other MSS offer this reading.

Differences between V^b and P^c in Eunuchus

7 easdem scribendo $V^bpA\gamma$: eas descr. P^cN: eas conscr. $DGLP^b$
16 cesset V^bp^1: desinet $P^cGNP^bE^1v^1$: desinat
41 dictum sit V^bNAEv: sit dictum
70 ultro V^bA: ei ultro
98 excl. hunc $V^bNA\gamma$: hunc excl.
144 ego eam $V^bNpA\gamma$: eam ego
157 dicta est P^cpA: est dicta
164 claudier V^bpAG(?): interclaudier / -cludier
174 uti V^bNp: ut
211 carius est P^cN: est carius
239 contempsi prae me $V^bNpA\gamma$: prae me contempsi
240 sit V^bNpA: siet
268 hic V^bA: *om cett*
269 ludere $V^bNp^1C^1A$: eludere
273 equidem V^bNpLA: quidem
289 advenire $V^bA\gamma$: adventare
300 illum alterum $V^bNpA\gamma$: alterum illum
309 utilitatem in ea re V^bp: in ea re utilitatem
316 tamen P^cNP^b: tam
316 bona est $V^bA\gamma$: est bona
324 quemquam hominem esse $V^b\varepsilon$: quemquam esse ego hominem P^cDGLNP^b: ego quemquam hominem esse CPv: quemquam ego esse hominem pA: quemquam esse hominem E
341 dicit $V^bD^1Lp^1A$: loquitur
345 huc cum $V^bpA\gamma$: cum adhuc P^c: cum huc
349 ago equidem V^bpA: equidem ego P^c: equidem ago
356 illum $P^cD^1P^bC^1pv$: illumne
386 pati $P^cP^{b2}p^2G^2L^2$: patri
425 homo inquam $V^b\gamma$: inquam P^c: inquam homini A: inquam homo
474 agis $P^cP^{b1}DG^1v$: ais

494 istam $P^cDN\gamma$: istanc
571 tacitus sis citius $P^cP^bp^2$: tacitus citius
573 tantum $V^bp^2DL^1P^{b1}$: tandem
581 circa V^bGLpP^bE: circum
591 ego homuncio hoc $V^bNGA\gamma$: ego hoc homuncio
594 exspectans $V^bNGA\gamma$: spectans
595 sic $V^bNA\gamma$: si G: *om cett*
611 a rure $V^bNLP^{b2}E\eta$: rure
639 licet $V^bNp^2A\gamma$: potest
715 i $V^bp^1\gamma$: in A: *om cett*
725 tum $V^bNA\gamma$: tunc
729 resurrexi P^cP^b: surrexi
730 Chreme $V^bNpAC^2P^2EF$: Chremes
747 quid est sic est Chreme $V^bNpG^2P^{b2}$: quid est
814 ita *om* $P^cN\gamma$: ita
819 num P^cP^b: non
833 illic $P^cp^1P^2D^2G^2EFv$: illuc
837 faciam $P^cNP^bD^2p^2\gamma$: facias
865 hac contumelia $V^bNpA\gamma$: contumelia hac
909 Chremen V^bNA: Chremetem P^cP^b: Chremem
916 illi $V^bp^2A\gamma$(*praeter E*): isti *cett*
926 et *om* P^cP^b
933 cognoverit P^cDLP^bE: cognovit v: cognorit
952 eius $V^bAD^2\gamma$(*praeter E*): huius
965 hoc putant $V^bAD^2\gamma$: hoc ita putant
1000 iam diu $V^bNpA\gamma$: diu iam *cett*
1056 feceris V^bP^bA: efferis G: effeceris

Most of the variants found in V^b and P^c appear in other MSS or classes of MSS. Horizontal influence must therefore be the reason for most of the differences between the two MSS. But have both been contaminated to the same degree or is one more pure than the other? When these 55 examples are examined, it will be seen that V^b is in error on eleven occasions: 16, 157, 273, 309, 324, 425, 573, 581, 611, 747, and 909. P^c, however, is correct on only nine occasions – those lines just mentioned, with the exception of 324 and 909 where P^c has an error different from that in V^b. If 174 is included (since *uti* of V^bNP may be correct against *ut* of all other MSS), the proportion of good readings appearing in V^b is 44 of of 55 (80 per cent), the proportion in P^c being 9 out of 55 (16.5 per cent).

The performance of V^b is comparable to that of p when the γp readings were examined and it emerged that over 80 per cent of these readings were good ones. The same argument may be applied to V^b that was applied to p then. The very high proportion of good readings in V^b where it differs in this list from P^c indicates that most of these were *inherited* by V^b and not acquired horizontally. It is P^c, therefore, which has been the more extensively contaminated. Two additional factors support this view. First of all, many of the V^b readings in the above list are shared with N or p or with both, MSS to which V^b is related on the basis of other evidence. Secondly, it will be noted that where V^b and P^c differ, P^c almost always agrees with P^b. Particularly noteworthy are those instances where P^c and P^b stand together alone in error: 571 *tacitus sis citius* (with p²); 729 *resurrexi;* 819 *num;* 909 *cremetem;* 926 omission of *et*. A major reason then for the difference between V^b and P^c is that P^c has suffered contamination from the P^b tradition, contamination of which V^b is free. Most of the V^b readings in the above list were probably inherited from θ.

What of the errors shared by P^bP^cV^b and by DGLP^bP^cV^b? The most economical explanation is that θ itself was contaminated by a MS which was descended from β and which was an antecedent of P^b. This would explain the presence in θ of errors common to DGLP^b and of errors found in P^b alone of these four MSS.

The lines of extensive contamination in the stemma run from the β branch to θ and from P^b to P^c. But almost certainly none of the eight MSS is totally free of some contamination. N and θ share readings found in some γ MSS: 14 *fraudetur;* 44 *operam et cum;* 51 *perficies;* 588 *et per;* 595 *flabellum et ventulum;* 634 *vero me;* 663 *scias;* 722 *scias;* 750 *Thais a me ita;* 1093 *eloquentiam*. It is possible that these readings also appeared in the p tradition but were corrected in p. It is equally possible that the readings were acquired independently by N and θ from γ MSS. Sporadic contact may be shown by cases of agreement between N and P^c (7 *eas describendo;* 16 *desinet;* 47 *accessor;* 211 *carius est;* 358 *istum;* 494 *istam* – with γD²; 593 *conlocant* – with γP^b; 976 *a rure*) and NV^b agreements (41 *dictum sit;* 103 *abstringo* – with G; 105 *sum rimarum*). Likewise p shares a few readings with P^c and V^b, but these are not numerous and are not of great significance. There seems to have been more contact between p and the DGL branch of the tradition: 52 *potueris* (G); 197 *parum* (DGL); 489 *ego te* (L); 570 *eam erat submonuit* (DGLN); 719 *ubi ei referam* (DGP^b); 800 *habeant* (DL); 835 omission of *is* (DG); 1033 *congruerunt* (DLN); 1069 *volim* (DL).

It is time to summarize what the stemma tells us about the δ MSS and how they should be used by editors. The study of p alone in the earlier part of the chapter has resulted in the conclusion that many of its so-called γ readings are actually inherited readings rather than corrections from γ MSS. In terms of the stemma these readings must have appeared in Δ. The stemma is based on conjunctive errors. What of the good γ readings that are in p? Do they appear in NP^cV^b as well? When the 45 good γp readings in *Eunuchus* are considered, we find that all but six of them also appear either in both N and θ (26) or in N alone (11) or in θ alone (2). Four of the six that are not found occur in the section of the text which has been lost in N (383-470) and it is possible that they may have been present in N. These facts confirm the conclusion that many good γp readings were in Δ. It follows from this that in the δ tradition a major point of corruption was β where many good readings which have survived in the α branch were lost. It also follows that many so-called γ readings were also the readings of Δ.

Of the nine γp errors in *Eunuchus* (listed above p 103), only two are not found in N, P^c, or V^b. Most of them must therefore have appeared in α. It was probably α rather than Δ which was contaminated by a γ MS since the γp errors do not appear in DGL. Some of the good γ readings may have entered the α tradition at this point also.

The most difficult point to resolve concerns the number of good readings of p which were thought to be unique to that MS among the Calliopians. It has been shown that some of these also appear in members of the α branch of the tradition (ten of the twenty-two in *Eunuchus*). When it is remembered that θ was contaminated by β and that the individual MSS have also suffered contamination, I see no reason to doubt that most of the good p and pA readings were present in α. The problem is whether they originated in α or were already in Δ. If they were in Δ, the loss of these readings in β has to be explained by contamination of β from a γ MS. This is basically Lindsay's explanation. The alternative is to suppose that they first appeared in α, arising from contact with a non-Calliopian MS. The solution depends on how much weight is placed on errors shared by p and A. These are by no means overwhelming in number or in quality. Some contact at some point with a non-Calliopian MS, however, must have occurred. Some good readings will have entered the tradition at this point, probably in α, but the majority, I believe, were inherited from Δ.

In practical terms the impossibility of a definitive conclusion about the sources of all the good readings makes little difference to an editor. Of the four MSS descended from α, p has best preserved what was in α and Δ. Some of p's good readings have also survived in N, P^c, or V^b. Occasionally a good reading has been lost in p but has been preserved in one or more of the others. V^b offers *dabis ultro* at 69-70 and alone of the Calliopians has *hic homines* at 268. N alone offers *abi* at 221. Therefore p is worth reporting fully as the best representative of the α tradition but the other three MSS should be summoned as witnesses when they offer a potentially good reading.

It is apparent that certainty about every reading in Δ is impossible. The consensus of the eight MSS will naturally give us a fair number of the readings in the archetype. Of the two main branches the α-class will preserve the readings of Δ more faithfully than the β-class, which has suffered considerable corruption and which has been contaminated by γ MSS. Of the α-group the sub-branch χ will be more faithful to what was in α than θ, which has been contaminated by a MS of the β-class. None of the sub-branches, however, can be ignored.

It must be stressed that these conclusions pertain only to *Eunuchus*. They may also hold good for other sections of the text where N, P^b, P^c, and V^b are descended from Δ, but a fuller examination of these MSS is required for the other plays. One suspects that they will be of assistance at the beginning of *Andria* where D, L, and p lack sections of the text. In *Hecyra*, where for most of the play D and p have been the sole representatives of the δ branch, P^b may be valuable.

One final problem must be addressed, even if it cannot be solved – that of the order of plays in the eight MSS in the *Eunuchus* stemma. Of these DGLp exhibit the so-called δ order (*An – Ad – Eun – Ph – Haut – Hec*); in NP^bP^c the plays are in the γ order (*An – Eun – Haut – Ad – Hec – Ph*), as they are in the V^b-tradition, except that *Hec* and *Ph* are reversed (see above p 120). The simplest solution would be that the δ order originated in ρ, the hyparchetype of DGL, and that the same order in p resulted from contamination with the ρ branch. But since the γ order was by far the commonest sequence in the medieval MSS, it is not impossible that p, like ρ, retained the δ order which already existed in Δ and that the order of plays in $NP^bP^cV^b$ has resulted from the influence of the predominant γ order on these MSS or on antecedents of them. The problem, however, is more apparent than real, if we remember that the stemma worked out in this chapter applies only to *Eunuchus*. Some of these MSS have clearly a γ text for the other plays. Their antecedents may have had the γ order, which was retained even though for *Eunuchus* and other sections of the text an exemplar with the δ text and order was used. In a similar fashion L has the δ order of plays but is descended from a γ MS for most of *Hauton timorumenos* and all of *Hecyra*.

5

The Γ Branch of the Medieval Manuscripts

Lest the title of this chapter suggest a comprehensive study of the γ branch of the tradition, it should be made clear at the outset that such a study would take many years of uninterrupted examination and evaluation of hundreds of MSS, most of which are of no value for recovering the *ipsissima verba* of Terence. Moreover, since many of these MSS have a text which has been contaminated by other γ MSS and by MSS of the δ class, it is often impossible to establish relationships among them. This chapter has a less ambitious scope and will be devoted to a study of some of the purer γ MSS which are of most value to textual critics and editors. Even these show signs of some contamination, but this is not extensive enough to obscure the relationships among them.

The characteristics of the γ branch which have been recognized in the past are – apart from conjunctive errors in the text – (1) the order of plays (*An – Eun – Haut – Ad – Hec – Ph*), which is different from that in the Bembinus and in the leading members of the δ class, and (2) the presence in this branch alone of MSS which contain illustrations that go back to an ancient cycle of miniatures. It has been shown in the previous chapter that the order of plays is not itself decisive for establishing the class to which a MS belongs; several MSS with the γ order are derived at least in part from Δ, while L, in which the plays are in the δ order, has clearly a γ text for *Hecyra* and most of *Hauton timorumenos*. Nevertheless it seems to be true that most of the MSS with the γ order of plays are indeed descended from Γ, however much their text betrays intermingling with δ MSS. Most of these contaminated MSS are commonly termed 'mixed,' and as a class designated as the μ group. There is little reason, however, for supposing that any of these is derived from a hyparchetype that is not itself derived from Γ or Δ.[1]

The three purest and most important members of the tradition which have been used by modern editors were discussed in the second chapter in connection with the relationship between the original miniatures and the γ text. These are C, P, and F. C (Vatican, Vat lat 3868) was almost certainly written and illustrated at Corvey at some time between AD 822 and 856. These dates are based on the presence of the names Hrodgarius and Aldricus in lists of monks under the abbots Adelard (822-6) and Warinus (826-56). The scribe of C identifies himself as Hrodgarius and one of the artists of the MS was Aldericus.[2] Bischoff dates the MS to around 820 or 830 and rejects the view of Jones and Morey that the MS originated in Corbie.[3] P (Paris, BN lat 7899) is also of the ninth century. Jones and Morey (2.67) assign it a date 'not long after 820,' a date which is based to some extent on artistic considerations but also on their belief in the Corbie provenance of C. They believe that P was copied at Rheims from the same exemplar as C and that this exemplar probably left Corbie for Rheims after C was copied. Although the relationship between C and P is not as close as they suggest, the date may be close enough and the origin of P in Rheims seems certain.[4] In both C and P *An* 804-53 were omitted by the first hands and were added later. The prologue of *Eunuchus* was also omitted initially by C, while only lines 1-30 do not come from the first hand of P. The third MS, F (Milan, Ambros H 75 inf), is probably to be dated to the late ninth or early tenth century. Its provenance is uncertain: Orléans or the neighbourhood of Rheims have both been suggested.[5] All of the *Andria* and nearly half of the *Eunuchus* have been lost from this MS. This is unfortunate. Consideration of the text and the illustrations shows that F is not descended from the same hyparchetype as C and P. If F were intact, it would have been possible to see immediately whether the losses in C and P mentioned above were peculiar to the hyparchetype of these two MSS or whether the common ancestor of all three lacked these sections.

These three MSS will continue to be used by editors as good witnesses to the γ branch of the tradition. But what of the many other γ MSS which exist? Apart from some fragments and mutilated MSS, Kauer and Lindsay employed E (Florence, Ricc 528) and v (Valenciennes, bibl publ 448 [420]). The former betrays contamination with δ MSS and is a good representative of the large number of mixed MSS, though whether it actually is the best representative remains uncertain. The Valenciennes MS is closely related to F for much of its text.

Particularly striking are numerous coincidences in erroneous verse division in *Hecyra* and *Phormio*. But other γ MSS exist which have equal claim for inclusion as *testes* of the text.

In 1900 Charles Hoeing published an article in which he described in detail a MS in the Bodleian library (Auct F 2 13),[6] hereafter designated O. This MS (described as the codex Dunelmensis) had been used by Leng for his 1701 edition, and later by Richard Bentley, who referred to it in his commentary as 'codex veterrimus' or 'codex vetustissimus.' While it was recognized that Leng and Bentley had used the same MS, its identity and whereabouts were not revealed until after Umpfenbach's edition of 1870. The MS, however, is not as old as Bentley believed it to be (ca 900). It was written in the twelfth century and probably in the second half. The MS was in the abbey of St Albans in the thirteenth century as an anathema on fol 1^r informs us: 'hic est liber sancti Albani quem qui ei abstulerit aut titulum deleverit anathema sit. amen.' Hoeing refers to the activities of the nineteenth abbot, Simon (1166-83), as described by Thomas Walsingham in his *Gesta Abbatum Monasterii S. Albani*:

> non desiit libros optimos et volumina authentica ... quibus non vidimus nobiliora scribere ... (1.184 Riley)

> notandum quoque quod iste immortalis memoriae Abbas Simon duo vel tres electissimos scriptores continue in camera sua honorifice sustinuit, unde librorum optimorum copiam impretiabilem ad unguem praeparavit et in speciali almario reposuit. (1.192)

The MS certainly warrants the description 'liber optimus.' Its parchment is of high standard, the text is beautifully written, and the figures in the drawings of O 'contain among their number some passages of the best quality of medieval drawing.'[7] It is highly probable that this MS was one of those whose execution was encouraged by Simon, 'librorum amator specialis' (1.183 Riley). Jones and Morey (2.92ff) agree with Hoeing about a St Albans provenance, though they state at the same time that the drawings show some Winchester influence.

Here then is a MS written more than three centuries after C and P, whose text on examination reveals its close relationship with these two leading γ MSS. Hoeing argued that O was copied from a MS which was descended from the same hyparchetype as C and P and that the exemplar of O had been copied from the hyparchetype before it had lost *An* 804-53, since these verses appear in O without any immediate indication that they had ever been missing in ancestors of O. If this were correct, the readings of O in this section of the text would be extremely valuable since F lacks the whole of the *Andria*. We would have not only a representative of the text of *An* 804-53 as it must have appeared in the γ archetype but also representatives of the illustrations that appeared in this section. The relationship of these three MSS which Hoeing suggested does not, however, bear scrutiny, as R.H. Webb demonstrated in an important article in 1911.[8] He pointed to the large number of errors shared by P and O against C. P and O therefore must be derived from a hyparchetype which, because of errors shared by P and O with C, must go back to a MS from which C is descended. Since C and P lack *An* 804-53, this common ancestor of C, P, and O must also have lacked these lines. O could not therefore have inherited this section of the text from the γ archetype. Whence came the verses and the illustrations? The answer of Jones and Morey and of Webb is that the text and miniatures of this section were derived from an illustrated γ MS which was closely related to F and did not descend from the hyparchetype of C, P, and O. But Jones and Morey diverge from Webb on an important point. They argue strenuously (2.76ff) that O was in fact copied directly from P and that it was the scribe and illustrators of O who used this other illustrated γ MS to supply the missing sections and (on occasion) to replace the reading of the main model with that of this secondary source.

In his article Webb adduced another MS which he felt had been unduly neglected and which was of help in establishing the stemma of the γ MSS. This MS, now in Paris (BN lat 7900), is designated Y by Webb (J by Jones and Morey). According to Bischoff it was written in the second half of the ninth century at Corbie.[9] Later it was in the Benedictine monastery at Fleury as a couplet on fol 1ᵛ shows:

Floriacus datur esse iacus vel flos benedictus
A folio vel flore pio cognomine dictus.[10]

Spaces have been left for illustrations at the beginning of the scenes but these are left blank after *Eun* 643 (IV.3). Some of the earlier spaces are also blank. *An* 797-871 (ie IV.5 and V.1) were omitted by the first hand of Y, probably because in the exemplar lines 804-53 were missing. Webb pointed out that not only do P and O have common errors against C and Y but that C and Y too share errors against P and O. Since Y often has the correct reading where C is wrong, Y cannot be a descendant of C. Thus between the archetype of CPOY and each

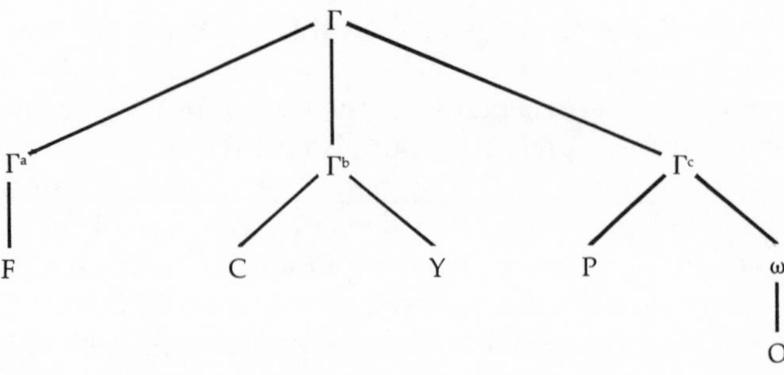

FIGURE 8

MS there must be at least one intermediate stage, the hyparchetype of P and O and the hyparchetype of C and Y. The stemma which emerged from Webb's study is shown in figure 8 (with some modification of the symbols he used). Thus the major γ MSS, C, P, and F, descend from three hyparchetypes. The number is reduced to two by Jones and Morey, since in their opinion O was copied from P and the MSS C, Y, and P were each descendants of Γ^b, independent of each other.

One issue, therefore, concerns the relationships among the four MSS C, P, Y, and O, and the value to editors of the last two. A second is the number and nature of the hyparchetypes of the γ MSS. Webb did not confront the question of whether the three hyparchetypes Γ^a, Γ^b, and Γ^c were written in antiquity or in the medieval period. He concluded, somewhat tentatively, that Γ was 'possibly written in capital script' (102), since on his reconstruction it had only eighteen lines to the page, and since common errors in P and O at *Ph* 619 (*pius* for *eius*) and 712 (*digesse* for *dicesse*) indicate that an antecedent of Γ^c (ie Γ) was written in majuscules. Once the stemma of the MSS is established, graphical errors may indicate how many illustrated γ MSS survived from antiquity into Carolingian times. A third issue is the source of the text and illustrations in *An* 804-53 in O. Were they copied from a γ MS as most seem to believe?

Before the relationships of C, Y, P, and O are examined, a brief list of errors shared by these four MSS against the correct reading in F is given. The lemmata are the readings of F.[11]

Eun 572 illoc] illic
Eun 849 me autem] mea autem
Eun 869 non possim] ne possim
Eun 1030 hic] hinc
Eun 1060 futurum] futuram

Haut 572 concedas] ut concedas
Haut 677 euge] *om CPYO*
Haut 682 audio] ut audio
Haut 936 malis] mavis
Haut 942 doti] dotis

Ad 520 prorsum] prosum

Hec 315 rursum prorsum] sursum prorsum
Hec 325 nunc te] te nunc
Hec 404 eius] *om CPYO*
Hec 408 idem] item
Hec 472 et benigno] *om CPYO*

The relationship of C and Y

C and Y can be separated from P and O by the following common errors of the first hands where P and O have the correct reading or a different error. For the most part I omit information about corrections of the four MSS.

An 275 inmutarier] immutareer
An 276 verear] vereor
An 496 re tulit] rem tulit
An 523 abi intro] abintro
An 589 vah] va
An 594 ibo] cibo C^1: #ibo *Y*
An 788 mi] mii C^1: mi# *Y*

Eun 333 quom minime] cum a minime C: cū#minime *Y*
Eun 379 quo trudis] quod rudis
Eun 381 istaec] estaec C^1: est haec *Y*
Eun 397 maxumas] maximus
Eun 519 mari] mare
Eun 624 facere contra] facere re contra
Eun 728 accubabam] accumbabam
Eun 889 quid ah] a quid
Eun 1052 fautrix] frautrix

Haut 67 vesperi] vespere
Haut 69 fodere] foedere
Haut 952 deridiculo] dericulo
Haut 967 semper erit] sempeperit

Ph 248 redierit] redierit dum mihi sunt omnia ... redierit
Ph 987 Nausistrata] Nausistra
Ph 1016 1016 *post* 1017 C^1: 1016-17 *in rasura Y*

Hec 235 odisse] odisse sese *CY*: odisse se *PO*
Hec 244 faciam] fagiam
Hec 269 se] si

Ad 412 phy] hy
Ad 432 numquid] nuncquid
Ad 975 hodie] hoc die

Most of the examples in the *Andria*, *Hauton timorumenos*, and *Phormio* are given by Webb. I have checked these examples in the four MSS and have added further material from the other plays, usually *Eunuchus* and *Adelphoe*. The list is not complete but is sufficient to show that C, Y, and P cannot be independent descendants of the same γ hyparchetype, as Jones and Morey suggest (2.195-6). C and Y must have a common hyparchetype, since the possibility of Y's being a copy of C is excluded by a large number of readings where Y is correct against uncorrected errors in C. I give examples from the *Eunuchus* and *Adelphoe* (unless otherwise indicated, the reading of Y is given first, that of C given second):

Eun 89 patent] pateant
Eun 126 cariam] caream
Eun 197 parvam] parum
Eun 291 et] *om C*
Eun 879 mage nunc] nunc magis
Eun 910 in mentem] in mente
Eun 1087 propino] propinabo (*ex* propinebo) C^1: prebebo C^2

Ad 23 i] hii C: ii *Y*
Ad 39 ipse est] ipse sit
Ad 65 quidem] equidem
Ad 124 in hac re] in hanc rem
Ad 179 habere] haberi
Ad 311 totam] *om C*
Ad 476 psaltriam] saltriam
Ad 734 certe est] est certe
Ad 779 paullulus] parvulus

If one were to add errors of C^1 which have been corrected by later hands, the list would increase in size. Y clearly shows itself to be a much more carefully copied MS than C. One could of course allege that some of these errors in C which do not appear in Y are obvious ones and could have been corrected by the scribe of Y if he was copying C. In addition the scribe of Y may have had access to a MS which did not contain these errors of C and which he may have consulted. But in the absence of any solid evidence for this procedure the natural and simpler inference is that C and Y descend from the same hyparchetype Γ^b and that Y has often preserved the correct reading.

What was the nature of the hyparchetype? Examination of the errors shared by C and Y shows that an antecedent of this hyparchetype was written in rustic capitals. The confusion of i and e at *An* 275 (*-mutareer* for *-mutarier*), *Eun* 381 (*estaec*/*est haec* for *istaec*), *Eun* 519 (*mare* for *mari*), *Haut* 67 (*vespere* for *vesperi*), *Hec* 269 (*si* for *se*) points to this. Further support for this is derived from other errors which would have occurred when a capital script was being copied: *fagiam* for *faciam* (*Hec* 244) and *sempeperit* for *semper erit* (*Haut* 967). Two of the examples in the list above (p 141) might at first sight point to an antecedent of the hyparchetype in minuscules, but *maximus* for *maximas* at *Eun* 397 has been prompted by the presence of the nominative *rex* close by, and the rather strange reading *cum a minime* at *Eun* 333, which could have been caused by the proximity of u in *cum* in minuscule could just as readily have resulted from the sequence VMM in rustic capitals being read as VMAM.

For the style of writing in the hyparchetype itself (Γ^b) recourse must be had to the graphical errors which are found separately in C and Y. Since each MS shows peculiar errors which must have occurred when a MS in rustic capitals was being copied, Γ^b itself must have been written in this style of writing. The most frequent error in C is the confusion of i and e. In *Eun* we find *restinguit* for *restinguet* (69), *caream* for *cariam* (126), *censio* for *censeo* (217), *munire* for *munere* (269), *ille* for *illi* (448), *frigit* for *friget* (732), *cavet* for *cavit* (782); in *Haut ille* for *illi* (199), *me* for *mi* (622), *investigare* for *investigari* (675); in *Ph quaerit* for *quaeret* (51), *nostre* for *nostri* (63), *bineficium* for *beneficium* (493), *uteri* for *utere* (527), *dicem* for *decem* (664), *benigni* for *benigne* (1051); in *Hec gravi* for *grave* (125), *possit* for *posset* (225), *agidum* for *agedum* (315); in *Ad haberi* for *habere* (179), *agis* for *ages* (226), *esse ne* for *es sine* (321), *dicet* for *decet* (506).[12] Other errors peculiar to C which indicate a hyparchetype in capitals are *attigam* for *atticam* (*An* 780), *cremium* for *gremium* (*Eun* 585), *redigat* for *re dicat* (*Ph* 444), *adungo* for *adunco* (*Haut* 1062), *inpotatam* for *indotatam* (*Ph* 120), *grationem* for *orationem* (*Ph* 783), *pape* for *rape* (*Ph* 882). All these errors are absent from Y, but this MS too has its own share of errors which have been caused by the misreading of rustic capitals: *poteres* for *poteris* (*Eun* 215), *vi* for *ut* (*Eun* 220), *mi* for *me* (*Eun* 715), *oli* for *oiei* (*Eun* 716), *intellexin* for *intellextin* (*Eun* 768), *dixitin* for *dixtin* (*Eun* 793), *ii* for *iit* (*Eun* 892), *posse* for *posset* (*Eun* 932) and *verum* for *virum* (*Ad* 564). Γ^b itself therefore was written in rustic capitals. Since the first hands of C and Y, which are both written as prose, omit different entire verses (*Ph* 242 and *Haut* 496 in C; *Eun* 850, *Ph* 374, and *Hec* 691-2 in Y), Γ^b was written in verse.[13]

It is more difficult to decide whether there were intermediaries in minuscule between Γ^b and C and between Γ^b and Y. Hoeing (332-3) pointed to *Haut* 746, where C^1 has *harunt* for *harunc*, as proof that 'the original of C ... was written in minuscules.' But if the scribe was copying from Γ^b, his eye might have jumped to the ending of *attulerunt* in the preceding line. There are indeed very few errors which can be imputed to the misreading of minuscule. At *Hec* 200 C offers *ullum* for *ullam*, but the scribe may have had in his mind *aliarum*, which he had just written. At *Eun* 738 we find *miseror* for *miror* which may have been prompted by reading r as s. A strange reading occurs at *Eun* 515, where C^1 has *eccum bene* for *accumbere*, caused perhaps by the misreading of the initial *ac-* as *ae-*. There is hardly enough evidence to convince one that C was copied from a MS in minuscules, but there is sufficient for the possibility not to be excluded. If C's exemplar was in minuscule, it had not been carefully corrected, since a very large number of errors which had been made when it was copied from Γ^b persisted in C. A scenario for this is not difficult to imagine. Perhaps a copy of Γ^b had to be made in haste (for transportation to Corvey?) and the artist added the miniatures immediately after the scribe had written each section of the text. This might have prevented careful correction of the text in the exemplar of C. The situation in Y is similar. There are only two errors in the *Eunuchus* and *Adelphoe* which may have been caused by the misreading of minuscules: *pollicitam* for *pollicitum* (*Eun* 308) and *abierant* for *abierunt* (*Eun* 702).[14] Again not very much evidence, but perhaps enough not to discount the possibility of a minuscule intermediary between Γ^b and Y.

Webb's view of the relationship between C and Y is substantially correct. What has been added is the conclusion that Γ^b was written in rustic capitals and was therefore an illustrated γ MS of antiquity, perhaps of late antiquity, which was still in currency in Carolingian times.

Finally, before the relationship between P and O is discussed, a few words may be said about the position in the γ stemma of the Lyon fragment (λ), which dates from the first half of the ninth century and contains only *Haut* 522-904.[15] There is no doubt that λ is descended from the γ archetype and that it is clearly related to the CPOY group of the γ MSS, since it shares errors with these MSS against F (572 *certe ut concedas*: 677 omission of *euge*; 682 *quantum ut audio*). Because of the comparatively short section and the high quality of the text which it contains, conjunctive errors shared by λ and other MSS are conspicuously absent. Some of its readings, however, betray a close affinity with Y:

595 ecquid] haecquid Y^1: ##ecquid λ
695 conloceter] collocetur λ: collicetur *Y*
733 dyonisia λY: dionysia *C*: dionisia *cett*
857 vah] va $C^1\lambda Y$

Y cannot be a direct descendant of λ, since the latter has errors not present in Y: 546 *adulescenti* for *adulescentuli*; 584 *id* for *hic*; 761 *fides* for *fide*. The two manuscripts are probably therefore descended from the same hyparchetype. An interesting error occurs in Y and λ at line 825 where Y^1 offers *fortunatus homo desum amo* (*fortunatus homo sum deamo* Y^2), and λ^1 reads *sum defor#tunatus homo amo* (*sum defor#tunatus homo sum deamo* λ^2, the correction possibly being made by the first hand). This seems to point to an error in the hyparchetype of λ and

Y relating to the omission of *de-* in *deamo*. The prefix was presumably added as an interlinear or marginal gloss and has been added to the wrong words in Y and λ.

The relationship of P and O

If the justifiable claim made by Webb for Y's inclusion among the witnesses to the text has been ignored by recent editors, the relationship between P and O, as explained first by Hoeing and then by Webb, has not passed unchallenged. Jones and Morey have argued that O was copied directly from P. If they are right, O is of little value to an editor, useful only for any readings which it has derived horizontally or (perhaps) for the text of sections lost in the other MSS which descend from Γ^b. If Webb is right, O may have as much right as P to an editor's attention. Common errors of P and O against C and Y are shown in the following list (not complete), in which the lemmata are the readings of C and Y:

An 79	dein] dehinc
An 151	praescripsti] praescripsisti/-ibsisti
An 171	sequor] sequar
An 345	opportune] oportune
An 495	certe] certi
An 659	illam] illum
An 700	haec] hae
An 864	ego] *om PO*
Eun 47	me] men
Eun 298	senem] se#nem *P*: semen *O*
Eun 381	istaec] ista#aec *P*: ista haec *O*
Eun 807	Thais] THA (*nota*)
Haut 217	facili me] facillime
Haut 487	illud] illum
Haut 528	gnatus] natus
Haut 545	fingit] figit
Haut 604	ea quae] eaque
Haut 620	quid siet] quod siet
Haut 675	tam] tamen
Haut 678[a]	argentum] argumentum
Haut 715	fiat] fiet
Haut 747	haud scit hoc] haud scit aut
Ph 78	advorsus] adversum
Ph 81	quandam] quondam
Ph 236	places] placet
Ph 275	iudicum] iudicium
Ph 490	adferres] adferes *P*: afferes *O*
Ph 610	volup est] voluptas est
Ph 619	eius] pius
Ph 621	sic] si
Ph 630	victum eum] victum #eum *P*: victum meum *O*
Ph 712	dic esse] digesse
Hec 532	adeon] adeo
Ad 697	te] *om PO*

Since the point at issue is whether O was copied from P or is descended from the same hyparchetype as P, ie from Γ^c, the following list of instances where O is correct against P (or retains what was probably the reading of the archetype of CYPO where it has been corrupted in P) takes account only of uncorrected errors in P.

An 301	hodie *O*: *om* P
An 515	accersitum *O*: arcessitum *P*
An 665	hoc est *O*: est hoc *P*
An 881	hanc *O*: *om P*
Eun 306	neque quorsum *O*: ne quorsum *P*
Eun 546	hoc *O*: *om P*
Eun 689	est *O*: *om P*
Eun 1094	et *O*: *om P*
Haut 235	te *O*: *om P*
Haut 563	modo *O*: *om P*
Haut 782	est *O*: *om P*
Haut 853	ita *O*: ita ut *P*
Haut 1048	te obsecro *O*: obsecro te *P*
Ph 62	dico: *O* dabo *P*
Ph 129	fuerit *O*: erit *P*
Ph 175	in eum incidi infelix locum *O*: infelix incidi in eum locum *P*
Ph 178	nunc] nunc nunc *O*: nunc *om P*
Ph 243	rediens *O*: regrediens *P*
Ph 249	esse *O*: est *P*
Ph 270	in se *O*: ipse *P*
Ph 291	facere voluisti *O*: voluisti facere *P*
Ph 406	bis iudicium *O*: iudicium bis *P*
Ph 436	satis *O*: satin *P*
Ph 586	si fit *O*: si scit *P*
Ph 603	esse *O*: est *P*
Ph 665	ancillula *O*: ancilla *P*
Ph 669	etiam inrideat *O*: et me inrideat *P*
Ph 754	duasne is uxores habet *OCY*: duas uxoresne is habet *P*
Ph 773	ut *O*: *om P*
Hec 154	tu *O*: *om P*
Hec 193	nisi *O*: ni *P*
Hec 197	quod agas *O*: quod agis *P*
Hec 239	magis *O*: *om P*
Hec 483	te *O*: *om P*
Hec 543	est *O*: *om P*
Hec 554	is *O*: id *P*
Hec 784	tute ipse *O*: tu ipse *P*
Hec 851	me *O*: memet *P*
Hec 865	dixti *O*: dixisti *P*
Hec 872	eventuram *O*: venturam *P*
Ad 225	hoc scio *O*: hic scio *P*
Ad 251	dices *O*: dicis *P*
Ad 395	tu *O*: *om P*
Ad 451	hac *O*: hoc *P*
Ad 468	est (*alterum*) *O*: *om P*
Ad 491	nobis *O*: nos *P*
Ad 697	te *O*: *om P*
Ad 958	suo *O*: et suo *P*

The obvious conclusion to be drawn from this evidence is that P and O descend independently from the same hyparchetype. Both Hoeing and Webb, however, have pointed to elements in the text of O which betray contamination from a mixed or possibly a δ MS. An intermediate MS (ω) is postulated by Webb between the hyparchetype and O to account for this influence. If one excludes cases where the agreement of O and this 'alien' MS may be illusory and caused by the presence of variants in the hyparchetype of P and O (ie if one excludes agreements of O and P^2), the number of instances is not very large:

An 709	incipit mihi *CPY*: mihi incipit *ODEG*
Eun 303	illum flocci C^1P^1Y: illum non flocci OC^2p^2: non illum flocci P^2DGE
Eun 337	heus (*semel*) OD^1: heus heus *cett*
Eun 404	coeperat *ODG*: ceperat *cett*
Eun 582	noviciae et puellae OYF^1A: noviciae puellae *cett*
Eun 705	istic *Op*: isti *cett*
Haut 174	quisnam $OD^1F^2E^1$: quinam *cett*
Haut 925	esse ut sentiat OD^1GpE: esse sentiat *cett*
Haut 985	qui istuc $CPYE^2F^1$: quid istuc *O et rell*
Ph 73	usus C^1PYD^1: usu *O et rell*
Ph 262	me *om* $ODGLp^2EFv$
Ph 475	feci $OFvE^2$: fecit *cett*
Ph 478	eheu $OEFC^2$: eu *vel* heu *cett*
Hec 134	istoc OD^1: isto *cett*
Ad 756	ut *OF*: et *P*: ac *cett*

Except for the *Eunuchus*, this list is not complete, but the number of examples would not be increased appreciably, I believe, by full collations of O. My impression is the same as that of Hoeing (329), that the influence in O (through ω) from this other source is fairly slight. Some of the examples given above could have arisen independently in O and its contaminating source (eg *Eun* 337, 404, 705; *Haut* 985; *Ph* 478). Compared with these examples, the number of instances where O is correct against errors in P is quite astonishing if O was copied from P, as Jones and Morey claim. The textual evidence clearly vindicates the relationship established by Webb.

The view of Jones and Morey about the relationship between O and P is based primarily on the alleged dependence of the illustrations in O on those in P. There is no doubt that there are close similarities between the two sets of miniatures, but that is to be expected even if both were derived independently from the same hyparchetype. The most important coincidence between the miniatures of P and O occurs in the illustrations of *Haut* II.4 (line 381); see plates 22 and 23. Bacchis is shown on the extreme left, apparently carrying a ring. On the ring there is a quite disproportionate setting of a fleur-de-lys. The same motif occurs in O. Neither in C nor in F does Bacchis hold anything (see plate 2) and there is nothing in the scene which justifies its presence. In a later scene (IV.1), however, Sostrata is portrayed in C, P, and F as holding the ring which she mentions at line 614: *nisi me animus fallit hic profecto est anulus quem ego suspicor / is quicum expositast gnata*. In O the ring has been transformed into some kind of flower, which may indeed have been what the artist drew in the miniature at line 381 (see plates 24 and 25). Jones and Morey think that the error in the illustrations at 381 originated with the artist of P 'by his having mistaken in his model (perhaps in resuming work after an interruption) the miniature of IV.1 for the miniature at II.4' (59). Later in their discussion of O they state: 'it is barely conceivable that O's mistake here [ie in the miniature at IV.1] is not due to a direct copy from P, but that the mistake occurred in a common archetype from which it was copied independently by both manuscripts, but the Rheims fleur-de-lys makes it far more probable that the error was original with P and was copied, therefore, directly by O from the Paris manuscript' (78). The presence of the Rheims fleur-de-lys is indeed significant. It occurs elsewhere in P and O on the summit of the *aedicula* of the *Andria* (see plates 28 and 29). Its presence shows that the error in the miniatures at IV.1 in P and O originated in Rheims, but not necessarily that it originated with the illustrator of P. Since the provenance of P is Rheims, without the evidence of the text the conclusion of Jones and Morey might be acceptable. But when the textual evidence conflicts so strongly with the explanation of Jones and Morey, another explanation must be sought. The obvious one is that the *hyparchetye* of P and O was executed at Rheims and that P and O have inherited the error from this hyparchetype.[16] This hyparchetype would have been written in minuscules. Since, however, Γ^b, the hyparchetype of C and Y, has been shown to have been written in rustic capitals, and since P and O must be descended from a MS independent of Γ^b, we must postulate another illustrated γ MS from which P and O are descended by way of the hyparchetype in minuscules.

This reconstruction is supported by the graphical errors which are found in P and O. Of the errors shared by these two MSS very few can be imputed to graphical causes. The few that do exist, however, indicate that the hyparchetype of P and O had an ancestor in capitals and more particularly in rustic capitals. We find *digesse* for *dic esse* at *Ph* 712 and *certi* for *certe* at *An* 495. The very strange error of *pius* for *eius* at *Ph* 619 is inexplicable in terms of minuscule writing but could have arisen from a misreading of capitals if I were written so that it touched the top and middle horizontals of the initial E. At *An* 659 *illum* for *illam* need not point to a prearchetypal MS in minuscules since *illum* could have been caused by the following word (*ducturum*).

Since P has been corrected by the first and later hands, only a few errors which may have been caused by confusion of similar letters remain. Umpfenbach reports two which seem convincing proof that P was copied from a MS in minuscules: *ducas nullam* for *ducas tu illam* at *An* 349, and *imperare* for *impertire* at *Ad* 320. In the second case, however, the reading of P is definitely *impertire*; in the first there is less certainty, but what Umpfenbach has read as *nu* looks more like *tui*. A certain error occurs at *Ad* 70, where *rescitum in credit* has been written by P^1 for *rescitum iri credit* (so P^2). This must point to an antecedent in minuscules, as do probably the errors at *Haut* 435 (*a#dacta* for *adaucta*), *Ph* 868 (*animam* for *animum*), and *Hec* 612 (*feruntur* for *ferantur*).

Overall, therefore, the evidence clearly contradicts the view that O was copied from P. Acceptance of such a relationship oversteps the bounds of credibility. An extraordinary amount of organization would have had to be done before O was actually written if its prime exemplar were P. To take but one example, the scribe of O has copied at the same time as the text itself prefaces to some of the scenes. For the *Andria*, at least, not one of these prefaces appears in P, although some are found in C.[17] Moreover we have to assume that the scribe continuously consulted other MSS from which he was able, with enviable discrimination, to choose mostly correct readings in preference to those which he found in P. The relationship between P and O which Webb has suggested is surely the correct one.

The text and miniatures of O at *An* 804-53

C, P, Y, and O all contain *An* 804-53 but the verses have been added by later hands in C, P, and Y. Examination of these additions shows that the verses in the three MSS have been culled from different sources. One must conclude that the lines had been lost in both Γ^b and Γ^c. Whence came this section of the text in O and the two miniatures for V.1 and V.2? There is no indication in the margins of O that the lines were not taken from its exemplar or that they had ever been lost. The opinions of Hoeing, Webb, and Jones and Morey are that the verses and illustrations are derived from an illustrated γ MS in which this section had not been lost and that accordingly both text and miniatures descend ultimately from Γ itself. The obvious source is Γ^a or a descendant. Unfortunately, however, the *Andria* has been lost from F, the prime witness to what was in Γ^a.

An attempt to solve the problem must begin with the text of *An* 804-53 in O. If the nature of the MS which was the source of these lines can be established, then light may be cast on the source and on the authenticity of the illustrations in O at V.1 and V.2. To this end I have examined the text of *An* 804-53 in over thirty MSS (other than those used in the OCT) which date from the twelfth century or earlier. The results of this collation are given for the most important features of the text of O in this section. Some of the MSS examined share only one or two features with O and these agreements have not been noted. Only MSS which agree with O on at least three occasions are cited.[18] The sigla listed below are assigned to MSS not used in the OCT:

E^c Erlangen, Univ 392
E^s El Escorial S-III-23
L^f London, BL Harl 2750
O^b Oxford, Bodl Auct F 6 27
T Florence, Med-Laur 38 27
V^b Vienna, Nationalbibl Pal 85

804 sic *$ODpL^f$*: *om cett*
809 semper eius dicta *$OD^1L^1pE^cE^sO^bV^b$*: semper enim eius dicta *L^f*: semper dicta eius *G*: semper enim dicta *cett*
809 esse *om $OD^1LpE^cE^sO^bT$*
811 id *$OL^1p^1E^cL^fO^bTV^bE^1$*: hic *vel* hic id *cett*
813 ei *$Op^2E^sL^fV^{b2}$*: eius *cett*
817 o optume *$ODTV^b$*: o *om cett*
830 in (*alterum*) *om $OD^1pE^cL^fV^bv^1$*

It is notable that at least one of the major δ MSS always agrees with the reading of O. The others cited above are either δ MSS (so T, which has the δ order of plays, and probably V^b) or have elsewhere a high proportion of δ readings.[19] It is reasonable to conclude therefore that the text of O for *An* 804-53 is derived (probably originally in ω) from a δ MS.

It may be asked in what sense one can talk about δ readings in *An*

804-53 when the three leading γ MSS (CPF) are not witnesses to this section of the text. Were not the readings really readings of Σ? But the very fact that most of the MSS examined are mixed and have a text which differs strongly from the δ MSS indicates that there was a branch of the γ tradition in which *An* 804-53 was transmitted. Webb argued that all of the mixed MSS descend from Γ^a and are more closely related to F than to C or P. The history of all the mixed MSS is not, I believe, quite as simple or as unified as Webb suggests, but many of them do seem to be closer to F than to C or P and probably do descend from Γ^a. It is possible therefore that *An* 804-53 were present in Γ^a and accordingly were also present in F before the *Andria* was lost from that MS. But this possibility will be re-examined after the miniatures in O at *An* V.1 and V.2 are discussed.

If it can be said with some confidence that the text of O at *An* 804-53 was drawn at some point from a δ MS, less certainty is attainable concerning the origin of the miniatures in O at V.1 and V.2 (plates 26 and 27). Since there is no evidence that the δ class ever contained illustrations, the artist of ω or O did not have models for his miniatures in the MS which was the source of the text. The miniatures were therefore either concocted by an artist or taken from an illustrated γ MS. There is nothing in the two illustrations which leads one to suspect their authenticity. But, conversely, it was not beyond the abilities of an artist to improvise with two miniatures of his own.[20] The illustration at V.1 shows Chremes and Simo facing each other in conversation – a frequent and obvious depiction when a scene consists of a dialogue between two characters. There is certainly a similarity between this miniature and the one which appears in the illustrated Tours MS of the twelfth century but the coincidence is hardly striking. The miniatures which appear at V.2 in O and the Tours MS are quite different (although it should be said that the artist of the latter or of an ancestor considerably modifies and deviates from the miniatures that appear elsewhere in C, P, and F). What evidence there is favours the conclusion that the two miniatures in O at V.1 and V.2 are owed to the originality of a medieval artist. The possibility that they are the sole representatives of the miniatures which once stood in these places in the illustrated γ archetype cannot be completely excluded. Conceivably the scribe of ω took the text of *An* 804-53 from a δ MS, leaving spaces for illustrations at the beginning of the two scenes, just as the scribe who copied the missing part of the text in C left spaces. The artist(s) of ω or O copied the miniatures which were in the γ exemplar, but had no illustrations for V.1 and V.2. Later, however, some artist may have found an illustrated MS which contained the two missing miniatures and added copies of these to ω or O.[21]

An 804-53 and Γ^a

I have said above that *An* 804-53, omitted in Γ^b and Γ^c, may have been present in F and Γ^a. This would account for the difference in the text of this passage between the δ MSS and the mixed MSS. There is, however, some evidence which runs counter to this hypothesis.

El Escorial S-III-23 (E^s), one of the MSS used when the text of O at *An* 804-53 was being examined, is an eleventh-century MS, written in Spain.[22] It contains *Andria, Eunuchus, Hauton timorumenos,* and *Adelphoe* (up to 970), but lacks *Hecyra* and *Phormio*. It is a γ MS and is most closely related to F, as is pointed out by Rubio in the introduction to his edition (1.lxx). In the Terence text which is common to both E^s and F the degree of similarity between them is approximately 95 per cent in each of *Eunuchus, Hauton timorumenos* and *Adelphoe* on the basis of an examination of 220 places in the text. By contrast the degree of similarity between the Escorial MS and C is somewhat smaller for the same three plays (approximately 86 per cent). In the list of errors shared by CPYO against F given above (pp 140-1) the Spanish MS agrees on every occasion with F, and the two MSS agree on a few occasions in distinctive errors in verse division (eg *Ad* 122, 343, 798). The Escorial MS, therefore, does not descend from either Γ^b or Γ^c. *In this MS, however, An 804-53 was omitted by the first hand. An* 854ff have been written immediately after 803 and a double folium containing 804-53 has been inserted between fol 50^v (ending with *An* 794) and fol 53^r (beginning with *An* 854.) If the ancestry of the text of *Andria* in this MS is the same as that of the other plays, we must conclude that *An* 804-53 were also missing in F and in Γ^a.

In *Andria* E^s offers a γ text, having most of the readings shared by all or most of the major γ MSS: eg, *te haec* (293), *vita est* (347), *videatur esse iniurius* (377), *suam mutet* (393), *homini cuiquam* (425), *malle melius esse* (427), *ipse* (442), *impetrare a me* (544), *sum pollicitus* (613), *me nunc* (614), *satis scio fuisse iratos* (664), *pedibus* (676), *periculum adire* (677), *putavi* (717), *hinc sume* (726), *puerum positum* (773), omission of *iam* (784), *vir sit* (915), *sese Atticam esse* (927). The question, however, is whether the text for *Andria* in E^s descends from Γ^b or Γ^c. If it does, the omission of 804-53 is explained and there is no need to suppose that these lines were absent in F and Γ^a. But E^s stands apart against the agreement of CPYO in error too frequently for descent from Γ^b or Γ^c to be possible:

106 ei] *om CPYOv*
194 hem] *om CPYO*
238 hodie] *om CPYOv*
281 hanc] *om CPYO*
360 ipsus] ipsius *$E^{s}p$*: ipse *CPYO*
408 qui] qua *CPYOLp, schol v*
583 deluderes] luderes *CPYO*
630 paullum] paulullum *E^{s}: om CPYO*
786 hinc] *om CPYO*
857 severitas] veritas *CPYOp*
882 hem] *om CPYOp* (*recte*?)
915 arbitrere] arbitrare *CPYO*
922 ego] *om CPYO*
971 eam uxorem] iam uxorem *CPO* (*non legitur* Y)

Since E^{s} is independent of Γ^{b} and Γ^{c},[23] it almost certainly descends from Γ^{a}, and it follows that *An* 804-53 were missing from Γ^{a} as well as from Γ^{b} and Γ^{c}. If this is the case, the source of the text of *An* 804-53 in the mixed MSS must have been a γ MS which was independent of Γ^{a}, Γ^{b}, or Γ^{c}.

Conclusion and the stemma

This examination of the major γ MSS has led to a somewhat surprising conclusion. It has emerged that three illustrated γ MSS survived from antiquity into the medieval period. That in itself is not beyond belief. But that all three were defective in not containing *An* 804-53 may prompt scepticism. How much more convincing would be a reconstruction in which the defect was transmitted in one ancient illustrated MS! To achieve such a reconstruction one would have to discount completely the graphical errors which pointed to *any* of the hyparchetypes being written in rustic capitals. For if Γ^{a} was an ancient MS, then at least one other ancient MS must have survived as the ancestor of the hyparchetypes of CY and PO. If either Γ^{b} or Γ^{c} dated from late antiquity, the other must also be ancient, as must Γ^{a}, which is independent of both.

It is often tempting to make too much of graphical errors and to impute to similarity in letter forms errors which occurred for other reasons – the momentary wandering of the scribe's eye to a different word or line or the similar pronunciation of different letters. But the evidence adduced above (p 142) to show that Γ^{b} was written in rustic capitals is not easily cast aside. The weight of the evidence supports the hypothesis that this hyparchetype was an ancient MS. It follows that Γ^{a} and Γ^{c} also dated from antiquity.

The stemma of the purer γ MSS is shown in figure 9. In summary, the conclusions we have reached about the problems stated above (p 140) are as follows. First, the relationships of the four MSS C, P, Y,

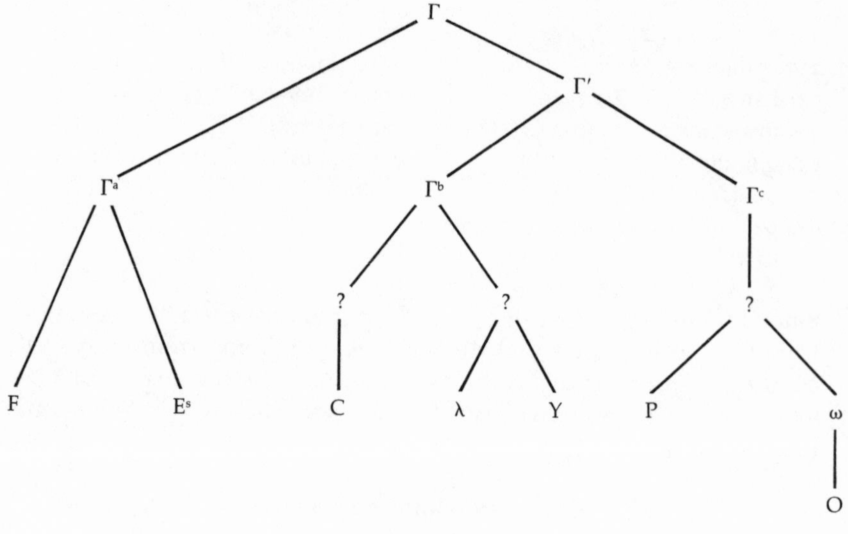

FIGURE 9

and O are very similar to those claimed by Webb. All four MSS deserve citation in a critical apparatus, since O and Y often retain correct readings against P and C respectively and sometimes O or Y alone has the correct reading against the other three. Secondly, there were three ancient illustrated γ MSS which survived into the Carolingian era and in all three *An* 804-53 were missing. Thirdly, the text of these lines in the μ MSS was drawn from a γ MS which descended from another ancient MS. Finally, it is probable, though not certain, that the miniatures in O at *An* V.1 and V.2 are the fabrications of a medieval artist.[24]

22 *Hauton timorumenos* 381 (P): Jones and Morey no. 361

23 *Hauton timorumenos* 381 (O): no. 363

24 *Hauton timorumenos* 614 (P): no. 386

25 *Hauton timorumenos* 614 (O): no. 388

26 *Andria* 820 (V.1) (O): no. 142

27 *Andria* 842 (V.2) (O): no. 145

28 *Aedicula* of *Andria* (P): no. 6

29 *Aedicula* of *Andria* (O): no. 8

6

Stemmatic Principles and the Manuscript Tradition

In this final chapter attention will be focused on the applicability of stemmatic principles to the textual tradition of Terence for recovering the readings of the archetype. In specific terms the question is whether agreements between A and Δ against Γ and agreements between A and Γ against Δ will provide the readings of Φ. The question can be answered in part if we examine instances where either the Bembinus and Γ or the Bembinus and Δ share *errors* against the correct reading in Δ or Γ respectively. If a large number of such common errors is found, then contamination has occurred between one of the branches of the Calliopian tradition and a MS related to the Bembinus or the correct reading found in Γ or Δ has been drawn from a source independent of Φ, though neither of these possibilities excludes the other.

The preceding chapters have established working procedures for determining the readings of Γ and Δ. Agreement of CPF will give the reading of Γ, agreement of DGLp will usually provide the text of Δ. Some *caveats* have to be noted. In places F shows signs of having been contaminated by a δ source, while p has been contaminated to some extent by a γ MS. This means that sometimes the text of Γ will be reflected by the agreement of C and P (or, more accurately, by the evidence of the four MSS CPYO) and sometimes the readings of Δ will be preserved in DGL.[1] Since the hyparchetype of DGL has suffered extensive γ influence, sometimes p and the δ MSS independent of the hyparchetype of DGL (ie NP^cV^b) will preserve what was in Δ.

Common errors in AΓ against Δ

1 *Eun* 854

TH. num meam saevitiam veritus es. CH. non. TH. quid igitur?

es *om Aγ*

2 *Ph* 656

quae debeo: et etiamnunc si volt Demipho

et *om Aγ*

3 *Eun* 1061 (trochaic septenarius)

o Thraso. TH. salvete. GN. tu fortasse quae facta hic sient

sint *Aγ* (*praeter E*)

4 *Ad* 635 (trochaic septenarius)

prodit nescioquis: concedam huc. MI. ita uti dixi, Sostrata

ut *Aγp*

5 *Haut* 436 (senarius)

ME. non tu illi dixti ut essem. CH. non. ME. quam ob rem, Chreme?

dixisti *Aγ*D^{2}*L*

6 *Haut* 1061

filiam Phanocratae nostri. CL. rufamne illam virginem

nostrae *AC*$P^{1}F^{1}$

7 *Hec* 349

nam si remittent quidpiam Philumenae dolores

Philumenam *AγL*

8 *Hec* 849

egon pro hoc te nuntio qui donem? qui? qui? nescio.

quid donem *AγL* qui qui D^{1}*p*E^{2}: quid qui *L*E^{1}*F*: quid quid *cett*

9 *An* 962

sed quem ego mihi potissumum optem, quoi nunc haec narrem dari?

nunc cui *Aγ*: cui nunc δ

10 *Haut* 902

est mihi ultimis conclave in aedibus quoddam retro:

in ultimis conclave aedibus *AγL*

11 *Hec* 562

quam ob rem incendor ira esse ausam facere haec te iniussu meo.

te *post* ira *AγL*

12 *Ph* 881

denique ego sum missus te ut requirerem atque adducerem AN. em

missus sum *ACPE*

13 *Eun* 936

quae cum amatore quom cenant ligurriunt.

amatore suo quom *AγD*²: amatores vocant *L*

Most of these errors are trivial and could have occurred independently. Examples 1 and 2 are simply graphical errors; examples 3-9 display different forms of the same word, in two cases (3 and 4) a modern form for an archaic, while examples 10-12 spring from the tendency to 'regularize' word order, instances of which abound in all branches of the tradition. In example 9 there seems to be no good reason for the aberration in word order, but since this is the only example of this kind, and since divergence from the correct word order is one of the most common of scribal errors, it is of little significance. The final example (*Eun* 936) points to the presence of *suo* as a gloss in Φ. It is quite unnecessary to postulate contamination.

The above list contains certain or near-certain errors common to the Bembinus and Γ. There are other examples where, with less certainty, the δ MSS may have the correct reading against AΓ:

Haut 600

vah vide quod inceptet facinus. fuit quaedam anus Corinthia

inceptat δ

Haut 869

ut istam rem video istius obsaturabere.

istanc *DGp*

Ph 293

neque testimoni dictio est. DE. mitto omnia;

est dictio δ

Ph 634

tibi in manum, ut erus his desistat litibus

erus tu δ

Ph 732

nam quae haec anus est exanimata a fratre quae egressast meo?

est anus δ

Hec 363

partim quae perspexi his oculis, partim quae accepi auribus:

hisce *Dp*

Ad 632

nunc hoc primum ad illas ibo ut purgem me. accedam ad fores.

me ut purgem δ

At these points the δ MSS offer the more unusual form or order of words. The immediate inclination is to print *istanc* at *Haut* 869 and *hisce* at *Hec* 363. It is worth remembering, however, that on occasions archaic forms have been wrongly incorporated into the text in all branches of the tradition: so *siet* for *sit* at *Ad* 723 (δ) and *Hec* 878 (A); *siem* for *sim* at *An* 619 (Σ); *istunc* for *istum* at *Eun* 777 (γ); *noscier* for *nosci* at *Hec* 573 (Σ except p); and *sollicitarier* for *sollicitari* at *An* 689 (Σ).[2] The readings at *Haut* 869 and *Hec* 363 may be correct, but if so, the readings in A and Γ could well have occurred independently. The same is true for *Ph* 634 and *Ad* 632 where the more unusual word order in the δ MSS is attractive.

Before the evidence can be evaluated, some more problematic instances where the Bembinus and the γ MSS stand in agreement against the δ group have to be examined.

Eun 781

THR. tu hosce instrue; ego hic ero post principia: inde omnibus signum dabo.

hic ego *Aγ*

The Aγ reading is unmetrical, while the text offered by the δ MSS scans. But the latter is unattractive, since *hic* and *inde* can hardly refer to the same spot. The Aγ reading makes better sense; *hic* has to be taken with *instrue* and separated from *ego* by punctuation. Thraso is telling Gnatho to draw up the men at the spot where he is standing at that moment. He will then move away *post principia* and from there (*inde*) will direct operations. Since, however, the Aγ reading will not scan, some change has to be made. Umpfenbach and Dziatzko deleted *hic* as an interpolation (see the critical apparatus of the OCT at *Eun* 893, *Ph* 548), but in this instance it is preferable to keep the antithesis of *hic* and *inde* and delete *ego* (cf *An* 538, *Eun* 813): read *tu hosce instrue hic; ero post principia*. The reading of Aγ may well preserve an error in Φ. Alternatively *ego* may have been a gloss in the archetype.

Eun 931

id verost quod ego mi puto palmarium
me repperisse quo modo adulescentulus (931)

931 men *A* (*corr Iov*),*C*[1]*P*[1]

Almost all editors have printed *me*, but it is difficult to understand why *me* would be corrupted to *men*. Over a century ago Minton Warren defended *men* and adduced as parallels Ennius 46-7 Ribbeck[2] (39-40 Jocelyn) *hoc dolet, men obesse, illos prodesse* and *Pseud* 371 *ten amatorem esse inventum inanem quasi cassam nucem*. Warren, I believe, is correct.[3]

Eun 977

PA. quis homost? ehem salvom te advenire, ere, gaudeo.
SE. quem praestolare? PA. perii: lingua haeret metu. SE. hem?
quid est? quid trepidas? satine salve? dic mihi.

977 hem *om* $AC^1P^1EF^1$

Most editors print *hem*. I would take it as another instance of an interpolated exclamation.[4] It is not as appropriate here as it is at *Eun* 986 for the *senex* to utter the interjection. Was *hem* perhaps a marginal gloss on *perii* which has been incorporated into the text of Δ?

Eun 1074

tu hercle cum illa, Phaedria,
ut lubenter vivis (etenim bene lubenter victitas) (1074)
quod des paullumst et necessest multum accipere Thaidem.

1074 ut] et $A\gamma D^2p^1$: *om* Gp^2

Only D^1 and L have the correct reading here and it is probable that *ut* was the reading of Δ. The error in the other MSS is a strange one and unlikely to have been made independently. It should be noted, however, that Y (Paris, BN lat 7900), one of the leading witnesses to the γ tradition, which has been discussed in the previous chapter, also offers *ut*. *ut* and *et* may have been variants in Σ, and since the Bembinus offers *et*, the history of the variants may go back to Φ. This example is therefore insufficient by itself to show contamination between a MS related to the Bembinus and the γ archetype.

Haut 1050

SO. mi vir, te obsecro
ne facias. CL. pater, obsecro, mi ignoscas. ME. da veniam, Chreme:
sine te exorem. CH. egon mea bona ut dem Bacchidi dono sciens? (1050)

exorem $C^2\delta EF^2\upsilon\eta\varepsilon$: exorent *cett*

If *exorem* is read, the verse is metrical; if *exorent*, it is not. Both make good sense but the preference should be given to *exorent*. This form is more likely to have been changed to *exorem* (so that the subject of the verb was the speaker) than for the reverse to have occurred. Most editors do indeed print *exorent* and exclude *egon*, following Guyet.[5] The personal pronoun, however, gives appropriate emphasis. What should be omitted is *te*; compare *Ph* 515 *Dorio, exoret sine*. Scan *sin(e) ĕxorent*.[6]

Ph 311

DE. abi, Phaedria, eum require atque hic adduce. PH. eo:
recta via quidem – illuc. GE. nempe ad Pamphilam.
DE. ego deos Penatis hinc salutatum domum (311)
devortar.

at ego $A\gamma pD^2L^2$

Of modern editions only Dziatzko-Kauer and Marouzeau have printed *at ego* (*at* being placed at the end of line 310). The gloss *at* is not an obvious one in this context, and it is more likely to have been lost than to have been added. I therefore follow Dziatzko-Kauer and Marouzeau; cf *An* 226 *sed Mysis ab ea egreditur. at ego hinc me ad forum*; see also *Ph* 463.

Hec 523

PH. atque eccam: video. quid ais, Myrrhina? heus tibi dico. MY. mihine, vir? (523)
PH. vir ego tuus sum?

523 vir $ACPLE^1Fv$: mi vir *Iov, cett*

Kauer-Lindsay and Marouzeau print the verse as given, correctly, I believe. Although the more intimate tone of *mi vir* suits Myrrhina's assumed air of innocence, *mi* is probably an intrusive gloss, prompted by the rejoinder of Phidippus *vir ego tuus sum*? If *mi vir* is read, some other change has to be made (the verse as printed by Bentley and Umpfenbach is unmetrical). Dziatzko, for example, deletes *video* (cf *An* 957, *Eun* 455, and the reading of the Calliopian MSS at *Eun* 738).

Hec 842

vide, mi Parmeno, etiam sodes ut mi haec certa et clara attuleris,
ne me in breve coniciam tempus gaudio hoc falso frui.

coniciam *scripsi*: conĭcias *codd* breve hoc conicias $A\gamma L$

Almost all editors have taken *hoc* of AγL to be an intrusive gloss. They may be correct, and in that case there is another common error of AΓ to be added to the above list. Yet *hoc* is not a gloss which one would naturally expect here, since the phrase *in breve tempus* normally appears without any qualifying demonstrative.[7] *hoc* here would give more specificity to his present *gaudium*: 'for this brief period of time.' There is no metrical difficulty, as *hoc* would be shortened after *brev(e)*. On balance, I think this should be considered an error of AΓ, though a less certain one than the one at *Eun* 936 (*amatore suo*).

Ad 299

nunc illud est quom, si omnia omnes sua consilia conferant

quod *Aγ,schol D,v²*: quod cum *G*

quom has won the support of almost all modern editors, but there is nothing wrong with *quod* in a temporal sense: cf Plaut *Amph* 302 *iam diu est quod ventri victum non datis; Haut* 54 *inde adeo quod agrum in proxumo hic mercatus es;* Cic *Q fr* 1.2.12 *de pactione statim quod audieram, iracundus scripseram.* See LHS 2.580, where these last three examples are given, and Kühn-Steg 2,2.271.

The number of errors shared by the Bembinus and the archetype comes then to between thirteen and twenty-one. If we were dealing with a short piece of text, the cumulative effect of these examples would suggest some contact between the class to which the Bembinus belongs and Γ. But that is not the case. These Aγ agreements form an extremely small number when the differences between A and Σ and between Γ and Δ are considered. At a rough count the total of such disagreements comes to over 2300. In comparison with this, the thirteen or even twenty-one errors shared by A and Γ seem insignificant. Moreover all of these common errors are trivial in nature. Not one of them could not have occurred independently. The conclusion must be that we cannot assume either that there was any contact between the class to which the Bembinus belonged and Γ or that Δ derived its correct readings from a source independent of Σ.[8]

Common errors in AΔ against Γ

The number of errors shared by A and the δ MSS against the γ MSS is certainly larger than the common errors of AΓ. In the following list of twenty errors, examples 1-7 are graphical errors, 8-11 have arisen from the intrusion of glosses, 12-13 are the result of modernizing, in 14-16 the word order has been regularized, and in 17-20 we find the wrong form of a word.

1 *An* 916

itane adtemperate evenit, hodie in ipsis nuptiis
ut veniret

venit AD^1GLVv^2: veni p^1

2 *Haut* 1033

CL. quos? CH. si scire vis, ego dicam, gerro iners fraus helluo

si *om* AD^1Gp

3 *Ph* 615

nam hercle ego quoque id quidem agitans mecum sedulo

quidem *om AGLp*: id quoque *GLp* (588-633 *desunt in D*)

4 *Ph* 666

supellectile opus est; opus est sumptu ad nuptias:

opus est *semel* $AD^1G^1LpF^1v$

5 *Hec* 229

sola hic fuisti: in te omnis haeret culpa sola, Sostrata.

sola (*alterum*) *om* AD^1Gp

6 *Hec* 853

sinam sine munere a me abire? ah, nimium me ignavom putas

a me *om* AD^1Gp

7 *Eun* 371 (iambic octonarius)

PA. pro illo te deducam. CH. audio. PA. te esse illum dicam. CH. intellego.

ducam *ADGLEvε*: deducam *cett*

8 *Eun* 519

rus Sunii ecquod habeam et quam longe a mari.

haberem *Aδ*

9 *Eun* 955-6

quidnam fecit? PY. conligavit primum eum miseris modis.
PA. conligavit?

956 hem conligavit *ALpE,D*(hem *superscriptum)*

10 *Ad* 325

actumst. SO. eloquere obsecro te quid sit. GE. iam ... SO. quid 'iam,' Geta?

eloquere ergo obsecro *Aδ*(*praeter p*)

11 *Ad* 906

vin tu huic seni auscultare? AE. quid? DE. missa haec face.

haec] istaec *A*(*corr Iov*),δ(haec D^2)

12 *Ph* 290

inmerito et me omnium horunc inmeritissumo.

horum *AδEF*

13 *Ad* 755

tuam istanc iracundiam atque ita uti decet

istam *Aδ*

14 *Eun* 769

TH. fac animo haec praesenti dicas. CH. faciam. TH. attolle pallium.

haec animo *Aδ*

15 *Haut* 415

quom illi pericli nihil ex indicio siet?

nihil pericli *ADGp*

16 *Ad* 299

nunc illud est quod, si omnia omnes sua consilia conferant

omnes omnia *Aδv*

17 *Eun* 797 (trochaic septenarius)

tibi illam reddat aut tu eam tangas, omnium ... ? GE. ah, quid agis? tace.

eam] illam *AD¹Gp*

18 *Ph* 456

rescindi posse et turpe inceptust. dic, Crito.

inceptumst *A*: inceptum est *DG²pv*

19 *Ph* 526

vanitatis? DO. minime, dum ob rem. GE. sterculinum. PH. Dorio!

sterculinium *ADGpEF²vC²,schol P*

20 *Hec* 860

semper sit. BA. at tu ecastor morem antiquom atque ingenium obtines

siet *ADpv*

With few exceptions the Aδ readings above give unmetrical lines. In example 8 *haberem*, giving a split anapaest, (*-quod habé-*) is probably admissible (cf *Ad* 877 *ecquíd ego póssiem*) but the present tense is preferable. It is the *lectio difficilior* in that it interrupts the historic sequence (*evasit ... essent ... periisset ... habuisset*). In example 9 Kauer-Lindsay printed *hem* (*extra metrum*). I prefer to believe that the interjection was a gloss in Φ. The iambic *nihil* at *Haut* 441 is doubtful, since the word is only disyllabic at verse end or the equivalent (cf *Haut* 896, *Ph* 940).[9] The same is true for *siet* at *Hec* 860.[10] The most striking common error is the unmetrical *istaec* for *haec* at *Ad* 906. But in the context a gloss of *istaec* for *haec* would not be surprising. Demea seems to be rejecting what Aeschinus has just mentioned, and *istaec*, with its second-person connotation, would be appropriate (cf *Eun* 90). It should be noted that the δ MSS (and E) offer *missa istaec faciamus* against *missa haec faciamus* of the others at *Eun* 864.

To the above examples of errors shared by A and the δ MSS others can be added, though there is less certainty about whether or not the shared reading is an error.

Eun 803

CH. diminuam ego caput tuum hodie, nisi abis. GN. ain vero, canis?

ego tibi caput tibi hodie *A*: ego caput tibi hodie *DL*: ego caput hodie *p*

The note in the Donatus commentary (*rusticius dixit 'caput tuum diminuam' quasi dicat 'diminuam tibi caput'*) gives strong support for *tuum* against *tibi* in ADL (also in E[1]). The replacement of *tuum* by *tibi* may have been prompted by the note in Donatus or by a similar one in an earlier commentary.

Haut 605

CH. quid tum? SY. Cliniam orat sibi uti id nunc det: illam illi tamen post daturum

id *om* *AD[1]G[1]L[2]pE[2]*

Syrus is telling Chremes that Bacchis is asking Clinia to pay her the money which she is owed by Antiphila's mother and for which Antiphila was given as *arrabo*. Antiphila will give him the money later. Most editors print *id* in line 605. If they are correct, the pronoun may have been omitted because of the proximity of *illam* which was taken as the object of *det*. But *id* could readily be an intrusive gloss in the γ MSS.

Haut 693

CL. deorum vitam apti sumus. SY. frustra operam opinor sumo.

opinor hanc sumo *AD[1]Gp*

The reading of AD[1]Gp will not scan. *hanc* can be retained if *opino* is read (so Kauer-Lindsay), but there is no certain example of *opino* in Terence and *opinor* is required at *Hec* 598 and 845. Most editors have printed the verse as above. An alternative is to read *frustra, opinor, operam hanc sumo*, with *sumus* being scanned as a pyrrhic. If *hanc* is an interpolated gloss, it is in a rather odd position; one would expect it to appear immediately beside *operam*.

Haut 953

non, ita me di ament, auderet facere haec viduae mulieri
quae in me fecit.

hoc facere *A*: facere hoc *D*^{1}*p*

Editors print *facere haec* but the agreement of AD^{1}p in offering *hoc* against the other MSS is odd. There is no persuasive explanation for *haec* being replaced or glossed by *hoc* when the relative clause in line 954 points naturally to a plural antecedent. The paradosis points to *facere hoc* (*hoc facere* is unmetrical) and this may well be correct; cf *Hec* 97-8 *sed quid hoc negotist modo quae* (so Σ and Donatus: *quod* A) *narravit mihi / hic intus Bacchis*, where most editors print *quod*, although Kauer-Lindsay retained *quae* and punctuated *sed quid negotist? modo quae ...* (see above p 94). These are two extreme cases of the violation of concord in Terence but it is wrong to exclude them when they have good MS support. Similar cases occur involving the neuter singular and plural: cf Plaut *Poen* 542 *per iocum itidem dictum habeto quae nos tibi respondimus; Men* 990-1; Turpilius *com* 70 Ribbeck: see LHS 2.431.

Ph 182

GE. nullus es, Geta, nisi iam aliquod tibi consilium celere reperis,
ita nunc inparatum subito tanta re inpendent mala;
quae neque uti devitem scio neque quo modo me inde extraham,
quae si non astu providentur me aut erum pessum dabunt; (181a)
nam non potest celari nostra diutius iam audacia, (182)
AN. quid illic commotus venit?
GE. tum temporis mihi punctum ad hanc rem est: erus adest. AN. quid illuc malist?

182 iam diutius *L*: iam *om ADGp*^{1}

Line 181a is a doublet of *An* 208 and has been regarded as an interpolation here by almost all editors, though it is retained by Kauer-Lindsay. In the context of the *Andria* the disjunctive *me aut erum* makes perfect sense. The speaker there, the slave Davos, goes on to say (210-11) that, if he abandons his young master, he fears for his life (ie he thinks the young man may commit suicide). But if he helps him, he fears what he himself will suffer at the hands of the old master. In the context of the *Phormio* the disjunctive is inappropriate. Indeed any reference to his young master is out of place at this point.

It is only at line 187 that the speaker goes on to think of Antipho (*quom mihi paveo, tum Antipho me excruciat animi*). Moreover, the repetition at 181a of the connecting relative *quae* is awkward. *Ph* 181a must be an interpolation.

Line 182 is an iambic octonarius. The line will not scan, however, if *iam* is omitted as in ADGp, the sixth foot consisting of a pyrrhic *-tĭŭs*.[11] Here then there seems to be a significant error shared by the Bembinus and the δ branch of the tradition – an omission which cannot have been caused by the confusion of similar letters or by the presence of the same letters as in *iam* in the immediate context. Such an omission is unlikely to have occurred independently.

The line, however, is probably interpolated. As the passage is transmitted, line 182 goes closely with 181a. If 181a is excised, the connection of thought between 179-81 and 182 is more tenuous but not objectionable. It is the presence of 184 which suggests the expulsion of 182. The adverb *tum* in 184 should introduce a new point, namely the shortage of time at Geta's disposal, but after 182 *tum* makes little sense.[12] If both 181a and 182 are removed, the sequence of thought in the passage is as follows. Line 179 makes two points: the need for a plan and the need to find one quickly. Line 180 gives the reason for this in general terms. In line 181 Geta says that he does not have a plan, thus picking up one of the points in 179. In line 184 the second point in 179, the need for promptness in finding a plan, is further developed.

It might be argued that the spuriousness of the verse does not affect the significance of the common error in *ADGp*, particularly if the verse was interpolated at an early stage in the transmission. But that argument carries weight only if the verse originally contained *iam*. It is just as possible that the verse as transmitted in *ADGp* was the original form and that *iam* in the γ MSS is an intrusive gloss. If an actor was responsible for the verse, he may not have felt that there was anything objectionable metrically about the line ending *diutius audacia*.[13]

Ph 724 (iambic octonarius)

non sat tuom te officium fecisse si non id fama adprobat:

satis est tuom *A*δ

The Aδ reading is unmetrical, unless *id si non* is read in the second half of the verse (so most editors, following Guyet). Kauer-Lindsay and Marouzeau read *non sat est*, a conflation of the two readings in the transmission. It is difficult to decide what should be read. The γ reading could easily have arisen from miscopying of *satisesttuom*, with the omission of *isest* between the final t of *sat* and the initial t of *tuom*. The preference of most editors sounds better rhythmically.

Ph 828

rogem quod tempus conveniundi patris me capere iubeat?

iubeat] suadeat *Aδ*

The γ reading gives an iambic septenarius, the metre of the rest of the monologue. With *suadeat* 828 is an iambic octonarius. A parallel for this sequence, pointed out by Dziatzko-Hauler, occurs at *Ad* 707-12, where 712 is a final iambic octonarius after septenarii. *iubeat* may have been a gloss on *suadeat* to remove the syntactic 'irregularity' of the infinitive following *suadeat*. The variants occur also at *Haut* 786 where the Calliopian MSS offer *iusseras* against *suaseras* of the Bembinus. I find it impossible to choose with confidence between the two verbs at *Ph* 828.

Ph 1040 (trochaic septenarius)

CH. hem, quid ais? NA. adeo hoc indignum tibi videtur, filius

adeo *CPv*: adeon *cett* hoc indignum *A*: indignum *CPv*: indignum hoc *cett*

For the verse to scan one must read either *adeon indignum hoc* or *adeo hoc indignum*. The latter is more probable. We have here, therefore, an error of AΔ, though the addition of the interrogative particule *-ne* is hardly of great significance.

Hec 485

quibus iris pulsus nunc in illam iniquos sim

inpulsus: *AD*[1]*Lp,schol E,Fv*

The line will scan if *inpulsus* is read (with 'shortening' of the first syllable of *illam*), but the resulting spondaic word-ending in the third foot is rare in Terence. A better possibility would be *quibus iris nunc impulsus* (so Dziatzko, following a suggestion in *PhilAnz* 8.403). I give preference to *pulsus*. The corruption to *inpulsus* is not unexpected after the preceding line: *verum vide ne inpulsus ira prave insistas, Pamphile.*

Ad 5

indicio de se ipse erit, vos eritis iudices
laudin an vitio duci factum oporteat.

duci id factum *Aδ* (*praeter* p^1)

Ad 236

iamne enumerasti quod ad te rediturum putes?

quod CPF^1: id quod *cett*

In both these examples it is more likely that *id* is an intrusive gloss.

To the initial list of twenty AΔ errors, then, we may add *Eun* 803, *Ph* 1040, *Hec* 48, *Ad* 5, *Ad* 236. In addition there are a few examples where the γ MSS offer the archaic form for a 'modern' one in Aδ: *necessum* for *necesse* at *Ph* 296, *quicum* for *quocum* at *Ph* 759, *hisce* for *his* at *Hec* 450, and *illuc* for *illud* at *Ad* 228. As in those cases where the δ MSS had archaic forms against Aγ (above p 163) one cannot be certain that the archaic forms are correct. Even if they are, corruption could have occurred independently.

Other γ readings have won the support of some editors, but in no case is the γ reading definitely correct, and apart from possibly two examples the alleged errors shared by the Bembinus and the δ MSS do not indicate contamination.[14] These two examples occur at *Eun* 1052 and *Ph* 747.

Eun 1052

CH. nil est Thaide hac, frater, tua (1051)
dignius quod ametur: ita nostrae omnist fautrix familiae. PH. hui,
mihi illam laudas?

1052 PH. *om* C^1P^1F hui *om* AD^1p 1053 PH. mihi C^1P^1F

This is as printed by Kauer-Lindsay. If they are correct, we have a common omission of Aδ. It is significant, however, that C^1P^1F give *hui* as the last word spoken by Chaerea in 1052. This is nonsense and indicates that *hui* was originally an interlinear gloss which has not been correctly integrated into the text. The reading of AD[1]p is to be preferred.

At *Ph* 747 the γ MSS read *em* (or *hem*) *istoc pol* against the other MSS. With Umpfenbach and Dziatzko I would reject *em* as an interpolation.

While AΔ share a larger number of errors than AΓ, the quantity is still very small when seen against the large number of differences between A and Σ and between Γ and Δ. The nature of the errors shared by AΔ is similar to that of the AΓ errors. There is not one which could not have occurred independently. The common omissions in examples 1-7 are explicable in graphical terms. The omissions of *id* at *Haut* 605, of *iam* at *Ph* 182, of *hui* at *Eun* 1052, and of *em* at *Ph* 747 would be much more significant for indicating contamination between Δ and a MS related to the Bembinus, but in these four examples the γ reading is, I believe, wrong. The conclusion must be the same as that drawn for the relationship between Γ and a Bembinus-type MS in the first part of this chapter. There is no strong evidence to assume any contact between Δ and an ancient MS which was independent of Σ and related to A. Editors must make allowance for independent errors and the presence of glosses in Σ and Φ but for the most part the agreement of AΓ and AΔ will provide the reading of Φ.

APPENDIX

Selected Readings from Manuscripts of Terence

Over the past several years I have partially collated a large number of Terence MSS. Some of these were inspected in the libraries which house them, some have been collated from microfilm. In each play I examined more than sixty places where differences among the major MSS had already been noted by previous editors. A vast amount of data has been gathered and some of it is offered here in the hope that the information will be helpful and time-saving to those who are or will be engaged in the study of the Terence tradition in the medieval and Renaissance periods. I have selected thirty places in each play where variants occur. The information about the variants has been coded and put in tabular form for the six plays. Except where two closely related MSS are adjacent in the listing, as, for example, Milan, Ambros D 79 sup and F 92 sup in the listing for *Andria*, it will take some effort and time to detect those MSS which share a large number of readings. In the long run, however, time may be saved. For *Phormio* and *Adelphoe* I have given the collations of the 1475 edition (Milan, Antonio Zarotto), in his copy of which Poliziano added notes based on his knowledge of the Bembinus. The text of this edition for the *Adelphoe* will be seen to be very close to that found in three MSS: Florence, BNC II IV 689; Oxford, Magd 23; and Paris, BN lat 7910. Collations of other editions and MSS and comparisons with the information given in this appendix should cast some light on the sources for early printed editions of Terence.

Like a scribe whose work he is examining a collator makes errors, particularly when collation is done for several hours. Errors there will be in this appendix, as it has been impossible to check many of the readings and I have had to trust in my notes. My hope is that the errors will be few enough not to deceive the enquirer in his search for MSS which are closely related. At any rate, the information given here is only the starting point and closer collation and inspection of MSS will be needed.

In the tables an asterisk denotes a lacuna in the text or some deficiency in my notes. In the variants minor spelling differences have for the most part been ignored, as have other divergences which were not relevant to the point at issue. The first variant, which is usually the text of the OCT, should be viewed as the lemma against which the subsequent variants are reported. Only readings of the first hand have been recorded.

Andria

1 (50): 1. in hac re te 2. te in hac re 3. te *om* 4. in hac te re 5. te ... in hac re 6. in hac re ... te

2 (121): 1. quid obstat 2. quid igitur obstat 3. quid ergo obstat

3 (181): 1. interoscitantes 2. interea oscitantes 3. inter mi obsitantes 4. inter *om* 5. inter sociantes 6. interea obs(c)itantes 7. inter obs(c)itantes

4 (237): 1. pro deum fidem 2. pro deum atque hominum fidem 3. pro deum fidem atque hominum

5 (252): 1. ego dicam 2. ego nunc dicam 3. nunc ego dicam 4. dicam ... ego 5. ego nunc (dicam *om*) 6. ego dicam nunc

6 (269): 1. sunt constitutae 2. sunt *om* 3. constitutae sunt

7 (293): 1. haec te 2. te haec 3. te *om*

8 (320): 1. ad auxilium 2. auxilii 3. ad auxiliandum 4. auxiliandi 5. auxilium

9 (348): 1. etsi scio 2. et id scio 3. et scio 4. etsi sint scio 5. id scio 6. et hoc scio 7. et scio id 8. etsi id scio

10 (349): 1. paves 2. praecaves 3. cave 4. caves 5. praecaves paves 6. times 7. praecave

11 (353-4): 1. dare hodie 2. dare se(se) hodie 3. dare hodie se(se) 4. se(se) dare hodie

12 (377): 1. esse iniurius videatur 2. videatur esse iniurius 3. videatur iniurius (esse *om*) 4. iniurius esse videatur 5. iniurius videatur (esse *om*) 6. esse iniurius (videatur *om*)

13 (378): 1. tuum ut se(se) habeat animum 2. tuum animum ut se habeat 3. tuum ut habeat se animum 4. tuum animum habeat ut se 5. tuum ad se habeat animum 6. tuum se ut habeat

animum 7. ut tuum animum se habeat 8. tuum in se habeat animum 9. animum tuum se ut habeat

14 (427): 1. malle melius esse 2. esse melius malle 3. melius esse malle 4. malle melius (esse *om*) 5. esse melius (malle *om*) 6. melius malle (esse *om*) 7. malle (melius esse *om*)

15 (422): 1. ipsus 2. ipse 3. ipsius 4. ipsus *om*

16 (484): 1. iussi dari 2. iussi ei dari 3. iussi ei dare 4. iussi dare ei 5. iussi ei date 6. iussi ei da 7. iussi dari ei 8. iussi date ei 9. iussi date

17 (530): 1. haud dubium est mihi id 2. haud d. est id mihi 3. haud d. mihi est id 4. haud d. id mihi est 5. haud d. mihi est (id *om*) 6. haud est id mihi d. 7. haud d. est mihi (id *om*) 8. haud d. mihi (id *et* est *om*) 9. haud d. id mihi (est *om*) 10. haud d. mihi id est 11. haud d. id est mihi 12. id mihi haud d. est

18 (532): 1. obviam 2. obviam Chremen(-em) 3. obviam Chremetem(-en)

19 (544): 1. a me impetrare 2. impetrare a me 3. apud me impetrare 4. me impetrare (a *om*)

20 (614): 1. nunc me faciam 2. nunc de me faciam 3. me nunc faciam 4. de me nunc faciam 5. de me faciam (nunc *om*) 6. nunc faciam de me 7. me *om*

21 (614): 1. nec me quidem 2. nec quidem me 3. nec de me quidem 4. nec quid(em) de me 5. ne quidem de me 6. nec quid me

22 (664): 1. satis scio fuisse iratos 2. fuisse ir. satis scio 3. satis fuisse scio ir. 4. satis fuisse ir. (scio *om*) 5. satis scio fuisse (ir. *om*) 6. scio satis fuisse ir.

23 (664): 1. auscultaverim 2. ei ausc. 3. ausc. ei 4. huic ausc.

24 (676): 1. pedibus 2. pedibusque 3. et pedibus 4. pedibus et manibus

25 (717): 1. putabam 2. putavi

26 (726): 1. hinc sume 2. sume hinc 3. sume *om* 4. hinc *om*

27 (773): 1. positum puerum 2. puerum positum 3. puerum *om*

28 (784): 1. audivi iam omnia 2. iam *om* 3. aud. omnia iam

29 (927): 1. se(se) esse atticam 2. se civem esse att. 3. se att. esse 4. se esse att. civem 5. se att. esse civem 6. se civem att. esse 7. att. se esse civem 8. civem esse se att. 9. se att. (esse *om*) 10. se att. civem (esse *om*) 11. att. se esse 12. se att. civem esse 13. se att. fuisse 14. se att. fuisse civem

30 (938): 1. tanto tam repentino hoc bono 2. tanto hoc tam rep. bono 3. hoc tanto tam rep. bono 4. hoc tanto et tam r.

bono 5. hoc tanto bono (tam rep. *om*) 6. ex hoc tam rep. bono 7. hoc tanto rep. bono (tam *om*)

Eunuchus

1 (7): 1. easdem scribendo male 2. easdem conscribendo male 3. eas describendo male 4. easdem male (de)scr. 5. descr. male (easdem *om*) 6. eas male descr. 7. easdem descr. bene

2 (144): 1. nunc ego eam 2. nunc eam ego 3. nunc eam (ego *om*) 4. nunc etiam ego 5. ego nunc eam 6. nunc ego (eam *om*)

3 (152): 1. ni(hi)l respondes 2. ni(hi)l mihi respondes 3. mihi ni(hi)l respondes 4. ni(hi)l respondes mihi

4 (208): 1. eius fratrem spero 2. eius spero fratrem 3. fratrem eius spero 4. spero eius fratrem

5 (238): 1. noti me 2. me noti 3. mei noti 4. noti mei 5. noti (me *om*) 6. me *ante* deserunt 7. me *post* deserunt

6 (239): 1. quid homo 2. quid a(g)is homo 3. quid ego homo

7 (255): 1. advenimus 2. adventamus 3. convenimus 4. venimus

8 (277): 1. Parmeno hos mensis 2. Parm. mensis hos 3. Parm. hos (menses *om*) 4. mensis Parm. hos 5. Parm. mensis (hos *om*)

9 (302): 1. senium perdant 2. omnes senem perd. 3. senem omnes perd. 4. omnes perd. (senem *om*) 5. omnes perd. senem 6. omnes senium perd.

10 (316): 1. bona est 2. est bona 3. est *om* 4. bonum est

11 (324): 1. quemquam ego esse hominem 2. ego qu. hominem esse 3. qu. esse ego hominem 4. qu. esse hominem (ego *om*) 5. qu. hominem esse (ego *om*) 6. qu. esse hominem ego 7. qu. hominem esse ego 8. qu. esse (ego *et* hominem *om*)

12 (354): 1. fratris partes praedicas 2. partes fratris praedicas 3. partes praedicas fratris

13 (355): 1. dono contra 2. contra dono 3. dono *om*

14 (445): 1. par pro pari 2. pro *om*

15 (454): 1. vocem visa sum modo militis 2. visa sum vocem modo mil. 3. visa sum modo vocem mil. 4. vocem modo visa sum mil. 5. modo vocem visa sum mil. 6. vocem modo mil. visa sum 7. vocem mil. visa sum modo 8. modo visa sum vocem mil. 9. sum visa modo vocem mil. 10. vocem militis modo visa sum

16 (490): 1. huic animum adsentari 2. ads. huic animum 3. huic ads. animum 4. animum ads. huic
17 (491): 1. petere te cibum 2. te cibum petere 3. te petere cibum 4. tibi cibum (petere *om*) 5. te cibum ... petere 6. petere cibum (te *om*)
18 (519): 1. habeam 2. haberem 3. habeo 4. habebam
19 (565): 1. ego 2. ego *om* 3. ergo
20 (588): 1. atque in alienas 2. et per al. 3. atque per al. 4. perque al. 5. ac per al.
21 (639): 1. licet 2. potest 3. licebit 4. posset 5. possi
22 (673): 1. ornarat 2. adornabat 3. adornarat 4. adornat 5. adornavit 6. adornaverat 7. adornabit
23 (694): 1. hoc mi(hi) 2. hoc nunc mi(hi) 3. hoc mi(hi) nunc 4. mihi nunc (hoc *om*) 5. mihi hoc
24 (721): 1. utrum taceam an praedicemne 2. utrum taceamne an praedicam 3. utrumne taceam an praedicem 4. utrum taceam an praedicem
25 (727): 1. verba mihi sunt 2. mihi verba sunt 3. verba sunt mi(hi) 4. sunt verba mi(hi)
26 (770): 1. ipsi est opus patrono 2. ipsi opus est patr. 3. ipsi opus patr. est 4. opus est patr. (ipsi *om*)
27 (781): 1. ego hic 2. hic ego 3. hic *om* 4. hos ego
28 (894): 1. dum venit 2. dum is venit 3. dum venit is 4. dum venerit
29 (945): 1. ne viderem 2. ne id viderem 3. ne viderem id 4. ne videam 5. ne *om*
30 (1071): 1. non facere 2. non id facere 3. id non facere 4. non facere id

Hauton timorumenos

1 (18): 1. factum id esse 2. id esse factum 3. id factum esse
2 (18): 1. hic 2. hic *om*
3 (72): 1. at enim dices 2. at enim dices me 3. at dices enim me 4. at dices etenim me
4 (75): 1. ab re tua est 2. est ab re tua 3. est *om*
5 (81): 1. est usus homini 2. est homini usus 3. usus homini (est *om*) 4. hominum est usus 5. homini est usus 6. est utile homini 7. homini opus est
6 (108): 1. in te sit 2. sit in te 3. sit *om* 4. te (in *et* sit *om*) 5. in te me sit
7 (156): 1. ille est credere ausus 2. ille cr. est ausus 3. est ille cr. ausus 4. ille *om* 5. est *om* 6. cr. ille ausus (est *om*) 7. cr.

ille est ausus 8. ille est ausus cr. 9. ille cr. ausus est 10. ille ausus cr. (est *om*) 11. est cr. ausus ille

8 (170): 1. ibo visam 2. ibo ut visam 3. ibo visum 4. ibo et visam

9 (192): 1. miserum se(se) esse 2. se(se) miserum esse 3. miserum esse se(se) 4. miserum esse (se *om*) 5. esse miserum

10 (211): 1. nobis quid in cena siet 2. nobis cenae quid siet 3. cenae quid nobis siet 4. nobis quid cenae siet 5. cenae nobis quid siet

11 (261): 1. monuisse frustra 2. mon. frustra dolet 3. dolet mon. frustra 4. mon. me se frustra dolet 5. doluisse mon. frustra

12 (368): 1. hoc 2. hoc *om* 3. ob hoc

13 (426): 1. ibo adloquar 2. adibo atque adl. 3. ibo atque adl. 4. ibo et adl. 5. adibo atque illi adl. 6. adibo atque eloquar 7. adibo adl. 8. adibo atque conloquar

14 (430): 1. domi 2. domi est 3. est ... domi 4. domi *om*

15 (498): 1. paul(ul)um negoti 2. paul. hoc negoti 3. paul. hic negoti 4. paul. hoc mihi negoti 5. paul. mihi negoti hoc 6. paul. negoti hic

16 (520): 1. visa vero est 2. visa est vero 3. visa vero in te est 4. vero visa est 5. visa non est 6. est *om*

17 (572): 1. concedas 2. concedas hinc 3. ut concedas 4. cedas

18 (609): 1. inesse in ea lucrum 2. in ea esse lucrum 3. esse in ea lucrum 4. in ea lucrum esse 5. esse ei lucrum 6. ei esse lucrum 7. esse lucrum in ea(dem) 8. in ea magnum esse 9. esse lucrum (in ea *om*)

19 (610): 1. nunc tibi ego respondeo 2. ego nunc tibi resp. 3. nunc ego tibi resp. 4. ego nunc resp. tibi 5. ego nunc resp. (tibi *om*) 6. ego tibi nunc resp. 7. ego tibi resp. (nunc *om*) 8. nunc tibi resp. (ego *om*) 9. tibi ego nunc resp.

20 (669): 1. hac re 2. hercle 3. hac re hercle 4. hercle hac re

21 (669): 1. nunc meae coguntur copiae 2. meae nunc cog. copiae 3. meae *om* 4. nunc cog. copiae meae 5. nunc me cog. copiae

22 (677): 1. euge 2. euge *om*

23 (678): 1. opinor ad me idem illuc(-d) 2. il. opinor ad me idem 3. il. opinor ad me (idem *om*) 4. idem il. (ut) opinor ad me 5. ad me idem il. ... opinor 6. opinor ad me il. idem 7. opinor *om* 8. opinor ad me il. (idem *om*) 9. opinor ad me idem (illuc *om*)

24 (716): 1. me aetatem censes 2. me tandem censes 3. tandem censes (me aet. *om*) 4. me censes (aet. *om*) 5. tandem me censes

25 (812): 1. mihi res semper 2. semper mihi res 3. res mihi semper 4. mihi semper res 5. res *om* 6. semper *om*

26 (825): 1. sum homo fortunatus 2. fort. homo sum 3. homo fort. sum 4. fort. sum homo 5. homo sum fort. 6. fort. homo (sum *om*) 7. fort. sum (homo *om*) 8. sum fort. homo 9. sum homo *om* 10. fort. homo desum

27 (842): 1. nunc me 2. me nunc 3. me *om* 4. nunc *om* 5. nunc me *om* 6. me ... nunc

28 (909): 1. decem dierum vix mi(hi) 2. decem vix dierum mihi 3. decem dierum mihi vix 4. vix est decem dierum (mihi *om*) 5. decem dierum est mihi vix 6. decem dierum vix est mihi

29 (939): 1. si minus 2. si minus est 3. si est minus 4. si quid minus 5. si nihil minus 6. si minus *om* 7. si quid minus est

30 (1001): 1. ad Menedemum hunc pergam 2. hinc nunc ad M. pergam 3. ad M. hinc pergam 4. ad M. hinc (pergam *om*) 5. ad M. (hunc pergam *om*) 6. ad M. hinc nunc pergam 7. hic nunc ad M. pergam 8. hinc ad M. pergam

Phormio

1 (13): 1. vetus si poeta non 2. vetus poeta si non 3. vetus non si poeta 4. si poeta vetus non 5. si *om*

2 (73): 1. usu 2. usus 3. per usum 4. usum 5. usu *om*

3 (130): 1. mater qui 2. mater unde qui 3. qui *om* 4. mater quae 5. mater qua

4 (161): 1. adimat hanc mi(hi) 2. hanc mihi ad. 3. hanc ad. mihi 4. ad. mihi hanc 5. mihi hanc ad.

5 (178): 1. is est ipsus 2. is est ipsus est 3. is ipsus est 4. ipsus is est 5. is est (ipsus *om*) 6. ipsus est (is *om*)

6 (182): 1. diutius iam 2. iam *om* 3. iam diutius

7 (221): 1. hic nos 2. nos hic 3. hic *om* 4. id nos 5. nos *om*

8 (284): 1. ibi 2. ibi *om* 3. illi 4. ubi

9 (323): 1. senis 2. patris 3. patris senis 4. senis *om*

10 (345): 1. hunc 2. eum 3. hunc *om* 4. illum

11 (392): 1. istoc 2. isto 3. ex hoc 4. hoc 5. illo

12 (451): 1. aequum est et bonum 2. aeq. ac bonum est 3. aeq. esse et bonum 4. aeq. et bonum est 5. aeq. ac bonum esse 6. aeq. est ac bonum 7. aeq. esse ac bonum est 8. aeq. ac bonum (est *om*)

13 (474): 1. ni(hi)l etiam 2. nihil adhuc etiam

14 (491): 1. idem ego metuo 2. idem et ego metuo 3. idem et

metuo 4. metuo *om* 5. idem metuo 6. idem metuo ego 7. ego idem metuo

15 (521): 1. et ni(hi)l ferentem flentem 2. flentem et nihil ferentem 3. et *om* 4. flentem *om* 5. et mihi ferentem flentem 6. et in his ferentem flentem

16 (548): 1. ignotum a(b)ducet 2. ign. hinc abducet 3. ign. abducet locum hinc 4. ignotum (abducet *om*) 5. ign. deducet 6. incognitum ducet 7. ign. ducet

17 (588): 1. mihi res 2. res mihi 3. res *om* 4. mihi *om*

18 (589): 1. usque 2. usquam 3. umquam 4. inquam 5. numquam

19 (662): 1. minas inquit 2. minas est inq. 3. inquit *om*

20 (679): 1. adeo argentum nunc mecum 2. adeo nunc arg. mecum 3. adeo nunc mecum arg. 4. nunc adeo arg. mecum 5. adeo arg. mecum (nunc *om*)

21 (703): 1. sunt dabunt 2. sunt argentum dabunt 3. sunt dabunt argentum 4. argentum dabunt (sunt *om*) 5. sunt argentum (dabunt *om*)

22 (729): 1. unde auxilium 2. unde mihi aux. 3. unde aux. mihi 4. mihi aux. (unde *om*)

23 (759): 1. et 2. atque 3. et atque 4. et *om* 5. aut

24 (806): 1. siet 2. est 3. sciet 4. sit

25 (876): 1. quae inter se(se) ipsi 2. ipsi quae inter se 3. quae intus se ipsi 4. ipsi *om* 5. inter se quae ipsi 6. inter quae se (ipsi *om*)

26 (930): 1. in hinc malam rem 2. in hinc in malam rem 3. hinc in malam rem 4. i hinc in malam rem 5. in malam rem hinc 6. i in malam rem 7. i hinc malam (rem *om*) 8. i nunc in malam rem 9. i in malam rem hinc 10. in malam rem hinc i

27 (953): 1. dixisse nemini 2. dix. id nemini 3. nemini dix. id 4. dix. nemini id 5. id dix. nemini

28 (992): 1. hicine ut tibi 2. h. ut tibi nunc 3. h. nunc tibi ut 4. h. quaeris ut tibi 5. h. nunc ut tibi 6. h. tibi ut 7. h. tibi nunc (ut *om*)

29 (1040): 1. adeo(n) hoc indignum 2. adeo indignum (hoc *om*) 3. adeo indignum hoc 4. hoc indignum *om*

30 (1043): 1. meam iam 2. iam meam 3. iam *om* 4. etiam meam 5. meam *om*

Hecyra

1 (23): 1. atque a(b) labore 2. ac labore 3. a labore 4. atque labore

2 (62): 1. ducturum uxorem 2. uxorem ducturum 3. uxorem *om*

3 (73): 1. captent eadem 2. captent illi eadem 3. captent ipsi eadem

4 (110): 1. tu non 2. non tu 3. non *om* 4. tu nam 5. tu *om*

5 (111): 1. percontor 2. perconter 3. percuncter 4. percunctor 5. percunctetur

6 (139): 1. potus sese illa 2. potus se illa 3. potus sed illa 4. potis se illa 5. potis se ab illa 6. potens se illa 7. potes se illa 8. potis se (illa *om*) 9. potuisse illa 10. potis se ipsa 11. potus se ab illa 12. potis ab illa (se *om*)

7 (164): 1. esse ingenio 2. ingenio esse

8 (238): 1. lassam oppido 2. lassam eam oppido 3. eam lassam oppido 4. lassam eam (oppido *om*)

9 (262): 1. ille redeat 2. ille huc redeat 3. ille ut redeat 4. ille redeat huc

10 (277): 1. expurgatu 2. expurgatum 3. excusatu 4. accusatum 5. expurgari 6. expurgata

11 (300): 1. nisi porro 2. porro nisi 3. nisi ut porro 4. nisi *om*

12 (368): 1. me repente 2. me derepente 3. derepente me 4. derepente (me *om*)

13 (396): 1. partus eveniat 2. eveniat partus

14 (404): 1. amor me graviter 2. me amor graviter 3. me *om* 4. amor graviter me

15 (472): 1. et benigno 2. et benigno *om*

16 (505): 1. iam 2. iam *om*

17 (538): 1. posse filiam tuam 2. filiam posse tuam 3. filiam tuam posse

18 (579): 1. exoptem 2. exopto 3. opto 4. optem 5. expecto 6. opta

19 (594): 1. iam tenet 2. iam me tenet 3. me tenet (iam *om*) 4. me iam tenet

20 (609): 1. idem hoc nunc si 2. idem nunc si non (hoc *om*) 3. idem hoc modo si (nunc *om*) 4. idem nunc hoc si 5. idem hoc si nunc 6. id nunc si non 7. idem hoc nunc (si *om*) 8. idem hoc ne si

21 (643): 1. natum tibi illam salvam 2. natum illum tibi et illam s. 3. natum illum et tibi illam s. 4. natum illi tibi et s. illam 5. natum illum tibi illam s. 6. illum natum tibi et s. illam

22 (676): 1. sit id quod 2. sit hoc id quod 3. sit hoc quod

23 (693): 1. falsas causas 2. causas falsas

24 (758): 1. nolo esse falsa fama 2. esse falsa fama nolo 3. nolo esse fama falsa 4. nolo falsa fama (esse *om*)

25 (779): 1. tua se uxor credidisse 2. tua se uxor falso cred. 3. se tua uxor falso cred. 4. tua uxor falso cred. (se *om*) 5. uxor tua se falso cred. 6. se uxor falso cred. (tua *om*)

26 (787): 1. coge 2. coge *om* 3. et age

27 (828): 1. in via nescioquam compressise 2. in via virginem nescioquam compr. 3. in via nescio virginem quam compr. 4. in via quam compr. 5. nescioquam compr. in via virginem 6. in via vi virginem nescioquam compr.

28 (849): 1. pro hoc te 2. te pro hoc 3. pro hoc munere te 4. te *om* 5. pro homo te

29 (849): 1. qui qui 2. quid qui 3. quid quid 4. qui qui *om* 5. qui 6. qui quid 7. quid negem qui 8. quicquam 9. quod qui

30 (868): 1. autem aequom est scire 2. autem est aeq. scire 3. autem scire aeq. est 4. autem aeq. est (scire *om*) 5. autem scire est aeq. 6. autem erit aeq. scire

Adelphoe

1 (5): 1. duci factum 2. duci id f. 3. factum duci 4. duci *om* 5. factum id (duci *om*) 6. duci (factum *om*) 7. id factum duci 8. duci id (factum *om*)

2 (38): 1. in animo instituere 2. inst. in animo 3. inst. aut in animo 4. in animo *om* 5. in animo constituere 6. in animum inst. 7. in animo instruere

3 (64): 1. aequumque et bonum 2. -que *om* 3. bonum et aequum

4 (140): 1. gravius dicere 2. gravius quicquam dic. 3. quicquam gravius dic. 4. gravius dic. quicquam 5. quicquam dic. (gravius *om*) 6. quicquam dic. gravius 7. dic. gravius quicquam

5 (168): 1. nunc iam 2. iam nunc tu 3. nunc tu iam 4. nunc iam tu 5. iam tu nunc 6. nunc iam *om* 7. nunc tu (iam *om*) 8. tu nunc iam 9. iam nunc (tu *om*) 10. tu iam nunc

6 (200): 1. homini 2. o homini 3. heu homini 4. et homini 5. ve homini 6. hei homini

7 (208): 1. puto 2. deputo 3. reputo 4. disputo

8 (235): 1. quam hic nunc 2. quam aut hic nunc 3. quam aut hic 4. quam aut nunc 5. quam nunc hic 6. quam hic 7. quam nunc 8. quam haud id nunc

9 (256): 1. nunc te 2. te nunc 3. te *om*

10 (281): 1. obsecro hercle te 2. te *om* 3. obsecro te hercle 4. hercle te *om* 5. hercle *om* 6. te obsecro hercle

11 (294): 1. mearum miseriarum est remedium 2. mearum est mis. rem. 3. mis. mearum est rem. 4. mearum mis. rem. est 5. mearum est rem. (mis. *om*) 6. est mearum rem. mis. 7. mearum mis. rem. (est *om*) 8. est mearum mis. rem.
12 (304): 1. inpium 2. impurum
13 (348): 1. conscia mihi sum 2. conscia sum mihi 3. mihi conscia sum 4. sum conscia mihi 5. mihi *om*
14 (366): 1. quicquam vidi laetius 2. vidi quicquam laetius 3. quicquam *om* 4. quicquam laetius vidi
15 (390): 1. haecin(e) fieri 2. h. fieri flagitia 3. h. fieri sinit 4. h. fieri sinit flagitia 5. h. flagitia 6. h. sine flagitia
16 (468): 1. quid est etiam amplius 2. quicquam est etiam amplius 3. quidem etiam est amplius 4. quicquam est amplius (etiam *om*) 5. quicquam etiam est amplius 6. quid est amplius (etiam *om*) 7. quidem etiam amplius (est *om*)
17 (507): 1. hic 2. hoc 3. haec 4. hic *om*
18 (518): 1. nunc cum maxume 2. nunc autem m. 3. nunc eum m. 4. nunc autem eum m. 5. cum *om* 6. nunc autem cum m. 7. nunc etiam m.
19 (538): 1. pater est 2. p. adest 3. est *om* 4. paterne (est *om*) 5. p. estne 6. paterne adest 7. paterne est
20 (560): 1. hinc modo 2. hinc mihi 3. modo *om* 4. hinc *om* 5. hinc modo *om* 6. hinc mihi modo
21 (631): 1. iam 2. nunc iam 3. nunc 4. nam 5. non
22 (632): 1. ut purgem me 2. me ut purgem 3. me *om* 4. ut me purgem 5. ut expurgem me 6. me ut expurgem
23 (698): 1. eo 2. ideo 3. id 4. immo 5. eo *om* 6. idem
24 (711): 1. ne imprudens forte faciam 2. ne forte impr. faciam 3. forte *om* 4. ne impr. faciam forte 5. ne forte impudens faciam
25 (762): 1. non potest(-erit) hanc familiam 2. hanc familiam non pot. 3. non hanc familiam pot. 4. non potis est hanc familiam 5. hanc non pot. familiam
26 (808): 1. hoc facito 2. facito hoc 3. facito haec 4. hoc *om* 5. haec facito
27 (877): 1. possiem 2. possim 3. possem 4. possum 5. possiem *om* 6. posse
28 (878): 1. hoc (huc) 2. eo 3. huc eo 4. illuc 5. ego 6. hoc *om*
29 (892): 1. te esse 2. esse te 3. esse *om* 4. te *om*
30 (905): 1. cantent 2. cantet 3. canat 4. cantitet 5. cantat 6. canant 7. amat.

ANDRIA

		1	2	3	4	5	6	7	8	9	10	11	12	13	14	15	16	17	18	19	20	21	22	23	24	25	26	27	28	29	30
Bamberg	Staatsbibl Class 48	3	2	1	2	1	1	2	2	2	2	2	2	2	4	2	3	1	3	2	4	4	1	3	1	2	1	2	1	11	3
	Class 49	2	2	1	2	1	1	1	2	2	1	2	2	2	1	1	9	3	2	1	2	3	2	2	2	1	2	1	1	2	2
Barcelona	BC 1743	1	2	2	3	1	1	2	2	*	2	2	2	2	1	2	2	2	1	2	4	4	6	2	1	2	1	1	2	3	2
Brussels	BR 5329	*	*	*	*	*	*	*	2	8	1	2	2	2	1	2	2	2	1	2	4	4	1	2	2	2	1	2	2	6	3
	BR 9705	1	2	2	1	1	1	2	3	1	2	3	2	2	3	1	2	2	1	2	3	2	1	2	1	2	1	2	2	3	3
Cambridge	UL Add 3024	1	2	1	3	2	1	1	2	2	2	2	1	1	3	1	7	2	2	1	2	3	1	3	2	*	*	*	2	5	5
	UL Add 3109	1	2	2	3	1	1	2	2	2	5	2	1	1	2	1	4	10	2	1	5	3	1	3	1	1	2	1	2	5	3
	CCC 231	1	1	2	3	1	1	2	3	2	1	2	*	*	1	2	3	2	2	2	4	4	4	2	3	2	1	1	2	3	3
	Peterhouse 253	1	2	6	3	6	1	1	3	2	2	2	2	9	1	1	7	12	1	2	4	4	1	2	2	1	1	3	2	2	7
Edinburgh	NL Adv 18.2.10	1	2	5	3	2	1	1	2	5	1	2	1	1	2	1	3	2	3	1	2	3	1	3	2	1	2	1	3	4	4
	NL Adv 18.7.2	*	2	2	2	*	*	*	*	*	*	*	*	*	1	2	3	2	4	2	4	3	2	3	3	2	1	2	2	6	3
Erlangen	Univ 391	2	2	1	2	2	2	1	3	2	1	2	1	3	2	1	1	1	2	1	2	1	1	1	3	1	1	2	2	3	3
	Univ 392	*	*	*	*	*	*	*	*	*	*	*	*	*	2	1	3	4	2	*	2	3	1	3	1	*	*	1	2	*	*
Escorial, El	S.III.23	4	1	1	1	1	1	2	2	2	2	1	2	2	1	2	2	2	1	2	3	2	1	2	1	2	1	2	2	3	3
Florence	Med-Laur 38.15	1	2	7	3	2	1	1	2	2	1	2	1	1	6	1	2	7	3	1	1	3	1	3	2	1	2	1	1	10	4
	38.19	1	2	7	2	2	1	2	2	2	1	2	5	7	3	1	8	10	3	1	1	4	4	2	2	1	1	2	2	6	4
	38.20	1	1	2	3	1	1	2	2	4	2	2	1	2	1	2	5	2	1	2	4	1	1	2	1	2	1	2	2	3	3
	38.21	1	2	1	3	2	1	2	3	3	1	2	1	1	2	1	2	2	1	1	4	3	2	3	2	2	1	1	1	13	3
	38.23	1	2	7	3	2	3	1	2	5	6	4	1	1	2	1	2	11	1	1	4	3	4	3	2	1	1	1	2	5	4
	38.24	2	*	1	2	2	2	1	3	1	1	2	1	3	*	*	1	3	2	1	1	1	2	1	2	1	2	1	1	2	2
	38.27	1	2	1	2	2	1	1	2	2	1	2	4	3	2	1	3	4	2	1	2	3	1	3	2	1	2	1	2	8	4
	38.28	1	2	1	2	1	1	1	2	2	1	2	1	1	6	*	2	7	2	1	2	3	6	3	2	1	2	1	2	10	3
	38.31	6	2	1	3	2	1	1	2	2	1	4	1	1	3	1	2	2	2	1	2	3	1	3	2	1	2	2	1	10	4
	91 sup 13,1	1	2	1	2	1	1	1	2	2	1	2	1	6	6	1	2	7	2	1	2	3	6	3	2	1	2	1	2	10	4
	Marc 244	1	2	*	2	2	1	1	2	2	2	2	1	1	2	*	3	4	1	1	2	1	1	3	2	1	2	1	1	2	3

		1	2	3	4	5	6	7	8	9	10	11	12	13	14	15	16	17	18	19	20	21	22	23	24	25	26	27	28	29	30
	BN II.IV.6	1	2	7	2	2	1	1	2	5	1	2	1	1	5	1	5	9	3	1	2	3	1	3	2	1	2	1	1	12	4
	Ricc 528	1	1	2	3	1	1	2	2	1	2	2	2	2	1	2	2	1	1	2	2	1	1	2	1	2	1	2	2	3	3
	529	1	2	6	2	1	1	2	2	1	4	2	2	2	1	2	2	2	1	2	3	2	1	1	1	2	1	2	2	3	3
	530	1	2	7	3	2	*	*	2	2	1	2	1	1	2	1	2	7	2	1	2	3	1	3	2	1	2	1	1	10	4
	531	5	2	1	2	2	1	1	3	2	2	2	1	3	2	2	1	7	2	3	5	3	1	2	1	2	2	1	1	3	3
	532	*	*	*	*	*	*	*	2	7	2	2	*	*	*	*	*	*	*	*	*	*	*	*	*	*	*	*	*	*	*
	613	1	2	7	2	2	1	2	2	2	3	2	1	1	2	1	3	1	2	1	4	3	2	3	1	2	*	1	1	13	4
	614	1	2	1	2	1	1	1	2	2	2	2	1	1	4	1	3	7	2	1	2	3	6	3	2	1	2	1	2	3	4
	3608	1	2	7	2	2	3	1	2	2	1	2	1	1	5	1	5	7	3	1	6	3	1	3	3	1	2	1	1	4	4
Glasgow	UL Hunt 26	*	3	1	2	1	1	1	2	2	2	2	1	1	*	*	*	*	*	*	*	*	6	3	2	1	2	1	2	10	*
Hague, The	Kon Bibl 72.J.49	1	2	1	2	2	1	2	2	2	2	2	1	1	2	1	8	5	2	1	2	3	1	3	2	1	1	1	1	2	3
Halle	Marienbibl 65	2	2	2	1	1	1	2	3	1	2	3	2	2	1	1	2	2	1	2	3	2	1	1	1	2	1	2	2	3	3
Leipzig	Univ I.37	2	*	*	*	*	*	*	*	*	*	*	*	3	2	1	1	3	2	1	1	1	2	2	2	1	2	1	1	1	2
Leyden	Rijksuniv BPL 109	*	2	2	3	1	1	2	3	1	3	2	2	2	1	2	2	2	1	2	4	4	1	2	1	2	1	2	2	3	3
	Lips 26	1	1	2	3	1	1	2	3	1	2	1	2	2	4	2	3	2	1	2	4	4	1	2	1	2	1	2	2	6	3
	Voss lat O.31	1	1	1	1	6	1	2	2	2	1	1	2	2	1	2	2	2	1	2	3	4	1	1	3	2	1	1	2	3	3
	Voss lat Q.38	1	2	2	3	2	1	1	2	2	3	2	1	1	2	1	2	4	2	1	2	2	1	2	1	1	2	1	1	2	2
London	BL Harl 2455	1	2	1	2	2	1	1	2	3	1	2	1	1	3	1	5	2	1	1	4	3	2	3	2	1	1	1	2	5	3
	2475	1	2	1	2	1	1	1	2	2	7	2	5	1	3	1	4	2	2	1	6	3	1	3	2	1	2	1	2	7	3
	2524	1	2	2	3	1	1	1	2	1	1	2	2	2	1	2	3	2	1	2	3	4	1	2	1	2	1	2	2	3	3
	2525	3	2	1	2	1	1	1	2	2	1	2	1	1	2	1	2	2	2	1	1	2	2	3	2	1	2	1	1	2	3
	2526	1	2	1	2	2	1	1	2	2	1	2	1	1	2	1	3	2	3	1	2	3	1	3	2	1	2	1	1	4	4
	2656	1	2	2	1	1	1	2	2	4	3	2	2	2	1	1	7	2	1	*	2	4	1	2	1	2	1	1	2	2	3
	2670	1	1	2	3	1	1	3	2	2	2	2	2	4	4	2	6	2	1	2	4	4	1	2	1	2	1	2	2	3	3
	2750	1	1	1	3	1	1	2	3	2	2	2	2	2	1	2	2	2	1	2	4	4	1	2	1	2	1	2	2	3	3

Andria *(continued)*

		1	2	3	4	5	6	7	8	9	10	11	12	13	14	15	16	17	18	19	20	21	22	23	24	25	26	27	28	29	30
	5000	1	2	7	2	2	1	1	2	2	1	2	1	1	4	1	6	7	1	1	2	3	1	3	2	1	1	1	1	5	3
	5443	1	2	1	2	2	2	1	2	2	1	2	1	1	2	1	3	2	3	1	2	4	2	3	2	1	2	1	1	2	3
	Roy 15.A.VIII	1	2	2	3	4	1	2	2	1	2	2	2	2	1	2	2	2	1	2	4	4	1	2	2	1	1	2	2	3	3
	15.A.XII	2	2	1	3	5	1	1	3	*	2	2	1	3	2	2	1	7	3	4	5	3	1	2	1	2	2	1	2	3	4
	15.B.VIII	1	2	1	2	2	1	2	2	2	1	2	4	1	2	1	3	8	3	1	2	4	1	3	2	1	1	2	2	5	3
Lucca	1420	1	2	3	2	3	1	1	3	2	6	2	2	1	4	1	2	6	3	2	4	4	1	2	2	1	1	2	2	4	3
Madrid	BN Vitr 5-4	*	*	6	3	1	1	2	2	3	1	2	2	2	1	2	2	2	1	2	4	4	1	2	1	2	1	2	2	3	3
Milan	Ambros A.33 inf	1	2	2	3	2	1	1	2	2	2	2	1	2	6	1	2	2	1	1	1	3	1	3	2	1	2	1	1	4	4
	D.79 sup	1	2	1	3	2	1	1	2	2	1	2	1	1	3	1	2	2	2	1	2	3	1	3	2	1	2	1	1	2	4
	F.92 sup	1	2	1	3	2	1	1	2	2	1	2	1	1	2	1	2	2	2	1	2	3	1	3	2	1	2	1	1	4	4
	F.142 sup	1	2	1	3	2	1	1	2	2	1	2	3	1	1	1	2	2	2	2	1	3	1	3	2	1	2	1	1	4	4
	G.130 inf	*	*	*	*	*	*	*	*	*	*	*	*	*	*	*	*	*	*	*	*	*	1	3	2	1	4	1	1	2	3
	H.135 inf	1	2	1	2	1	1	1	2	2	1	2	1	5	6	1	3	9	2	1	2	3	1	3	2	1	2	1	2	10	4
	I.5 sup	1	2	4	3	2	1	2	3	3	2	2	1	1	2	1	2	2	1	1	4	4	2	3	2	1	1	1	1	13	3
	Triv 663	6	2	2	3	2	1	2	2	2	1	2	2	1	1	1	2	2	3	2	4	4	1	2	2	2	1	2	1	13	3
	727	1	2	1	3	2	1	1	2	2	1	2	1	1	2	1	2	2	2	1	2	3	1	3	2	1	2	1	2	14	4
Oxford	Bodl Auct F.2.13	1	1	2	1	1	1	2	2	1	4	1	2	2	1	2	2	2	1	2	3	2	1	1	1	*	*	2	2	3	3
	F.6.27	1	2	1	1	2	1	2	2	2	5	2	1	1	2	1	4	4	2	1	2	3	1	3	1	1	2	1	2	5	3
	Brasenose 18	1	2	2	3	1	1	1	2	1	1	2	2	2	1	2	3	2	1	2	3	4	1	2	3	2	1	2	2	3	3
	Clarke 28	1	2	7	3	2	1	1	2	2	1	4	1	1	2	1	2	7	2	1	2	3	6	3	2	1	2	1	2	10	4
	D'Orville 155	1	2	1	3	2	1	1	2	2	1	2	1	1	2	1	2	7	2	1	2	3	1	1	2	1	2	1	1	10	4
	Laud 76	1	*	1	3	1	1	2	2	1	3	2	3	2	1	2	7	4	2	1	2	3	1	1	2	1	4	2	2	3	7
	Magd 23	1	2	2	2	2	3	2	2	2	2	2	2	2	3	1	2	4	2	1	2	3	1	3	2	2	2	1	1	4	4
	Rawl G.135	1	2	1	3	2	1	1	2	2	1	2	5	1	2	1	3	2	3	1	2	3	1	3	2	1	2	1	1	4	4
Paris	BN lat 7899	1	1	2	1	1	1	2	2	1	3	1	2	2	1	2	2	2	1	2	3	2	1	1	1	2	1	2	2	3	3

		1	2	3	4	5	6	7	8	9	10	11	12	13	14	15	16	17	18	19	20	21	22	23	24	25	26	27	28	29	30
	7900	*	1	1	1	1	1	2	2	1	1	1	2	2	1	2	2	2	1	2	3	2	4	1	1	2	1	2	2	*	*
	7900A	1	2	1	1	2	1	1	2	2	5	2	1	1	2	1	2	2	1	1	2	2	2	1	2	1	2	1	1	2	3
	7901	1	2	4	2	1	1	2	4	1	2	3	2	2	1	2	2	2	1	2	3	2	1	1	2	1	1	2	2	3	3
	7903	1	1	2	2	1	1	2	2	1	2	2	2	2	1	2	2	2	1	2	3	2	1	2	2	2	1	2	2	6	3
	7904	5	2	2	3	1	1	2	2	2	4	2	2	2	1	2	7	2	1	2	7	4	1	2	1	2	1	2	2	3	3
	7905	1	2	2	2	1	1	1	2	2	2	2	5	1	1	2	8	9	1	2	1	2	1	2	1	1	1	2	2	9	3
	7906	1	1	2	1	1	1	2	2	2	2	3	3	2	4	2	5	2	1	2	*	*	1	2	1	2	3	2	2	3	3
	7907	1	2	1	3	1	1	1	2	2	4	2	1	1	2	1	2	2	1	1	2	1	1	2	2	1	2	1	1	4	4
	7912	1	2	1	2	2	1	2	2	2	2	2	1	1	2	3	4	5	2	1	2	3	1	1	2	1	2	3	2	5	3
	9345	1	1	1	2	2	1	1	2	2	2	2	1	3	2	1	2	3	1	1	2	4	2	3	2	2	2	1	1	2	2
	10304	*	*	*	*	*	*	*	3	2	1	2	1	3	2	1	1	4	2	1	1	1	1	2	2	1	2	1	1	2	3
	14755	1	3	2	3	1	1	2	2	2	2	2	2	2	1	2	3	1	2	2	4	4	1	2	1	2	1	2	2	3	3
	16235	1	1	1	2	1	1	2	2	1	1	2	2	2	1	1	2	2	1	2	3	4	1	1	1	2	1	2	2	3	3
	18544	1	2	2	2	1	1	2	2	2	2	2	3	2	2	2	1	2	2	1	1	3	1	2	2	2	1	2	2	6	3
Rome	Angel 1407	6	2	2	2	2	3	1	2	2	1	2	2	2	3	1	3	2	2	1	2	3	1	3	2	1	2	1	1	2	4
	Casan 416	1	2	7	2	2	3	1	2	2	1	2	1	1	5	1	5	7	3	4	6	3	1	3	2	1	2	1	1	4	4
	Vallic F.67	1	2	1	2	1	1	1	2	2	1	2	1	1	7	1	2	7	2	1	2	3	6	3	2	1	2	1	2	10	4
Valenciennes	BM 448	3	2	2	3	1	1	2	2	1	2	2	2	2	1	2	3	2	1	2	4	5	1	2	1	2	1	2	2	6	3
Vatican City	Arch S Pietro H.19	1	1	2	2	1	1	2	2	1	3	2	2	2	1	2	3	2	1	2	3	2	1	1	1	2	1	2	2	3	3
	Barb lat 82	1	2	1	2	2	1	1	2	6	2	1	1	1	4	1	6	7	1	1	2	3	1	3	2	2	1	1	1	3	3
	83	1	2	1	3	2	1	1	2	2	1	2	1	1	2	1	2	2	3	1	2	3	1	3	2	1	2	1	1	4	4
	133	1	2	1	3	2	1	1	2	8	1	2	1	1	2	1	2	7	1	1	2	3	1	3	2	2	2	1	2	12	4
	Ottob lat 1367	1	2	1	2	1	1	1	2	2	2	2	1	8	2	1	2	2	3	1	1	2	2	3	2	1	2	1	1	2	3
	1468	6	1	2	3	2	1	2	2	2	1	2	2	1	1	2	1	2	1	2	7	4	1	2	2	2	1	2	2	2	2
	Pal lat 1620	1	2	1	2	2	2	1	2	2	1	2	5	1	1	4	5	9	1	2	3	5	1	4	4	1	1	2	2	3	3

Andria *(continued)*

		1	2	3	4	5	6	7	8	9	10	11	12	13	14	15	16	17	18	19	20	21	22	23	24	25	26	27	28	29	30
	1621	1	2	7	2	1	1	1	2	2	1	2	1	1	2	1	3	7	3	1	2	3	1	3	2	1	2	1	1	4	4
	1623	1	2	1	3	2	1	1	2	2	1	2	1	1	2	1	3	2	2	1	2	3	1	3	2	1	2	1	1	3	4
	1627	1	2	7	2	2	1	2	2	2	1	2	3	2	1	2	5	2	1	2	4	4	1	2	2	1	1	2	2	14	6
	Rossi 445	1	2	1	2	2	1	2	2	2	1	2	1	1	3	1	8	5	3	1	4	3	4	3	2	1	2	1	2	5	3
	506	1	2	1	3	2	1	2	2	7	1	2	2	2	1	2	2	7	2	1	4	4	1	2	3	1	1	2	1	3	3
	928	1	2	1	2	2	1	1	2	2	1	2	6	1	2	1	2	2	2	1	2	3	*	*	*	1	2	1	2	4	4
	Vat lat 1634	1	2	1	2	2	1	1	2	2	2	2	1	1	2	1	2	9	2	1	4	4	4	2	3	2	1	2	2	6	3
	1640	2	2	2	3	2	2	1	5	1	2	1	1	3	2	2	1	3	2	1	2	2	2	3	2	1	2	1	1	2	2
	3305	1	2	2	2	6	1	1	2	2	3	2	2	2	1	2	2	2	1	2	4	2	1	2	4	2	1	2	2	3	3
	3306	1	2	6	2	1	1	2	2	1	4	2	2	2	1	2	2	2	1	2	3	6	1	2	1	2	1	2	2	3	3
	3868	1	1	1	1	1	1	2	2	1	3	1	2	2	1	2	2	2	1	2	3	2	1	1	1	2	1	2	2	3	3
	3869	1	1	1	3	1	1	2	2	4	2	2	2	2	1	2	2	2	1	2	4	4	1	2	1	2	1	2	2	3	3
	6728	1	2	1	3	2	3	1	2	2	1	2	1	1	2	1	2	7	2	1	2	3	1	3	2	1	2	1	1	4	4
Vienna	lat 85	5	2	1	2	2	1	2	2	2	2	2	1	1	2	1	4	4	2	1	2	3	1	2	1	2	2	1	1	3	3
Wolfenbüttel	Gud lat 193	1	2	2	3	1	1	2	3	2	2	2	2	2	1	2	2	2	1	2	4	4	3	2	1	1	2	1	1	2	2
Zwettl	Stiftsbibl 313	1	1	1	3	1	1	2	3	2	2	2	2	2	1	2	*	7	1	2	4	4	5	2	1	1	2	2	1	1	2

EUNUCHUS

		1	2	3	4	5	6	7	8	9	10	11	12	13	14	15	16	17	18	19	20	21	22	23	24	25	26	27	28	29	30
Bamberg	Staatsbibl Class 48	1	1	2	1	1	2	3	1	2	2	3	1	2	2	2	2	1	2	1	2	2	2	2	3	2	2	1	1	2	2
	Class 49	1	1	4	1	1	2	3	2	2	2	3	1	2	2	3	2	1	*	1	1	2	2	1	3	1	3	2	2	2	2
Brussels	BR 5329	3	1	2	1	1	1	3	1	3	1	2	2	1	1	1	1	2	1	2	2	1	6	2	2	2	3	2	2	2	1
Cambridge	UL Add 3024	3	2	2	1	1	1	1	1	2	2	4	1	2	2	3	3	1	1	2	2	1	2	2	3	2	2	3	2	2	2
	Add 3109	3	1	1	2	1	1	2	1	2	1	5	2	2	2	3	2	1	1	2	2	1	2	2	3	2	2	*	2	2	2
	CCC 231	5	1	1	1	1	1	1	1	3	1	2	2	1	1	1	1	2	1	2	2	1	3	1	4	1	3	2	1	1	1
Edinburgh	NL Adv 18.2.10	3	1	1	1	1	1	3	1	3	1	5	2	1	2	7	2	4	1	2	2	2	2	1	3	1	1	2	3	4	2
	Adv 18.7.2	*	1	2	1	1	1	2	1	3	1	2	2	1	2	1	1	2	1	2	2	1	3	5	4	1	3	2	1	2	1
Erlangen	Univ 391	2	3	2	1	2	2	4	2	5	1	3	1	2	2	2	2	1	2	1	1	1	3	2	3	2	2	2	2	1	2
	392	1	1	2	2	*	*	*	*	*	3	1	1	1	*	*	*	*	*	2	2	1	3	2	3	2	*	2	*	1	3
Escorial, El	S.III.23	*	1	1	1	1	1	1	1	3	1	5	2	1	1	1	1	2	1	2	2	1	3	2	2	1	3	2	1	2	1
Florence	Med-Laur 38.21	3	1	*	1	5	1	2	4	2	1	5	1	1	2	1	1	1	1	2	2	1	2	3	3	1	1	3	2	2	2
	38.24	2	2	1	2	2	2	1	2	2	2	3	1	2	2	2	2	1	2	1	1	2	2	2	3	2	2	1	2	1	2
	38.27	2	2	1	2	2	2	2	1	2	2	3	1	2	2	2	2	3	2	1	3	2	2	2	3	2	2	1	2	2	1
	38.28	3	1	2	2	1	1	2	1	2	1	5	2	1	2	1	3	1	1	1	3	2	2	1	3	1	1	2	2	1	2
	Marc 244	1	1	3	2	1	1	2	1	2	1	7	2	1	2	1	3	1	1	2	2	2	2	1	3	2	2	3	2	2	2
	BN II.IV.689	*	*	*	*	*	*	*	*	2	1	5	2	1	2	1	3	6	1	1	5	2	2	1	3	1	1	2	2	2	2
	Ricc 528	4	1	2	2	1	3	3	1	4	1	4	2	1	1	3	1	2	1	2	2	1	4	2	2	1	3	2	2	1	3
	529	3	1	1	1	1	1	1	1	2	1	2	2	1	1	1	1	2	1	2	2	1	3	1	1	1	3	2	1	5	1
	530	3	2	3	1	5	1	2	1	1	1	5	2	1	2	1	3	3	1	1	3	2	4	1	3	1	1	2	2	2	2
	532	3	2	2	2	2	*	*	*	2	1	5	2	1	2	3	4	2	1	2	2	1	2	3	3	2	3	2	2	3	3
	614	3	1	2	2	5	1	2	1	2	1	5	2	1	2	4	3	2	1	1	3	2	2	1	3	1	1	2	2	2	2
	3608	3	2	3	2	1	1	2	1	2	1	5	2	1	2	1	3	3	1	1	3	4	2	1	4	1	1	2	2	1	2
Hague, The	Kon Bibl 72.J.49	3	4	1	2	1	1	2	1	2	2	1	1	2	2	3	2	2	1	2	2	1	2	2	3	2	2	2	2	2	2
Leipzig	Univ I.37	2	2	2	2	2	2	1	2	2	2	3	1	2	2	2	2	1	2	1	1	2	2	2	3	2	2	1	2	1	2

Eunuchus *(continued)*

		1	2	3	4	5	6	7	8	9	10	11	12	13	14	15	16	17	18	19	20	21	22	23	24	25	26	27	28	29	30
Leyden	Rijksuniv BPL 109	3	1	2	1	1	1	3	1	3	1	5	2	1	1	2	2	1	1	2	2	1	4	2	2	1	3	2	2	2	1
	Lips 26	3	1	1	1	1	1	1	1	3	1	2	2	1	1	1	1	2	1	2	2	1	3	2	2	1	3	4	1	2	1
	Voss lat Q.38	3	1	2	1	2	2	2	1	2	2	3	1	1	*	*	2	1	2	1	2	1	5	3	2	1	3	2	2	1	3
London	BL Harl 2455	3	1	1	2	4	1	3	4	2	1	4	2	1	2	1	1	2	1	2	2	1	2	2	2	1	2	2	2	2	2
	2475	3	2	2	4	2	2	2	2	2	2	3	1	2	2	1	3	1	1	1	3	3	2	1	3	2	1	2	2	1	2
	2524	3	5	1	1	1	1	3	1	3	1	5	2	1	1	6	1	2	1	2	2	1	3	2	4	1	3	2	1	1	1
	2525	3	2	2	4	2	1	2	2	2	1	2	2	1	2	3	1	2	1	2	2	1	3	2	3	2	3	2	2	3	2
	2526	3	1	2	2	1	1	2	1	2	1	5	2	1	2	1	3	1	1	3	3	2	2	1	3	1	1	2	2	1	2
	2656	3	1	2	1	4	1	3	1	3	1	5	2	1	1	6	1	2	1	2	2	1	3	2	2	1	2	2	1	2	1
	2670	3	1	2	3	1	1	4	1	3	1	5	2	1	1	3	1	2	1	2	4	1	3	1	2	1	4	2	1	1	1
	2750	1	3	2	1	4	2	1	1	3	1	5	2	1	1	1	2	2	2	1	2	1	2	1	3	1	3	2	1	1	1
	5443	3	1	3	2	2	1	2	3	2	1	6	1	2	2	2	3	1	1	1	1	2	2	1	3	1	1	2	3	2	2
	Roy 15.A.XII	3	1	1	1	1	2	2	1	3	1	2	2	1	1	1	1	2	1	2	2	1	3	1	2	1	3	2	1	2	1
Lucca	1420	3	3	2	1	1	1	2	1	2	1	3	2	2	2	8	2	1	1	1	2	2	2	1	3	4	2	2	2	2	2
Milan	Ambros A.33 inf	3	1	2	2	1	1	2	1	6	1	5	2	1	2	1	3	1	1	1	3	2	2	1	3	1	1	2	3	1	2
	D.79 sup	3	1	2	2	6	1	2	1	2	1	1	2	1	2	2	3	1	1	1	3	2	2	2	3	1	2	2	2	2	2
	G.130 inf	3	1	2	2	1	1	2	1	2	1	7	2	1	2	1	2	1	1	2	2	2	2	2	2	2	2	3	2	2	2
	H.75 inf	*	*	*	*	*	*	*	*	*	*	*	*	*	1	*	1	2	1	2	2	1	3	2	2	3	3	2	1	2	1
	I.5 sup	3	1	2	1	1	2	1	4	2	1	5	1	1	2	1	1	1	1	2	2	2	2	2	3	1	1	3	2	2	2
	Triv 727	3	1	1	2	1	1	2	1	2	1	4	2	3	2	3	2	5	1	2	2	1	2	2	3	2	2	3	2	2	2
Montpellier	FMéd 227	3	1	2	1	1	1	3	1	3	1	5	2	1	1	5	1	2	1	2	2	1	3	2	3	1	3	2	4	1	1
Oxford	Bodl Auct F.2.13	1	1	1	1	1	1	1	1	3	1	2	2	1	1	1	1	2	*	2	2	1	3	1	2	1	3	2	1	2	1
	F.6.27	1	1	2	2	3	2	2	1	2	3	1	1	1	2	1	2	1	1	2	2	1	3	2	3	2	2	2	2	1	3
	Brasenose 18	3	1	1	1	1	1	3	1	3	1	5	2	1	1	6	1	2	1	2	2	1	3	2	4	1	3	2	1	1	1
	Clarke 28	3	1	2	2	1	1	2	1	2	1	5	2	1	2	1	3	1	1	1	3	2	2	1	3	1	1	2	2	1	2

		1	2	3	4	5	6	7	8	9	10	11	12	13	14	15	16	17	18	19	20	21	22	23	24	25	26	27	28	29	30
	D'Orville 155	3	1	2	1	1	1	2	1	2	1	5	2	1	2	1	3	3	1	1	3	2	2	1	2	1	1	2	2	1	2
	Laud 76	3	1	1	1	1	1	1	2	3	1	2	2	1	1	1	1	2	1	2	2	1	3	2	2	1	3	2	1	1	1
	Magd 23	3	1	3	2	1	1	2	1	2	1	5	2	1	2	1	3	2	1	1	3	2	2	1	3	2	2	2	3	1	2
	Rawl G.135	1	1	2	2	1	1	3	5	2	1	5	2	1	2	1	3	1	1	1	3	2	2	1	1	2	2	2	3	1	2
Paris	BN lat 7899	*	1	1	1	1	1	1	1	2	1	2	2	1	1	1	1	2	1	2	2	1	3	1	2	1	3	2	1	*	1
	7900	*	1	1	1	1	1	1	1	3	1	2	2	1	1	1	1	2	1	2	2	1	3	1	2	1	3	2	1	2	1
	7900A	3	2	2	2	2	1	2	2	2	2	3	1	2	2	3	2	1	1	2	2	2	2	2	3	2	2	3	2	2	2
	7901	3	1	2	1	1	1	1	2	3	1	2	2	1	1	1	1	2	1	2	2	1	3	2	2	1	2	2	1	1	1
	7903	3	1	1	1	1	1	1	1	3	1	2	2	1	1	1	1	2	1	2	2	1	3	2	2	1	3	2	1	2	1
	7904	3	1	2	1	1	1	3	1	3	1	5	2	1	1	1	1	2	1	2	2	1	3	2	4	1	3	2	1	1	1
	7905	3	1	2	1	1	1	3	1	3	4	5	3	1	1	2	2	1	1	2	2	1	3	2	4	1	3	2	2	2	1
	7912	3	1	1	2	1	1	2	1	3	1	5	2	2	2	1	2	1	*	2	2	1	2	2	3	2	2	3	2	2	2
	9345	2	2	1	2	2	2	1	2	2	2	3	1	2	1	3	2	1	1	1	3	2	2	2	3	2	2	1	2	2	2
	10304	1	1	2	2	2	2	2	1	2	2	1	1	1	2	1	2	1	2	1	1	2	2	2	2	2	2	1	2	1	3
	16235	3	1	2	1	1	1	3	1	3	1	5	2	1	1	5	1	2	1	2	2	1	4	2	2	1	3	2	1	1	1
	18544	3	1	1	3	1	1	1	1	3	1	2	2	1	2	1	1	2	1	2	2	1	3	2	2	1	3	2	1	2	1
Rome	Angel 1407	3	1	2	2	6	1	2	1	2	2	4	2	1	2	8	3	1	1	1	3	2	2	2	3	3	2	2	2	1	4
	Casan 416	3	3	2	2	1	1	2	1	2	1	5	2	1	2	1	3	3	1	1	3	5	2	1	3	1	1	3	2	1	2
	Vallic F.67	3	1	2	2	1	1	2	1	2	1	5	2	1	2	1	3	1	1	1	3	2	2	1	3	1	1	2	2	1	2
Valenciennes	BM 448	3	1	1	1	1	1	1	1	3	1	2	2	1	1	1	1	2	1	2	2	1	3	2	2	1	3	2	1	2	1
Vatican City	Arch S Pietro H.19	3	1	1	1	1	1	1	1	2	1	2	2	1	1	1	1	2	1	2	2	1	3	1	4	1	3	2	1	1	2
	Barb lat 82	3	1	2	1	1	1	1	1	5	1	3	2	1	2	8	3	1	1	2	2	2	2	2	3	2	2	2	3	1	2
	83	3	1	1	4	1	1	2	1	2	1	5	2	3	2	9	2	4	1	2	2	1	7	2	3	2	2	3	2	2	2
	133	3	5	2	1	1	1	1	1	2	1	5	2	1	2	1	3	3	1	1	3	1	2	2	3	1	1	2	2	2	2
	Ottob lat 1367	3	2	2	4	2	1	2	4	2	2	3	1	2	2	3	2	1	1	2	2	2	2	2	3	2	2	3	2	2	2

Eunuchus *(continued)*

		1	2	3	4	5	6	7	8	9	10	11	12	13	14	15	16	17	18	19	20	21	22	23	24	25	26	27	28	29	30
	1468	2	2	2	2	2	2	1	2	2	2	3	1	2	2	2	2	1	2	1	1	2	2	2	3•	2	2	2	2	1	2
	Pal lat 1620	3	1	2	1	6	1	4	2	4	1	8	2	1	2	8	1	2	1	2	2	1	2	2	4	2	3	1	2	2	4
	1621	3	1	1	4	1	1	2	1	2	1	5	2	3	2	9	2	4	3	2	2	1	2	2	3	2	2	3	2	2	2
	1623	3	1	2	2	1	1	2	1	2	1	5	2	1	2	1	3	1	1	1	3	2	2	1	3	1	1	2	2	1	2
	1627	7	1	2	1	5	1	3	1	2	1	5	2	1	2	1	1	2	1	1	2	1	2	2	2	1	3	2	2	2	2
	Rossi 445	3	5	2	1	1	1	2	1	2	2	5	2	3	2	1	3	3	1	1	3	2	2	2	3	1	1	2	2	2	2
	506	4	1	2	2	5	1	3	1	2	1	1	1	1	2	1	4	1	1	2	3	2	3	2	3	1	1	2	2	1	2
	928	3	1	2	2	1	1	2	1	2	1	5	2	1	2	1	3	1	1	1	3	2	2	1	3	1	1	2	2	1	2
	Vat lat 1634	6	5	3	2	7	1	2	4	2	1	3	1	1	2	3	2	1	4	2	2	1	1	2	3	2	2	2	2	2	1
	1640	2	2	1	2	2	2	1	2	2	2	3	1	2	2	2	2	1	2	1	1	2	2	2	3	2	2	1	*	*	2
	3305	3	6	2	1	4	1	3	1	3	1	5	2	3	1	10	1	2	1	2	2	1	4	4	2	1	3	2	2	2	1
	3306	3	1	2	1	1	1	3	1	3	1	5	1	1	1	1	1	2	1	2	2	1	3	2	2	1	3	2	1	1	1
	3868	*	1	1	1	1	1	3	1	3	1	2	2	1	1	1	1	2	1	2	2	1	3	1	2	1	3	2	1	2	1
	3869	3	5	2	1	1	1	3	1	3	1	5	2	1	2	4	1	2	1	2	2	1	4	2	2	1	3	2	1	1	3
	6728	3	1	2	2	1	2	2	1	2	1	5	2	1	2	1	3	1	1	1	3	1	2	2	3	2	1	3	1	2	2
Vienna	lat 85	1	1	2	2	1	1	2	1	2	1	4	2	2	2	3	2	1	1	2	2	1	2	2	3	2	2	3	2	2	2

HAUTON TIMORUMENOS

		1	2	3	4	5	6	7	8	9	10	11	12	13	14	15	16	17	18	19	20	21	22	23	24	25	26	27	28	29	30
Cambridge	UL Add 3024	2	1	3	2	1	1	6	1	2	3	3	3	2	2	3	1	1	2	2	2	1	1	1	2	3	2	5	1	2	2
	Add 3109	2	1	2	1	1	1	3	1	2	3	3	2	2	2	2	1	1	2	7	2	1	1	1	2	1	2	2	3	2	2
	CCC 231	2	1	3	2	1	1	2	2	1	2	1	2	1	1	2	1	1	2	2	1	1	1	1	2	1	2	2	1	*	2
Edinburgh	NL Adv 18.2.10	2	1	2	1	1	4	5	1	2	3	2	3	2	1	2	5	1	5	2	2	1	1	1	2	1	6	2	5	5	2
	Adv 18.7.2	2	1	2	2	6	1	3	2	1	2	2	3	2	1	2	1	1	4	2	2	1	1	1	2	1	2	1	6	3	2
Erlangen	Univ 391	2	1	2	1	2	3	4	2	1	3	3	3	1	2	2	2	1	2	4	2	1	1	1	2	1	4	3	4	4	2
	392	3	2	2	1	1	2	1	1	2	3	*	*	*	*	*	*	*	*	*	*	*	*	*	*	*	*	*	*	*	*
Escorial, El	S.III.23	2	1	3	2	2	1	2	2	1	2	1	2	1	1	2	1	1	2	2	2	1	1	1	3	1	2	2	3	1	2
Florence	Med-Laur 38.19	2	1	3	2	2	1	9	4	1	2	2	3	1	1	4	1	1	2	7	2	1	1	1	2	1	2	2	1	3	2
	38.21	2	1	2	1	1	1	2	2	1	2	2	3	2	2	2	1	1	2	6	2	1	1	1	2	5	2	6	3	3	2
	38.24	2	2	2	1	2	1	1	1	2	3	3	2	2	1	*	2	2	3	3	1	2	1	3	1	2	1	3	2	2	3
	38.27	2	1	3	1	2	1	1	2	2	3	3	3	2	2	2	2	2	2	2	2	2	1	3	2	2	5	1	2	2	2
	38.28	2	1	2	2	1	1	9	1	2	3	2	3	2	1	2	1	1	6	2	2	4	1	8	2	1	7	2	3	1	2
	Marc 244	2	1	2	1	1	1	3	1	2	3	3	3	2	2	2	1	1	2	2	2	1	1	1	2	1	2	2	3	2	2
	BN II.IV.689	2	1	2	2	1	1	9	1	2	3	2	3	2	1	2	1	1	6	6	2	4	1	1	2	1	7	2	3	1	7
	Ricc 528	3	2	3	1	1	2	2	1	4	3	2	3	1	1	2	3	1	2	2	2	1	1	1	2	1	3	2	1	3	2
	530	2	1	2	2	1	1	9	1	2	3	2	3	2	1	2	1	3	6	6	2	4	1	1	2	1	8	2	3	1	2
	532	2	2	2	1	1	1	3	2	2	3	3	3	2	2	5	1	1	2	2	2	1	1	1	2	6	2	2	3	2	2
	614	2	1	2	2	1	1	5	1	2	3	3	3	2	1	2	1	1	6	2	2	4	1	8	2	1	7	2	3	1	2
	3608	2	1	2	2	1	1	5	1	2	3	2	3	2	1	2	1	2	8	6	2	4	1	1	2	1	2	2	1	2	2
Hague, The	Kon Bibl 72.J.49	2	1	2	1	1	1	3	1	2	3	3	3	2	2	2	1	1	2	2	2	1	1	1	2	1	2	2	3	2	2
Leipzig	Univ I.37	2	1	2	1	2	1	2	2	1	2	2	3	1	1	2	1	1	2	2	2	1	1	1	2	1	2	2	3	3	2
Leyden	Rijksuniv BPL 109	2	1	2	1	2	1	3	1	2	3	3	1	2	2	1	2	1	3	3	1	2	1	3	2	2	5	1	2	2	3
	Lips 26	2	1	3	2	2	1	2	2	1	2	2	3	1	1	2	1	1	2	6	3	1	1	1	2	1	2	2	3	1	2
	Voss lat Q.38	2	2	2	1	2	1	1	1	2	3	3	3	2	2	1	2	1	3	3	1	2	1	2	2	1	5	1	2	2	3

Hauton timorumenos *(continued)*

		1	2	3	4	5	6	7	8	9	10	11	12	13	14	15	16	17	18	19	20	21	22	23	24	25	26	27	28	29	30
London	BL Harl 2455	2	2	2	1	2	1	2	3	2	2	2	3	2	1	2	1	1	2	8	2	1	1	1	2	1	2	1	3	3	2
	2475	2	1	1	1	3	1	5	1	1	3	2	3	1	*	2	1	1	2	2	2	1	1	1	2	1	2	2	3	1	2
	2524	2	1	3	2	5	1	2	2	1	2	2	3	1	1	2	1	1	2	2	2	1	1	1	2	1	2	2	3	3	2
	2525	2	1	1	1	1	1	3	1	2	3	3	3	2	2	2	1	1	2	2	2	1	1	1	2	1	2	2	3	2	2
	2656	2	1	3	2	2	1	2	1	1	2	2	3	1	1	2	1	1	4	2	2	1	1	1	2	1	2	2	3	3	2
	2670	2	1	3	2	2	1	2	2	2	4	4	3	4	1	2	4	1	2	5	2	3	1	1	2	1	*	2	3	3	2
	2750	2	1	3	2	2	1	2	2	3	2	3	2	2	1	2	2	1	2	2	2	1	1	1	2	1	2	4	3	3	2
	5443	3	2	2	1	1	1	3	1	2	3	3	3	2	1	2	1	2	2	6	1	4	1	1	2	1	2	2	3	1	2
	Roy 15.A.XII	2	1	3	1	2	2	9	2	1	2	2	3	1	3	2	1	1	4	4	1	1	1	1	2	1	8	4	6	6	2
Lucca	1420	2	1	2	1	4	1	10	1	2	3	2	3	2	1	2	1	1	6	6	2	4	1	6	2	1	7	2	3	2	2
Milan	Ambros D.79 sup	2	1	2	1	1	1	5	1	2	3	3	3	2	1	2	1	1	2	5	2	1	1	1	2	4	5	1	3	2	2
	F.142 sup	2	1	2	1	1	1	5	1	2	3	2	3	2	1	2	1	1	3	2	2	2	1	1	2	1	2	2	3	1	2
	G.130 inf	2	1	2	1	1	1	3	1	2	3	3	3	2	2	2	1	1	2	2	2	1	1	1	2	1	2	2	3	2	2
	H.75 inf	2	1	3	2	2	1	2	2	1	2	1	2	1	1	2	1	1	2	2	2	1	1	1	3	1	2	2	3	1	2
	I.5 sup	2	1	2	1	1	1	2	2	1	5	2	3	2	2	2	1	1	2	2	2	1	1	1	2	5	2	6	3	3	2
Oxford	Bodl Auct F.2.13	2	1	3	2	2	1	2	2	1	2	1	2	1	1	2	1	1	2	2	1	1	2	1	1	1	2	2	1	1	2
	F.6.27	3	2	2	1	1	2	1	1	2	3	3	3	2	1	1	2	1	3	3	2	2	1	4	2	2	5	1	2	2	6
	Brasenose 18	2	1	3	2	2	1	2	2	1	2	2	3	1	1	2	1	1	2	2	2	1	1	1	2	1	2	2	3	3	2
	Clarke 28	2	1	2	2	1	1	5	1	2	3	2	3	2	1	2	1	1	6	6	2	4	1	3	2	1	7	2	3	1	2
	D'Orville 155	2	1	2	2	1	1	5	1	2	3	2	3	2	1	2	1	1	6	6	2	4	1	1	2	1	7	2	3	1	2
	Laud 76	2	1	3	2	2	1	2	2	1	2	2	3	1	1	2	1	1	2	2	2	1	2	6	2	1	2	2	3	3	2
	Magd 23	2	1	2	1	1	1	5	1	2	3	2	3	2	1	2	1	1	5	6	2	4	1	1	2	1	2	2	3	1	2
	Rawl G.135	2	1	2	1	1	5	5	1	2	3	2	3	6	1	2	1	1	5	4	2	3	1	3	2	1	9	2	3	1	2
Paris	BN lat 7899	2	1	3	2	2	1	2	2	1	2	1	2	1	1	2	1	1	2	6	1	1	2	1	1	1	2	2	3	1	2
	7900	2	1	3	2	2	1	2	2	1	2	1	2	1	1	2	1	3	2	2	1	1	2	1	1	1	10	2	3	1	2

		1	2	3	4	5	6	7	8	9	10	11	12	13	14	15	16	17	18	19	20	21	22	23	24	25	26	27	28	29	30
	7900A	2	1	2	1	1	1	3	1	2	3	3	3	2	2	2	1	1	2	2	2	1	1	1	2	1	2	2	3	1	2
	7901	2	1	3	2	2	3	2	2	1	2	*	*	*	*	*	*	*	*	*	*	*	*	*	*	*	*	*	*	*	*
	7903	2	1	3	2	5	1	2	2	1	2	2	3	1	1	1	1	1	2	2	2	1	1	1	2	1	2	2	3	1	2
	7904	2	1	4	2	2	1	2	2	1	2	2	3	1	1	2	6	1	2	6	2	1	1	1	2	1	2	2	3	3	2
	7905	2	1	2	1	5	2	1	2	2	3	5	3	2	2	4	2	1	3	3	4	2	1	3	5	3	5	1	1	2	3
	7912	2	1	3	1	1	1	3	1	2	3	3	3	2	2	2	1	1	*	7	2	1	1	1	2	1	2	2	3	2	2
	9345	2	1	2	1	2	1	1	1	1	3	3	3	2	2	1	2	2	3	2	2	1	1	1	2	1	5	1	2	2	5
	10304	3	2	2	1	1	2	1	1	2	3	3	1	2	2	1	2	1	3	3	1	2	1	3	1	2	1	1	2	2	4
	16235	2	1	3	2	2	1	2	2	1	2	2	3	1	1	2	1	1	2	2	2	1	1	1	3	1	2	2	3	3	2
	18544	2	1	3	2	5	1	7	2	1	2	2	3	1	1	1	1	1	2	5	2	1	1	1	2	1	2	2	3	1	2
Rome	Angel lat 1407	2	1	2	1	1	1	5	1	2	3	2	3	2	2	2	1	1	7	6	2	4	1	1	2	1	1	1	3	7	2
	Casan 416	2	1	2	2	1	1	5	2	2	3	2	3	2	1	2	1	2	8	6	2	4	1	1	2	1	8	2	1	2	2
	Cors Rossi 314	2	1	3	2	2	1	2	2	1	2	1	2	7	1	2	1	1	2	2	1	1	1	7	2	1	8	4	3	1	2
Valenciennes	BM 448	2	1	3	2	2	1	2	2	1	2	2	3	1	1	2	1	1	2	2	3	1	1	1	2	1	2	2	3	1	2
Vatican City	Arch S Pietro H.19	2	1	2	1	2	1	8	1	2	3	2	3	1	1	2	1	1	2	2	1	1	1	1	2	1	2	2	3	1	2
	Barb lat 82	2	1	2	1	1	1	5	1	2	3	3	3	5	2	2	1	1	2	2	2	4	1	1	2	1	2	4	3	2	2
	83	2	1	2	1	1	1	3	1	2	3	3	3	8	1	2	1	1	2	6	2	1	1	7	2	1	2	2	3	*	2
	133	2	1	2	2	1	1	5	1	1	3	2	3	2	1	2	1	1	9	2	2	4	1	1	2	1	2	6	3	4	2
	Ottob lat 1367	2	1	2	1	1	1	3	1	2	3	3	3	2	2	6	1	1	2	2	2	1	1	1	2	1	2	2	3	2	2
	1468	2	1	2	1	7	1	2	2	1	2	2	3	3	1	2	1	1	2	2	2	5	1	1	2	1	5	2	3	3	2
	Pal lat 1620	2	1	2	1	3	1	11	1	5	3	3	3	2	1	2	1	4	2	9	2	1	1	1	2	1	2	2	3	1	*
	1621	2	1	3	1	1	1	3	1	2	3	3	3	2	1	2	1	1	2	2	2	5	1	5	2	1	2	1	3	3	2
	1623	2	1	2	1	1	1	5	1	2	3	2	3	2	1	2	1	1	5	2	2	4	1	6	2	1	2	2	3	1	2
	1627	2	1	3	2	5	1	7	1	2	2	2	3	2	1	2	1	1	2	5	2	1	1	1	2	1	8	2	3	3	2
	Rossi 445	2	1	2	2	1	1	5	1	2	3	3	3	2	1	2	3	1	2	2	2	4	1	1	2	1	2	6	1	1	2

Hauton timorumenos *(continued)*

		1	2	3	4	5	6	7	8	9	10	11	12	13	14	15	16	17	18	19	20	21	22	23	24	25	26	27	28	29	30
	506	2	1	2	2	6	1	5	1	1	3	2	3	2	1	2	1	1	6	6	2	4	1	1	2	1	7	2	3	1	7
	928	2	1	2	1	1	1	5	1	2	3	2	3	2	1	2	1	1	5	6	2	4	1	1	2	1	2	2	3	1	2
	Vat lat 1634	2	1	2	1	1	1	2	2	2	2	2	3	2	2	2	1	3	2	2	2	1	1	1	2	1	2	3	3	2	2
	1640	*	*	*	*	*	*	*	*	*	*	*	1	2	2	1	2	1	3	3	2	2	1	3	4	2	5	3	2	2	3
	3305	2	1	3	2	2	1	2	2	1	2	2	2	1	1	2	2	1	2	2	2	1	1	1	1	1	2	2	6	1	2
	3306	1	1	3	2	2	1	2	2	1	2	2	3	1	1	2	1	1	2	2	2	1	1	1	2	1	7	2	3	3	7
	3868	2	1	3	2	2	1	2	2	1	2	1	2	1	1	2	1	1	2	2	1	1	2	1	1	1	2	2	3	1	2
	3869	2	1	2	1	2	1	5	4	1	2	2	3	1	*	1	1	1	3	3	1	1	1	9	2	1	2	2	3	2	3
	6728	2	1	2	3	1	1	9	1	1	3	2	3	2	1	1	1	2	3	6	2	4	1	1	2	4	5	1	3	3	8
	8200	2	1	3	2	2	1	7	1	2	2	2	3	6	4	2	1	1	2	5	2	1	1	1	2	1	8	6	1	3	2
Vienna	lat 85	2	1	2	1	1	1	4	1	2	3	3	3	3	2	2	1	1	2	5	2	1	1	1	2	1	2	2	3	1	2

PHORMIO

		1	2	3	4	5	6	7	8	9	10	11	12	13	14	15	16	17	18	19	20	21	22	23	24	25	26	27	28	29	30
Brussels	BR 9705	2	1	1	2	1	1	3	2	2	1	2	2	1	1	1	2	2	2	1	2	2	2	2	2	1	4	2	1	*	*
Cambridge	UL Add 3024	2	3	1	1	1	1	1	1	1	1	4	3	1	1	1	2	1	3	1	3	2	2	2	*	1	4	*	*	1	2
	3109	5	3	1	2	1	1	1	2	2	1	2	2	1	6	1	2	2	3	1	2	2	1	2	1	1	4	4	3	2	2
	CCC 231	2	1	1	2	1	1	1	2	2	1	5	2	1	1	1	2	2	3	1	2	2	2	2	2	1	4	*	*	*	*
Edinburgh	NL Adv 18.2.10	2	3	3	1	2	3	1	1	1	1	4	3	1	1	1	1	1	4	3	3	3	3	2	2	1	5	3	3	1	2
	18.7.2	1	1	1	2	1	1	2	2	2	1	2	2	1	1	1	2	2	3	1	2	2	2	2	2	1	4	2	1	2	4
Erlangen	Univ 391	2	1	1	4	2	2	3	1	1	2	1	4	1	4	1	2	2	3	1	4	2	1	2	1	1	4	2	1	1	1
	392	1	1	1	2	1	1	1	2	*	*	*	*	*	*	*	*	2	3	*	*	*	*	*	*	*	*	*	*	*	*
Florence	Med-Laur 38.21	1	1	1	2	1	1	1	2	2	1	2	2	1	5	1	1	2	3	1	2	3	1	*	2	1	3	5	1	2	2
	38.24	2	2	2	1	2	2	2	1	1	2	1	3	2	3	2	1	*	*	2	3	1	2	2	1	2	3	4	2	1	3
	38.27	2	4	2	1	3	2	2	1	1	2	1	1	1	2	2	1	1	2	2	3	1	2	2	1	2	4	4	2	1	2
	38.28	2	1	1	1	1	1	2	1	1	1	1	3	1	1	6	1	1	3	3	3	1	3	2	1	1	4	2	3	1	2
	BN II.IV.5	2	3	4	1	1	1	2	1	1	1	4	3	1	1	1	2	1	3	1	3	4	2	2	2	1	4	2	3	*	*
	II.IV.333	1	4	1	2	1	1	1	2	2	1	2	2	1	1	1	2	2	3	1	2	5	1	2	2	1	6	2	3	2	2
	II.IV.689	2	3	1	1	1	1	1	1	2	1	1	3	1	1	*	*	*	*	*	*	*	*	*	*	*	*	*	*	*	*
	II.VIII.52	1	3	1	1	1	1	1	2	2	1	4	5	1	1	1	2	1	3	2	4	2	1	2	2	1	4	2	1	1	2
	Ricc 528	1	3	1	2	1	1	2	2	2	1	*	2	1	6	1	2	2	3	1	2	2	1	2	2	1	*	*	*	*	1
	530	2	3	1	1	1	1	1	1	1	1	4	3	1	1	1	2	1	3	1	3	2	3	2	2	1	4	2	*	1	2
	532	1	1	1	2	1	1	1	2	2	1	2	5	1	1	1	2	2	5	1	4	5	2	2	2	6	8	2	3	2	2
Glasgow	Univ Hunt 26	2	3	1	1	1	1	2	1	1	1	1	3	1	1	1	1	1	3	3	3	1	2	2	*	*	*	*	*	*	*
	Gen 1189	2	1	1	1	6	1	1	1′	1	1	2	2	1	6	1	2	4	3	1	2	1	2	2	1	1	4	4	3	2	2
Hague, The	Kon Bibl 72.J.49	1	1	1	2	4	3	1	2	2	1	2	5	1	6	1	2	2	5	1	2	2	1	4	1	1	*	*	3	2	2
Leipzig	Univ I.37	2	3	1	1	2	3	2	1	1	2	3	3	2	2	2	1	1	2	1	2	3	1	1	2	1	2	4	2	1	3
Leyden	Rijksuniv BPL 109	1	1	1	2	1	1	1	2	2	1	2	2	1	5	3	2	2	2	1	2	2	1	2	2	1	4	2	1	2	2
	Lips 26	1	1	1	2	1	1	1	2	2	1	2	2	1	1	1	2	2	3	1	2	2	1	2	2	1	4	2	1	2	2

Phormio *(continued)*

		1	2	3	4	5	6	7	8	9	10	11	12	13	14	15	16	17	18	19	20	21	22	23	24	25	26	27	28	29	30
	Voss lat Q.38	1	1	1	2	1	1	1	2	2	1	2	2	1	5	1	1	2	3	1	2	2	2	2	2	1	4	2	1	4	2
London	BL Harl 2455	1	1	1	2	1	1	1	2	2	1	2	2	1	5	3	2	2	2	1	2	2	1	2	2	3	4	2	1	2	2
	2475	2	3	4	1	5	1	1	1	1	3	4	3	1	1	1	5	1	3	3	3	1	2	2	4	1	6	2	3	1	2
	2524	1	1	1	2	1	1	1	2	2	1	2	2	1	5	3	2	2	3	1	2	2	1	2	2	1	4	2	1	2	2
	2656	2	2	1	1	1	1	1	1	4	2	4	1	1	2	1	3	1	3	1	3	1	2	2	1	1	4	4	3	1	2
	2670	1	1	1	2	1	1	1	2	2	1	2	1	1	2	2	1	1	1	2	3	1	2	2	2	1	4	5	1	2	2
	2750	2	1	1	4	1	1	1	1	1	2	2	1	1	2	2	4	2	2	2	3	1	2	2	1	2	4	4	1	2	2
	5443	*	*	*	*	*	*	*	1	2	1	4	3	1	5	1	2	2	3	1	3	2	2	2	1	1	4	1	3	1	1
	Roy 15.A.XII	2	1	1	1	1	1	1	2	2	1	2	2	1	1	1	2	2	3	1	2	2	2	2	2	1	4	2	1	2	4
Lucca	1420	1	3	1	1	1	1	1	1	2	1	4	3	1	1	1	2	1	3	1	3	2	2	2	2	4	4	2	3	1	5
Milan	Ambros A.33 inf	2	3	1	1	1	1	1	1	1	2	4	3	1	1	1	7	1	3	1	3	1	2	2	1	1	10	4	*	1	2
	D.79 sup	2	1	1	2	1	1	2	2	1	1	4	3	1	1	1	1	1	3	1	3	2	2	2	2	1	4	2	7	1	2
	F.92 sup	2	3	1	1	5	1	1	4	1	2	4	3	1	1	1	7	1	3	1	3	1	3	1	2	1	9	2	3	1	2
	G.130 inf	2	3	1	1	5	1	1	1	1	2	4	3	1	1	1	1	1	4	3	3	1	2	5	2	1	8	2	3	1	2
	H.63 sup	2	1	1	4	3	2	2	2	1	2	1	1	1	5	3	2	1	3	2	3	1	2	2	1	1	7	2	*	1	2
	H.75 inf	1	1	1	2	1	1	1	2	2	1	2	2	1	6	1	2	2	3	1	4	2	1	2	1	*	*	*	*	*	*
	I.103 sup	2	1	1	2	1	1	5	2	2	1	2	2	1	1	*	*	2	3	1	2	3	3	2	1	5	4	2	5	2	2
	Triv 663	1	2	1	2	1	1	1	2	2	1	2	2	1	5	3	2	2	3	1	2	3	1	2	3	1	4	2	*	2	2
	727	1	5	5	2	1	1	3	2	2	1	2	2	1	6	3	2	2	3	1	2	2	1	2	1	1	4	4	3	2	1
Oxford	Bodl Auct F.2.13	1	1	1	2	1	1	1	2	2	1	2	*	1	1	1	2	2	3	1	2	2	2	2	2	*	*	*	*	*	*
	Auct F.6.27	1	1	1	2	1	1	1	2	2	1	1	2	1	6	1	*	2	3	1	2	2	1	2	1	1	4	4	3	2	2
	Brasenose 18	1	1	1	2	1	1	1	2	2	1	2	2	1	5	3	2	2	3	1	2	2	1	2	2	1	4	2	1	2	2
	Clarke 28	2	3	1	1	1	1	2	1	1	1	1	3	1	1	1	1	3	3	3	3	1	2	2	2	1	6	2	3	1	2
	D'Orville 155	2	3	1	1	1	1	1	1	1	1	4	3	1	1	1	2	1	3	1	3	2	2	2	2	1	4	4	3	1	2
	Laud 76	1	1	1	2	1	1	1	2	2	1	2	2	1	1	1	2	2	3	1	2	2	2	2	*	1	4	2	1	1	2

		1	2	3	4	5	6	7	8	9	10	11	12	13	14	15	16	17	18	19	20	21	22	23	24	25	26	27	28	29	30
	Magd 23	2	3	1	1	5	1	1	1	1	2	4	3	1	1	1	7	1	3	3	3	1	2	2	2	1	5	2	3	1	2
	Rawl G.135	2	3	1	1	5	1	1	1	1	3	4	3	1	1	1	1	1	3	3	3	2	2	4	1	1	5	1	3	1	2
Paris	BN lat 7899	1	1	1	2	1	1	1	2	2	1	2	2	1	1	1	2	2	3	1	2	2	2	2	2	1	2	2	1	1	2
	7900	1	1	1	2	1	1	1	2	2	1	2	2	1	1	1	2	2	3	1	2	2	2	2	2	1	2	2	1	2	2
	7900A	1	1	1	2	1	1	1	2	2	1	2	2	1	6	1	2	2	3	1	2	2	1	2	3	1	*	4	3	2	2
	7903	1	1	1	2	1	1	1	2	2	1	2	4	1	1	1	2	2	3	1	2	2	1	2	2	1	4	2	1	2	2
	7904	2	1	1	2	1	1	1	2	2	1	1	4	1	1	1	2	2	3	1	2	2	2	4	2	1	4	2	1	2	2
	7905	1	2	1	2	1	1	1	2	2	1	2	6	1	5	3	2	2	3	1	5	2	1	2	2	1	4	4	4	2	2
	7912	1	1	1	2	1	1	1	2	2	1	1	2	1	5	1	2	2	3	1	2	2	1	2	2	1	4	2	1	2	2
	9345	2	1	1	1	1	2	2	1	1	2	1	1	1	2	2	1	1	2	2	3	1	2	2	2	1	4	2	1	2	2
	10304	*	1	1	1	2	2	2	1	3	2	1	3	1	2	2	1	1	2	2	3	1	2	1	1	2	4	4	2	1	2
	16235	1	1	1	2	1	1	1	2	2	1	2	2	1	5	3	2	2	3	1	2	2	1	2	2	1	4	2	1	2	2
	18544	1	1	1	2	1	1	1	2	2	1	2	2	1	1	1	2	2	3	1	2	2	1	2	2	1	4	2	1	2	4
Rome	Angel 1393	1	4	1	4	5	1	1	3	2	1	4	*	1	1	1	2	1	3	3	3	2	2	4	2	1	4	2	*	1	2
	1407	2	3	4	1	1	1	1	1	1	2	4	3	1	1	1	7	1	3	1	3	1	2	5	1	1	5	4	*	1	2
	Casan 416	1	3	1	1	1	1	1	1	2	1	4	3	1	1	1	2	1	3	1	3	2	2	2	2	1	4	2	1	1	2
	Cors Rossi 63	2	3	1	1	1	1	1	1	1	4	4	3	1	1	1	5	1	3	3	3	1	2	2	2	1	5	2	3	1	2
	Rossi 314	5	1	1	2	1	1	1	2	2	1	2	2	1	1	1	2	1	3	1	2	2	1	2	2	1	4	2	1	2	3
	Vallic F.67	2	3	1	1	1	1	2	1	1	1	1	3	1	1	1	1	3	3	3	3	1	2	2	2	1	6	2	3	1	2
Valenciennes	BM 448	1	4	1	2	1	1	1	2	2	1	2	2	1	6	1	2	2	3	1	2	2	1	2	1	1	4	4	3	2	2
Vatican City	Arch S Pietro H.19	3	2	1	2	1	1	1	2	2	1	2	2	1	1	1	2	2	3	1	2	2	2	2	2	1	4	2	1	2	2
	Barb lat 82	2	1	1	4	1	2	2	2	1	2	1	1	1	7	3	2	1	3	2	3	2	2	*	1	1	4	5	1	2	2
	83	1	5	1	2	1	1	3	2	2	1	2	2	1	6	3	2	2	3	1	2	2	1	2	1	1	4	4	3	2	2
	133	2	3	1	1	1	1	1	1	1	*	4	3	1	1	5	2	2	3	2	3	2	4	2	2	1	4	2	3	1	2
	Ottob lat 1367	1	3	1	2	4	3	1	2	2	1	2	8	1	1	1	2	2	3	1	2	2	1	2	2	1	4	2	*	2	4

Phormio *(continued)*

		1	2	3	4	5	6	7	8	9	10	11	12	13	14	15	16	17	18	19	20	21	22	23	24	25	26	27	28	29	30
	Ottob lat 1468	2	3	1	1	1	1	1	1	1	1	4	3	1	1	1	2	1	3	3	3	2	1	2	2	1	4	2	3	1	2
	Pal lat 1621	4	5	4	2	1	1	3	2	2	1	2	2	1	6	3	2	2	3	1	4	1	1	2	3	1	4	4	3	2	2
	1622	1	1	1	2	1	1	1	2	2	1	2	2	1	5	1	2	2	3	*	*	*	*	*	*	*	*	*	1	2	2
	1623	2	3	1	1	5	1	2	1	1	2	4	3	1	1	1	6	2	3	3	3	1	2	2	2	1	5	2	3	1	2
	1627	2	1	1	5	1	1	1	2	2	3	2	7	1	1	1	1	2	3	1	4	3	3	2	1	1	4	2	5	2	1
	Rossi 445	2	1	1	2	1	2	1	2	2	3	2	3	1	1	*	1	2	3	1	2	3	3	2	2	1	4	2	5	2	2
	506	2	3	1	1	1	1	1	1	2	1	1	3	1	1	1	2	1	3	3	3	1	4	2	1	1	5	2	3	1	2
	928	2	3	1	1	5	1	1	1	1	2	4	3	1	1	1	1	1	2	3	3	1	2	2	2	1	9	2	3	1	2
	Vat lat 1634	2	1	1	4	1	2	2	2	1	2	1	1	1	5	3	2	1	3	2	3	1	2	2	1	1	4	2	1	2	2
	1640	2	3	2	1	3	2	2	1	1	2	1	3	1	2	2	1	1	3	2	3	1	2	2	*	*	*	*	*	*	*
	3305	1	1	1	2	1	1	1	2	2	1	2	2	1	1	1	2	2	2	1	2	2	1	2	2	1	4	2	6	2	2
	3306	1	1	1	2	1	1	1	2	2	1	2	2	1	5	3	2	2	3	1	2	2	1	2	2	1	4	2	1	2	2
	3868	3	2	1	2	1	1	1	2	2	1	2	2	1	1	4	2	2	3	1	2	2	2	2	2	1	2	2	1	2	5
	3869	1	1	1	2	1	1	4	2	2	3	2	2	1	5	3	1	2	3	1	2	2	1	*	2	1	4	2	1	2	2
	6728	2	1	1	1	5	1	1	2	1	2	4	3	1	1	1	1	1	3	3	3	1	2	2	2	1	5	2	3	1	2
	8200	2	3	4	2	1	1	5	2	2	1	2	7	1	1	1	2	2	3	1	2	3	3	2	2	1	4	5	5	2	2
Vienna	lat 85	2	3	1	3	1	2	2	2	2	1	1	2	1	2	2	1	1	3	3	3	2	1	3	2	2	*	3	*	*	*
ed 1475 Milan	A. Zarotti	2	1	1	1	1	1	1	2	1	1	1	4	1	1	5	2	1	3	1	3	3	3	2	2	1	4	2	3	1	1

HECYRA

		1	2	3	4	5	6	7	8	9	10	11	12	13	14	15	16	17	18	19	20	21	22	23	24	25	26	27	28	29	30
Cambridge	UL Add 3024	1	1	2	1	1	4	1	1	2	2	3	2	2	1	1	1	3	3	2	4	4	3	2	2	2	2	6	1	4	3
	Add 3109	1	1	2	1	2	2	1	2	1	3	2	2	1	3	1	2	3	2	2	1	2	2	2	2	2	2	2	2	8	3
	CCC 231	1	2	2	1	3	2	2	2	2	1	1	2	2	1	2	2	2	3	4	5	2	2	1	1	2	2	1	1	6	1
Edinburgh	NL Adv 18.2.10	1	1	2	1	4	2	1	2	2	4	2	4	1	1	1	1	3	2	2	1	2	3	2	2	2	2	2	2	4	3
	Adv 18.7.2	1	1	2	5	5	3	1	*	*	*	2	2	1	2	2	1	3	6	2	1	2	3	1	1	2	*	*	*	*	*
Erlangen	Univ 391	1	2	2	1	2	5	2	2	2	1	1	1	2	1	2	2	2	3	2	3	2	3	1	1	3	2	1	1	2	2
	392	2	1	2	2	1	6	1	2	2	1	2	1	1	2	1	2	1	2	2	1	2	2	2	2	2	2	2	2	2	3
Florence	Med-Laur 38.21	4	2	2	1	1	11	2	2	2	1	1	2	2	1	2	2	2	3	2	2	2	1	1	1	6	2	1	1	4	2
	38.24	2	1	1	2	1	2	1	1	3	2	2	1	1	2	1	1	1	2	2	1	*	1	2	2	4	1	2	2	1	3
	38.27	2	1	1	2	2	4	1	1	2	2	2	1	1	2	1	1	1	1	3	1	3	1	2	2	4	1	2	2	1	3
	38.28	1	1	2	1	1	*	*	2	2	2	2	2	1	3	*	*	*	*	*	*	*	*	*	*	*	*	*	*	*	*
	BN II.IV.5	1	2	2	5	1	4	2	1	2	2	4	1	2	1	2	2	3	3	2	1	2	3	1	1	2	2	1	1	3	6
	II.IV.689	1	1	2	1	1	4	1	2	2	3	2	2	1	2	1	*	3	2	2	1	2	3	1	2	2	1	2	2	4	3
	II.VIII.52	1	1	2	1	1	2	1	2	2	1	1	2	2	1	1	1	3	2	2	1	2	2	1	2	2	1	2	2	4	3
	Ricc 528	1	2	2	1	2	2	2	2	2	1	1	2	2	1	2	2	2	3	4	5	2	2	1	1	2	2	1	1	2	2
	530	1	1	2	1	1	5	1	2	2	3	2	2	1	2	1	1	3	2	2	1	2	3	1	2	2	1	2	2	4	3
Hague, The	Kon Bibl 72.J.49	1	3	2	2	1	2	1	2	2	3	1	2	2	1	2	2	3	3	2	1	2	1	1	1	2	2	1	1	3	2
Leipzig	Univ I.37	1	2	2	1	2	3	2	2	2	2	1	2	2	1	2	2	2	3	2	1	2	2	1	1	2	2	1	4	2	1
Leyden	Rijksuniv BPL 109	1	2	2	1	2	2	2	2	2	1	1	2	2	1	2	2	2	3	4	1	2	2	1	1	2	2	1	1	3	2
	Lips 26	1	2	2	1	2	4	2	2	2	1	1	2	2	1	2	2	2	3	2	1	2	3	1	3	2	2	1	1	6	2
	Voss lat Q.38	1	2	2	1	2	4	2	2	2	1	1	2	2	1	2	2	2	2	2	1	2	1	1	1	2	2	1	1	3	2
London	BL Harl 2455	4	1	2	4	2	4	1	2	2	3	2	2	2	1	2	2	2	3	2	3	2	2	1	1	2	2	1	1	8	2
	2475	1	1	2	1	2	2	1	2	1	1	2	2	1	3	1	2	3	3	2	1	2	3	1	2	2	1	2	2	3	3
	2524	1	2	2	1	2	4	2	3	2	1	1	2	2	2	1	2	2	3	2	7	2	2	1	1	2	2	2	1	3	2
	2656	1	2	2	1	2	7	2	2	2	1	1	2	1	2	1	1	3	2	2	1	2	3	1	2	2	2	2	2	3	4
	2670	4	2	2	2	1	4	2	2	2	1	1	2	2	1	2	2	2	3	2	1	2	1	1	1	*	2	4	1	3	2

Hecyra *(continued)*

		1	2	3	4	5	6	7	8	9	10	11	12	13	14	15	16	17	18	19	20	21	22	23	24	25	26	27	28	29	30
	2750	2	2	2	1	2	4	2	2	2	1	1	1	2	1	2	2	1	1	1	1	5	1	1	1	2	3	3	1	5	*
	5443	1	2	2	1	1	4	2	2	2	1	1	*	*	*	*	*	*	*	*	*	*	*	*	*	*	*	*	*	*	*
	Roy 15.A.XII	1	1	2	1	3	4	1	2	2	1	2	2	1	2	1	1	3	*	*	*	*	*	2	2	2	2	2	1	3	3
Lucca	1420	4	2	3	1	2	4	2	2	2	3	1	2	2	1	2	2	2	2	2	1	2	3	1	2	2	1	2	2	4	3
Milan	Ambros D.79 sup	1	2	2	1	2	4	2	2	2	1	2	2	2	1	2	1	3	3	2	1	2	3	1	2	2	2	2	2	2	3
	G.130 inf	1	1	2	1	2	5	1	2	2	3	2	2	1	2	1	1	3	2	2	1	2	3	1	2	2	1	2	2	2	3
	H.75 inf	1	1	2	2	2	2	1	2	2	3	2	2	1	2	1	1	3	2	2	1	2	2	2	2	2	2	2	2	2	3
Oxford	Bodl Auct F.2.13	1	2	2	1	2	9	2	2	2	1	1	2	2	1	2	2	2	3	1	1	2	3	1	1	2	2	1	1	3	2
	F.6.27	3	1	2	2	1	6	1	2	2	1	2	1	1	2	1	2	1	2	2	1	2	2	2	2	2	2	2	2	2	3
	Brasenose 18	4	2	2	1	2	2	2	2	2	1	1	2	2	1	1	2	2	3	2	1	2	2	1	1	2	2	2	1	3	2
	Clarke 28	1	1	2	1	1	3	1	2	2	2	2	2	1	2	1	1	3	2	2	8	2	3	1	2	2	1	2	2	4	3
	D'Orville 155	1	1	2	1	1	2	1	2	2	3	2	2	1	2	1	1	3	2	2	1	2	3	1	2	2	1	2	2	4	3
	Laud 76	1	2	2	1	1	10	2	3	2	1	1	2	2	1	2	2	2	3	1	1	2	3	1	1	2	2	1	1	3	2
	Magd 23	1	1	2	1	2	4	1	2	3	3	2	2	1	2	1	1	3	2	2	1	2	3	1	2	2	1	2	2	4	3
	Rawl G.135	1	1	2	1	4	4	1	2	2	3	2	2	1	3	1	2	3	3	2	1	2	3	1	2	2	1	2	2	4	3
Paris	BN lat 7899	1	2	2	1	2	4	2	2	2	1	1	2	2	1	2	2	2	3	1	1	2	2	1	1	2	2	1	1	3	2
	7900	1	2	2	1	2	2	2	2	2	1	1	2	2	1	2	2	2	3	1	1	2	2	1	1	2	2	1	1	3	2
	7900A	1	1	2	3	1	2	1	2	2	3	2	2	1	2	1	1	3	2	2	1	2	2	2	2	2	2	2	2	2	3
	7903	*	2	2	1	2	4	2	2	2	1	1	2	2	4	2	2	2	3	2	1	2	2	1	1	2	2	1	1	6	2
	7904	1	2	2	1	2	4	2	2	2	1	1	2	2	1	2	2	2	3	1	1	2	2	1	1	2	2	1	1	3	2
	7905	1	2	2	1	2	4	2	2	2	1	1	2	2	3	2	2	2	3	4	1	2	2	2	4	5	2	1	3	3	*
	7912	1	1	2	1	1	4	1	2	2	1	2	3	1	2	1	1	3	2	2	1	2	3	2	2	2	2	2	2	3	3
	9345	2	2	2	2	1	4	1	1	3	1	2	1	2	3	2	2	1	1	2	1	3	2	2	1	2	2	2	2	3	3
	10304	2	1	1	2	1	*	1	1	3	1	2	1	1	2	1	1	1	1	2	6	2	1	1	2	1	1	2	2	1	3
	16235	1	2	2	1	2	4	2	2	2	2	1	2	2	1	2	2	2	3	2	1	2	2	1	1	2	2	1	1	3	2

		1	2	3	4	5	6	7	8	9	10	11	12	13	14	15	16	17	18	19	20	21	22	23	24	25	26	27	28	29	30
	18544	1	2	2	1	2	4	2	1	2	2	1	2	2	1	2	2	2	3	2	1	2	1	1	1	2	2	1	5	3	2
Rome	Angel 1407	1	1	2	2	3	4	1	3	2	1	2	2	1	2	1	1	2	5	2	1	2	3	1	2	2	1	2	2	4	3
	Casan 416	1	2	2	1	4	4	2	2	1	6	2	2	1	2	1	2	3	2	2	1	2	3	1	2	3	1	6	2	4	3
	Cors Rossi 314	4	2	2	1	3	4	2	2	4	3	2	2	2	1	1	1	3	3	2	1	2	2	2	2	2	2	2	2	2	3
	Vallic F.67	1	1	2	1	1	3	1	2	2	2	2	2	1	2	1	1	3	2	2	8	2	3	1	2	2	1	2	2	4	3
Valenciennes	BM 448	1	1	2	1	4	4	1	2	2	3	2	2	1	2	1	1	3	2	2	1	2	2	2	2	2	2	2	2	7	3
Vatican City	Arch S Pietro H.19	1	2	2	1	2	4	2	2	2	1	1	2	2	1	2	2	2	3	1	1	2	2	1	1	2	2	1	1	3	2
	Barb lat 82	1	1	2	1	1	4	1	2	2	3	1	2	1	1	1	2	3	3	2	1	2	3	1	2	2	2	2	2	3	2
	83	1	1	2	1	4	8	1	2	2	1	1	2	1	2	1	1	3	2	2	1	2	2	2	2	2	*	2	2	2	3
	133	4	1	2	1	1	4	1	2	2	3	2	2	1	2	1	1	2	2	2	1	2	3	1	2	2	1	2	2	*	3
	Ottob lat 1367	1	2	2	5	4	4	2	2	2	5	1	2	2	1	2	2	3	3	2	1	2	3	1	1	2	2	1	1	2	2
	1468	4	2	2	2	4	12	2	2	2	2	1	2	2	2	2	2	3	2	4	1	2	2	1	1	2	2	1	4	9	1
	Pal lat 1621	1	1	2	1	4	8	1	2	2	1	1	2	1	2	1	1	3	2	2	1	2	2	2	2	2	2	2	2	2	3
	1623	1	1	2	5	1	4	1	2	2	3	2	2	1	3	1	1	3	3	2	1	2	3	1	2	2	1	2	2	4	3
	1627	1	2	2	*	*	*	*	4	2	1	1	2	2	1	1	2	3	2	2	1	6	3	2	2	2	1	2	2	4	5
	Rossi 445	1	2	2	1	4	4	2	3	2	1	2	2	2	3	1	2	3	2	2	1	2	3	1	2	2	1	2	2	4	5
	506	1	1	2	1	1	4	1	2	2	3	2	2	1	2	1	1	3	2	2	8	2	3	1	2	2	1	2	2	4	3
	Vat lat 1634	1	2	2	1	3	4	1	2	2	1	1	2	2	1	1	2	3	3	2	1	2	2	1	1	2	2	2	1	6	2
	1640	*	*	*	*	*	*	*	1	3	1	2	*	*	*	*	*	*	*	*	*	*	*	*	*	*	*	*	*	*	*
	3305	4	2	2	1	2	4	2	2	2	1	1	2	2	1	2	2	2	3	2	7	2	2	1	1	2	2	5	1	6	2
	3306	1	2	2	1	2	4	2	2	2	1	1	2	2	1	2	1	2	4	2	1	2	2	1	1	2	2	1	1	3	2
	3868	1	2	2	1	2	2	2	2	2	1	1	2	2	1	2	2	2	3	1	1	2	2	1	1	2	2	1	1	3	2
	3869	1	2	2	1	2	4	2	2	2	1	1	2	2	1	2	2	2	3	4	1	2	3	1	1	2	2	1	1	2	2
	6728	1	1	2	1	1	2	1	2	1	3	2	2	1	2	2	2	3	2	2	1	2	3	1	2	*	*	*	2	4	3

ADELPHOE

		1	2	3	4	5	6	7	8	9	10	11	12	13	14	15	16	17	18	19	20	21	22	23	24	25	26	27	28	29	30
Bamberg	Staatsbibl Class 49	2	1	1	1	3	2	1	2	2	6	2	2	1	2	6	4	2	2	2	2	3	1	2	2	2	2	3	2	2	3
Barcelona	BC 1743	1	6	1	1	2	2	2	1	1	3	1	1	1	1	1	2	2	2	1	1	2	1	1	2	1	3	2	1	1	1
Brussels	BR 5329	1	2	1	1	2	2	2	2	2	2	8	1	3	2	2	4	2	3	2	3	3	1	2	3	2	2	1	2	2	3
	9705	1	1	1	1	2	2	2	2	2	1	2	1	1	2	1	2	2	3	2	3	3	1	2	1	2	3	1	2	2	3
Cambridge	UL Add 3024	1	1	2	2	5	2	2	3	1	2	1	2	1	1	2	2	2	2	2	4	2	1	3	2	1	3	2	2	2	3
	Add 3109	1	1	2	2	3	2	2	2	1	2	7	1	2	1	1	2	2	2	1	3	3	3	2	1	1	3	1	2	2	3
	CCC 231	1	2	2	1	2	2	2	2	2	2	2	1	*	*	2	2	2	5	2	3	3	1	2	3	2	3	1	2	2	3
	Peterhouse 253	2	1	2	3	8	2	2	3	1	2	1	2	1	2	2	2	2	2	2	3	3	1	2	3	2	3	1	2	1	3
Edinburgh	NL Adv 18.2.10	1	1	2	2	5	2	2	4	1	2	1	1	1	1	2	2	2	2	3	2	2	2	2	1	1	2	2	2	2	3
	Adv 18.7.2	1	2	2	1	2	2	2	2	1	4	1	1	2	2	2	2	2	2	3	3	3	2	2	1	1	3	2	2	1	4
	UL 197	1	4	2	3	3	2	2	1	1	2	2	1	1	2	2	2	2	4	1	3	3	1	3	1	2	3	1	2	3	3
Erlangen	Univ 391	2	1	2	2	4	2	1	2	1	2	1	2	2	1	2	4	2	2	2	2	2	2	1	2	2	3	1	2	1	3
	392	*	*	*	*	*	*	*	*	*	*	*	*	*	*	*	*	*	*	*	*	*	*	*	*	*	*	3	4	1	3
Escorial, El	S.III.23	1	2	1	1	2	1	2	2	2	2	2	1	5	2	2	2	2	5	2	3	3	1	2	1	2	3	1	2	2	3
Florence	Med-Laur 38.19	1	2	2	2	2	1	2	2	2	*	8	2	1	2	2	2	2	2	2	3	3	4	2	1	2	3	2	2	2	3
	38.20	1	2	2	1	2	2	2	2	2	6	2	1	1	2	2	2	2	2	2	3	3	1	2	3	2	3	1	2	2	3
	38.21	1	2	1	3	2	2	2	2	3	4	7	1	3	2	2	2	2	2	2	2	3	1	2	2	2	3	3	2	2	3
	38.23	1	1	2	3	10	2	2	3	1	2	2	1	3	2	2	2	2	2	1	1	2	1	2	2	1	2	2	2	2	3
	38.24	2	1	1	2	3	2	1	1	1	2	1	2	2	1	2	4	1	2	1	2	2	2	1	2	1	2	2	1	1	2
	38.26	1	2	2	1	2	2	2	3	3	2	7	2	3	2	1	2	2	2	2	3	2	1	2	2	2	3	1	2	2	3
	38.27	2	1	2	1	3	2	2	2	1	2	1	2	2	1	2	4	2	3	2	2	2	4	2	2	1	3	2	2	1	3
	38.28	1	7	2	2	5	2	2	2	1	2	1	1	1	1	2	2	2	2	1	1	2	1	2	5	1	3	2	2	2	3
	38.30	1	1	2	2	5	2	2	3	1	2	1	1	1	1	2	2	3	2	1	1	2	1	2	2	1	2	2	2	2	3
	38.31	1	1	2	2	5	2	2	2	1	2	1	1	1	1	2	2	2	2	4	1	2	1	3	2	1	2	2	2	2	3
	38.32	1	1	2	2	3	3	2	2	1	2	1	2	1	2	2	2	2	3	2	2	2	1	2	3	1	3	4	6	2	3

		1	2	3	4	5	6	7	8	9	10	11	12	13	14	15	16	17	18	19	20	21	22	23	24	25	26	27	28	29	30
	91 sup 13,1	1	1	2	2	5	2	2	2	1	2	1	1	1	1	2	2	2	2	1	1	2	1	2	2	1	3	2	2	2	3
	BN II.IV.5	1	1	2	2	*	2	2	2	1	2	1	2	1	1	2	2	2	2	4	1	3	1	2	3	2	3	2	2	2	3
	II.IV.6	3	1	2	2	8	2	2	2	1	2	3	2	2	1	2	2	2	2	1	2	2	2	2	2	1	*	2	2	2	3
	II.IV.333	1	1	2	3	3	2	2	1	2	2	1	2	2	1	2	2	2	2	1	3	3	1	2	2	2	2	3	2	2	6
	II.IV.689	1	1	2	2	5	2	2	2	1	5	1	1	1	1	2	2	2	2	4	1	2	1	2	2	1	2	2	2	2	3
	II.VIII.52	1	2	2	1	2	2	3	2	2	2	7	2	1	2	2	2	2	2	4	1	3	1	2	3	2	3	1	2	2	3
	II.IX.127	1	2	2	1	2	2	2	3	3	*	*	*	3	2	2	2	2	2	1	3	3	1	*	2	2	*	1	2	2	3
	Ricc 528	1	2	1	1	2	2	2	2	3	2	2	1	1	2	2	2	2	5	2	3	3	1	2	3	2	3	1	2	2	3
	529	1	6	1	1	2	1	2	2	2	1	2	1	1	2	1	2	2	3	2	3	3	1	2	1	1	3	1	2	2	3
	530	1	1	2	2	5	1	2	2	1	2	1	1	2	1	2	2	2	3	2	1	3	1	5	2	1	2	2	2	4	5
	531	2	1	2	4	4	1	2	2	1	2	1	2	1	1	2	2	2	2	1	3	2	6	1	1	1	3	2	1	1	1
	532	1	1	2	2	4	2	2	2	1	2	3	2	2	1	2	2	2	2	7	3	2	2	2	2	1	2	2	2	1	2
	613	1	1	2	3	5	2	2	3	1	2	1	1	1	1	5	4	2	2	4	1	2	1	6	2	2	2	2	2	2	3
	614	1	1	2	2	5	2	2	2	1	2	1	1	1	1	2	2	2	2	3	1	2	1	2	2	1	3	2	2	2	3
	3608	3	1	2	2	5	2	2	2	1	2	1	1	2	1	2	3	2	2	2	1	1	1	2	2	2	2	2	2	2	3
Glasgow	UL Hunt 26	1	7	2	3	5	2	2	2	1	2	1	1	1	1	2	2	2	2	4	1	2	1	2	5	1	3	2	2	2	3
	Gen 1125	1	1	2	2	5	2	2	8	1	2	3	2	3	2	2	2	2	2	2	3	3	5	2	2	2	3	1	2	2	3
	1189	2	1	2	2	3	2	2	2	2	2	2	2	1	1	2	4	2	6	1	2	2	2	2	2	5	3	4	1	1	2
Hague, The	Kon Bibl 72.J.49	1	2	1	1	2	2	2	3	3	2	2	1	1	2	2	2	2	5	2	3	3	1	2	3	2	3	2	2	3	3
Leipzig	Univ I.37	2	1	1	2	3	2	1	1	1	2	3	2	2	1	2	4	2	4	1	2	2	2	1	2	1	2	2	2	1	1
Leyden	Rijksuniv BPL 109	1	2	1	1	2	2	2	2	2	6	2	1	1	2	2	2	2	2	2	3	3	1	2	3	2	3	1	2	2	3
	Lips 26	1	2	1	1	2	2	2	2	2	2	2	1	5	2	2	2	2	2	2	3	3	1	2	1	2	3	1	2	2	3
	Voss lat Q.38	2	1	1	1	2	2	2	6	2	1	2	1	2	2	2	2	1	2	2	3	3	1	2	3	2	3	1	2	2	3
London	BL Harl 2455	2	1	1	2	3	2	1	1	1	2	3	2	2	1	2	4	2	4	1	2	2	2	1	2	1	2	2	2	1	1
	2475	1	1	2	3	5	2	2	3	1	2	1	1	1	1	2	2	2	2	3	1	3	1	2	2	3	2	2	2	2	3

Adelphoe *(continued)*

		1	2	3	4	5	6	7	8	9	10	11	12	13	14	15	16	17	18	19	20	21	22	23	24	25	26	27	28	29	30
	2524	1	2	2	1	2	2	2	2	1	2	6	2	1	2	2	2	2	2	2	3	3	1	2	3	2	3	1	2	2	3
	2525	1	1	1	2	2	2	2	1	1	2	3	2	2	1	2	4	2	2	1	2	2	2	1	2	1	2	2	2	1	2
	2526	1	1	2	2	5	2	2	2	1	2	1	1	1	1	2	2	2	2	3	1	2	1	2	2	1	2	2	2	2	3
	2656	1	2	2	1	2	2	2	2	1	2	2	1	1	2	2	2	2	2	2	3	3	1	2	3	2	3	1	2	2	3
	2670	1	2	2	1	6	2	2	2	2	2	2	1	1	2	2	2	3	2	2	3	3	1	2	2	2	3	5	2	2	3
	2750	1	2	1	1	2	1	1	2	2	2	2	1	1	3	2	2	2	2	2	6	3	1	2	2	2	3	3	2	2	3
	5000	1	3	2	3	4	2	2	2	1	2	1	2	2	2	1	4	1	2	2	3	2	2	2	1	2	2	2	2	2	3
	5224	1	2	2	2	2	2	2	2	1	2	1	1	1	2	2	2	2	2	2	3	2	1	4	3	1	2	2	2	2	3
	5443	1	4	2	1	2	2	2	2	2	2	2	1	1	2	2	2	2	3	2	2	3	1	2	2	2	3	1	2	2	3
	Arun 247	2	1	2	5	3	2	2	7	1	2	1	1	1	1	2	2	2	2	2	1	2	1	2	2	1	3	2	2	*	3
	Burn 261	1	1	2	3	3	2	2	6	1	2	4	2	2	1	2	2	2	5	3	3	3	1	2	1	2	3	2	2	2	3
	262	1	1	2	2	5	1	2	1	1	2	1	1	1	2	2	2	2	4	3	3	3	1	2	2	2	3	2	2	2	3
	Roy 15.A.VIII	7	1	3	3	8	2	2	2	1	2	3	1	1	2	2	2	2	2	2	3	5	1	2	2	2	3	3	2	1	3
	15.A.XII	2	3	2	2	2	1	3	2	1	2	1	2	1	1	2	2	2	3	4	3	3	2	2	2	1	3	2	2	2	4
	15.B.VIII	1	1	2	3	3	2	2	3	1	2	1	2	1	2	2	2	2	2	2	3	3	1	2	2	2	3	1	2	2	3
Lucca	1420	1	1	2	2	4	2	2	2	1	2	1	1	2	1	2	2	2	2	1	3	2	2	5	2	1	3	2	2	2	3
Milan	Ambros A.33 inf	1	1	2	2	1	2	2	2	1	3	1	2	1	1	2	2	2	2	2	1	2	1	2	2	1	3	2	3	*	3
	D.79 sup	2	2	2	4	2	2	2	2	2	1	8	1	1	2	2	2	2	2	2	3	3	1	2	1	2	3	1	2	2	7
	F.92 sup	1	1	2	2	5	5	2	3	3	2	1	2	1	1	2	2	2	2	4	1	2	1	2	2	1	2	2	2	2	3
	F.142 sup	1	1	2	2	5	2	2	3	1	2	1	1	1	1	2	2	2	2	4	1	2	1	2	2	1	2	2	2	2	3
	G.130 inf	1	1	2	2	3	2	2	2	1	2	1	2	2	1	1	2	2	2	1	1	3	3	2	1	1	3	3	2	2	3
	H.63 sup	1	1	2	3	3	6	2	2	1	2	1	2	1	1	2	2	2	2	1	3	3	2	2	1	1	2	4	2	1	3
	H.75 inf	1	2	1	1	2	1	2	2	2	2	2	1	1	2	1	2	2	2	2	3	3	1	2	1	2	3	1	2	2	3
	H.135 inf	1	7	2	2	5	2	2	2	1	2	1	1	1	1	2	2	2	2	1	1	2	1	2	5	1	3	2	2	2	3
	I.5 sup	1	2	1	1	2	2	2	2	3	2	7	1	3	2	2	2	2	2	2	2	3	1	2	2	2	3	1	2	2	3

		1	2	3	4	5	6	7	8	9	10	11	12	13	14	15	16	17	18	19	20	21	22	23	24	25	26	27	28	29	30
	I.103 sup	1	2	2	2	2	4	2	3	1	2	1	2	1	2	2	2	2	2	2	3	3	1	2	2	2	3	1	2	1	3
	Triv 663	1	2	2	1	2	2	3	2	2	2	2	2	1	2	2	2	2	2	2	3	3	1	2	3	2	3	1	2	2	3
	727	1	1	2	2	4	2	3	2	1	2	1	2	1	1	2	2	2	2	2	1	4	2	2	2	1	2	3	2	2	2
Montpellier	FMéd 227	1	2	1	4	2	2	2	2	2	2	2	1	1	2	2	2	2	2	2	3	3	1	2	3	2	3	1	2	2	3
Oxford	Bodl Auct F.2.13	1	6	1	1	2	1	2	2	2	1	2	1	1	2	1	2	2	1	2	3	3	1	2	1	1	3	1	2	2	3
	Auct F.6.27	2	1	2	2	4	1	1	1	1	2	1	1	1	1	1	2	2	2	2	3	2	2	2	2	1	2	3	4	1	3
	Brasenose 18	1	2	2	1	2	2	2	2	2	2	2	1	1	2	2	2	2	2	2	3	3	1	2	3	2	3	1	2	2	3
	Clarke 28	1	7	2	2	5	2	2	2	1	2	1	2	1	1	2	2	2	2	5	1	2	1	2	5	1	3	2	2	2	3
	D'Orville 155	1	1	2	2	5	2	2	2	1	2	1	1	1	1	2	2	*	2	4	1	2	1	2	2	1	2	2	2	2	3
	Laud 76	1	1	1	1	2	1	2	2	2	1	2	1	1	2	1	2	2	2	2	3	3	1	2	1	1	*	1	2	2	3
	Magd 23	1	1	2	2	5	2	4	2	1	2	1	1	1	1	2	2	2	2	4	1	2	1	2	2	1	2	2	2	2	3
	Rawl G.135	1	1	2	2	5	5	2	3	1	2	1	1	1	1	2	2	2	2	4	1	2	1	2	2	1	2	2	2	2	3
Paris	BN lat 7899	1	6	1	1	2	1	2	2	2	1	2	1	1	2	1	2	2	1	2	3	3	1	2	1	1	3	1	2	2	3
	7900	1	6	1	1	2	1	2	2	2	1	2	1	1	2	1	2	2	*	2	3	3	1	2	1	1	3	1	2	2	3
	7900A	1	1	2	2	3	*	2	2	1	2	1	2	2	1	1	2	1	2	1	3	2	2	2	1	1	2	2	2	2	3
	7902	1	2	2	1	2	2	2	2	2	2	7	1	1	2	2	2	2	7	2	3	3	1	2	3	2	2	1	2	2	3
	7903	1	2	1	4	2	2	2	2	2	2	2	1	1	2	2	2	3	1	2	3	3	1	2	1	2	3	1	2	2	3
	7904	1	5	2	1	2	2	2	3	2	2	1	1	1	2	2	2	2	3	2	3	3	1	2	3	2	4	1	2	1	3
	7905	1	2	2	1	2	2	2	3	1	3	2	1	3	4	3	2	2	2	2	3	3	1	2	3	2	5	1	2	2	3
	7906	1	3	2	1	2	2	2	2	2	2	2	1	1	3	1	4	2	3	2	3	2	1	2	4	1	3	1	2	2	3
	7907	1	1	2	3	5	2	2	2	1	2	1	1	1	1	2	2	2	2	3	1	2	1	2	2	1	2	2	2	2	3
	7909	1	1	2	2	5	2	2	2	2	1	1	1	1	2	2	4	2	2	3	1	2	1	2	2	1	2	2	2	2	3
	7910	1	1	2	3	5	2	2	2	1	2	1	2	1	1	2	4	2	2	4	1	2	1	2	2	1	2	2	2	2	3
	7911	5	1	2	2	5	2	2	3	1	2	1	2	1	2	1	4	2	2	2	3	3	1	2	2	2	2	1	2	2	3
	7912	3	1	2	3	1	2	2	2	1	2	1	2	2	1	2	2	2	2	1	3	2	3	2	1	1	2	3	2	2	3

Adelphoe *(continued)*

		1	2	3	4	5	6	7	8	9	10	11	12	13	14	15	16	17	18	19	20	21	22	23	24	25	26	27	28	29	30
	7913	1	1	2	3	5	2	2	2	1	2	1	1	1	1	2	4	2	2	2	1	2	1	2	2	1	3	1	2	2	3
	7915	1	1	2	2	3	2	2	2	1	2	1	2	2	1	2	2	2	2	4	2	3	1	2	2	1	2	1	2	2	3
	7916	1	1	2	2	5	2	2	2	1	5	1	1	1	1	2	2	2	2	4	1	2	1	2	2	1	3	2	2	2	3
	7917A	1	1	2	1	3	2	*	1	2	2	2	2	1	2	2	2	2	3	2	3	3	1	2	1	2	3	1	2	2	3
	7918	1	1	2	3	5	2	1	2	1	2	3	2	1	1	2	4	2	2	4	1	2	1	2	2	1	2	2	2	2	3
	7919	1	1	2	3	2	2	2	3	2	2	2	2	1	2	2	7	2	2	2	3	3	1	2	1	1	3	1	2	3	3
	8191	1	2	1	3	2	2	2	2	1	2	2	2	1	2	2	2	2	2	2	3	3	1	1	1	2	3	1	5	2	3
	8192	1	2	1	7	2	4	2	2	3	2	1	1	2	1	2	5	2	2	2	3	2	1	2	1	2	3	1	2	2	3
	9345	2	1	2	2	3	2	2	1	2	2	2	2	2	1	2	2	2	2	1	3	2	4	2	3	2	2	1	2	2	2
	10304	*	1	1	2	3	1	1	1	1	1	1	2	1	1	1	3	1	3	1	2	2	2	1	2	1	2	2	1	1	1
	11306	1	1	2	6	3	2	2	1	1	2	1	1	2	1	2	2	2	2	4	3	3	1	2	2	2	2	1	2	2	6
	14755	2	1	1	1	2	2	2	2	2	2	2	1	1	2	2	2	2	4	2	3	3	1	2	3	2	3	1	2	2	3
	16235	1	2	1	1	2	2	2	2	2	2	2	1	1	2	2	2	2	2	2	3	3	1	2	3	2	3	1	2	2	3
	17895	2	1	2	2	8	2	2	2	1	2	1	2	2	2	2	2	2	2	1	3	3	2	2	4	1	3	2	2	2	3
	18544	1	2	1	2	2	2	2	2	2	2	2	1	1	2	2	2	2	3	2	3	3	1	2	1	*	3	1	2	2	3
Rome	Angel 1356	4	1	*	1	3	2	2	2	2	2	1	1	1	1	2	2	3	2	2	3	2	1	2	2	1	4	4	2	2	6
	1393	3	1	2	2	5	2	2	2	1	2	1	1	2	2	2	2	2	2	2	1	2	1	2	3	2	2	2	2	2	3
	1395	1	1	2	2	5	2	2	5	1	2	1	1	1	1	2	4	2	2	1	1	2	1	2	2	1	*	*	*	*	*
	1407	2	1	2	2	1	2	2	3	1	2	1	2	1	1	2	2	2	2	1	1	2	1	2	2	1	3	1	2	2	3
	2241	2	1	2	3	3	2	2	6	1	2	4	1	2	1	2	2	2	5	3	3	3	1	2	1	2	3	2	2	2	3
	Casan 58	1	1	2	6	3	2	2	1	1	2	1	2	2	1	2	2	2	2	4	3	3	1	2	2	2	2	3	2	2	3
	288	2	2	1	1	3	2	2	1	1	2	1	2	2	1	2	6	2	2	2	3	3	2	2	1	1	3	4	2	1	3
	416	1	1	2	2	5	2	2	2	1	2	1	1	2	1	2	2	2	2	2	2	4	1	2	2	2	3	2	2	2	3
	Cors Rossi 63	2	2	1	1	2	2	2	3	1	2	1	1	1	1	2	2	2	2	4	1	2	1	2	2	1	3	2	2	2	3
	300	1	1	2	3	3	2	2	2	1	2	1	2	2	1	2	2	2	2	1	1	3	1	2	2	2	3	2	2	2	3

		1	2	3	4	5	6	7	8	9	10	11	12	13	14	15	16	17	18	19	20	21	22	23	24	25	26	27	28	29	30
	Rossi 314	1	2	1	2	2	2	2	2	1	1	2	1	3	2	2	2	2	3	1	3	3	1	2	1	2	3	1	2	2	3
	Vallic F.67	1	1	2	2	5	2	2	2	1	2	1	1	1	1	2	2	2	2	1	1	2	1	2	5	1	3	2	2	2	3
Tours	BM 924	1	6	1	1	2	1	2	2	1	2	2	1	1	2	1	2	2	3	2	3	3	1	2	1	1	3	1	2	2	2
Valenciennes	BM 448	1	2	1	1	2	2	2	2	2	2	2	1	1	2	2	2	2	2	2	3	3	1	2	1	1	3	2	2	2	3
Vatican City	Arch S Pietro 19	1	1	1	1	2	1	2	3	2	1	2	1	1	2	1	2	2	3	2	3	3	1	2	1	1	3	1	2	2	3
	Barb lat 82	1	1	2	2	5	2	2	2	1	2	3	1	1	1	2	2	2	2	4	1	2	2	2	2	1	2	2	2	1	3
	83	1	1	2	3	3	2	3	3	1	2	1	1	1	1	2	5	2	2	2	1	2	2	2	1	1	2	2	2	2	2
	133	1	1	2	2	5	2	2	3	1	2	1	1	1	1	2	2	2	2	1	1	2	1	2	2	1	2	2	2	2	3
	Chig H.VIII.261	1	2	2	1	2	2	3	2	2	2	2	1	1	2	2	2	2	2	2	3	3	1	2	3	2	2	1	2	2	3
	Ottob lat 1367	1	2	1	2	2	2	2	2	1	2	1	2	1	2	2	2	2	3	2	2	2	1	2	3	2	2	2	2	1	3
	1468	1	1	1	2	2	3	2	2	1	2	1	2	1	2	2	2	2	2	3	1	2	1	2	2	1	2	2	2	2	3
	Pal lat 1621	2	1	2	3	3	2	3	3	1	2	1	1	1	1	2	3	2	2	2	1	2	2	2	1	4	2	2	2	2	2
	1622	1	1	2	2	9	2	2	2	1	2	1	2	2	1	4	2	2	2	2	5	3	5	2	3	2	3	*	2	2	3
	1623	1	1	2	2	5	2	2	1	1	4	1	*	1	1	2	2	2	2	2	1	2	1	2	5	1	2	2	2	2	3
	1625	1	2	2	2	4	2	2	2	1	2	1	2	2	2	2	5	2	2	2	3	3	2	2	1	1	3	6	2	1	3
	1627	1	2	2	4	2	1	2	2	1	2	1	2	1	2	2	2	2	2	6	3	3	1	2	2	2	3	1	2	2	3
	Reg lat 1842	2	1	2	2	3	2	2	2	2	1	2	1	1	2	2	2	2	2	2	3	3	*	2	3	2	1	3	2	2	5
	Rossi 445	1	1	2	4	2	2	2	3	1	2	2	2	1	2	2	2	2	2	2	3	3	1	2	1	2	2	1	2	2	3
	506	1	1	2	2	5	2	2	2	1	1	1	1	1	1	2	2	2	2	3	1	2	1	2	2	1	2	2	2	2	3
	928	1	1	2	2	5	2	2	2	1	2	1	1	1	1	2	2	2	2	3	1	2	1	2	2	1	2	2	2	2	3
	1021	2	1	1	2	2	2	2	1	1	2	1	2	2	1	2	4	2	2	1	3	3	1	2	3	1	2	2	2	2	3
	Val lat 1634	1	2	2	4	7	2	2	2	1	2	1	2	2	2	1	2	2	2	2	3	3	2	2	1	1	2	2	2	2	3
	1635	1	2	2	1	2	2	2	3	3	4	7	2	1	2	1	2	2	2	2	3	3	1	2	2	2	3	3	2	2	3
	1636	1	1	2	2	3	2	2	2	1	2	3	2	2	1	2	2	2	2	1	3	3	1	2	1	2	3	2	2	2	3
	1640	8	1	2	2	3	1	2	1	2	2	1	2	2	1	2	4	1	2	1	2	2	2	1	2	1	2	2	1	1	2

Adelphoe *(continued)*

		1	2	3	4	5	6	7	8	9	10	11	12	13	14	15	16	17	18	19	20	21	22	23	24	25	26	27	28	29	30
	3305	1	2	2	1	2	2	2	2	2	2	2	2	1	2	2	2	2	2	2	3	3	1	2	1	2	3	1	2	2	3
	3306	1	2	1	1	2	2	2	2	2	2	2	1	1	2	2	2	4	2	2	3	3	1	2	3	2	3	1	2	2	3
	3868	1	6	1	1	2	1	2	2	2	1	2	1	1	2	1	2	2	1	2	3	3	1	2	1	1	3	1	2	2	3
	3869	1	2	2	1	2	2	2	3	2	3	2	1	1	2	2	2	2	2	2	3	3	1	2	3	2	3	1	2	2	3
	6728	2	1	1	2	5	2	2	1	1	2	1	2	1	1	2	2	2	2	1	2	2	1	2	1	1	2	3	2	2	3
	8200	1	2	1	4	2	4	2	2	1	2	1	1	1	2	2	2	2	2	6	3	3	1	2	2	2	3	2	2	2	3
Vienna	lat 85	1	1	2	1	3	1	1	1	1	2	1	2	1	1	1	2	1	2	1	3	3	3	2	1	1	2	4	2	2	3
Wolfenbüttel	Gud lat 193	6	1	2	1	2	2	2	3	2	2	1	2	4	1	1	2	2	2	4	3	2	4	2	1	1	2	2	2	2	3
Zwettl	Stiftsbibl 313	2	1	2	2	3	1	2	5	2	2	5	2	1	2	2	2	2	2	2	2	3	1	2	2	2	3	1	2	2	3
ed. 1475, Milan	A Zarotta	1	*	*	2	2	2	2	2	1	2	1	2	1	1	2	2	2	2	4	1	2	1	2	2	1	2	2	2	2	3

NOTES

PREFACE

1 As is shown in the *didascaliae* by the mention of magistrates who held office after the death of Terence. See Dziatzko in his introduction to his commentary of *Phormio* (25). See also D. Klose *Die Didaskalien und Prologe des Terenz* (Diss Freiburg 1966) 12-13.

2 Ausonius includes Terence among the authors he had studied in his youth (*Protr* 58-60). See Heinrich Marti 'Zeugnisse zur Nachwirkung des Dichters Terenz im Altertum' in *Musa iocosa: Festschrift A. Thierfelder* (Hildesheim 1974) 158-78.

3 'Terenzio, Ildemaro, Petrarca' *IMU* 17 (1974) 1-60. See esp 43, 60.

CHAPTER 1

1 On the Munich MS Clm 14420 and the so-called *commentum Monacense* which it contains see B. Bischoff 'Das Güterverzeichnis des Klosters SS. Faustino e Giovita in Brescia aus dem Jahre 964' *IMU* 15 (1972) 53-61; John N. Grant 'The *commentum Monacense* and the MS tradition of Terence' *Manuscripta* 22 (1978) 83-90; Claudia Villa '"Denique Terenti dultia legimus acta ... ": una "lectura Terenti" a S. Faustino di Brescia nel secolo ix' *IMU* 22 (1979) 1-44. M.D. Reeve (in L.D. Reynolds ed *Texts and transmission: A survey of the Latin classics* [Oxford 1983] 420 n 59) notes that a comprehensive examination of the exegetical material in the medieval MSS is being conducted by C. Villa and G. Alessio.

2 R.H. Webb 'An attempt to restore the γ archetype of Terence manuscripts' *HSCP* 22 (1911) 55-110. His results were modified by L.W. Jones and C.R. Morey *The miniatures of the manuscripts of Terence prior to the*

thirteenth century (Princeton 1931) 2.195-221. The relationship of the major γ MSS will be discussed in ch 5 below. For a crude and in part quite erroneous grouping of MSS in stemmatic form see J. Marouzeau *Térence. Comédies* (Paris 1947) 1.87.

3 Umpfenbach used the codex Basilicanus (Vatican, Arch S Pietro H 19 = B) in his edition, although it is a direct copy of C (Vatican, lat 3868). In the Budé Marouzeau rarely cites p (Paris, BN lat 10304) or v (Valenciennes, bibl publ 448 [420]), MSS which were favoured by Kauer and Lindsay in the OCT, while Prete has used in his edition a fourteenth-century MS in Bologna.

4 The figure of 650 is quoted by Reeve (above n 1) 412 n 1, based on information given him by Claudia Villa.

5 Published in facsimile in S. Prete *Il codice di Terenzio Vaticano Latino 3226* (*Studi e Testi* 262 [Vatican City 1970]). See also *CLA* 1 no. 12; Chatelain 1 pl 6; R. Seider *Paläographie der lateinischen Papyri* (Stuttgart 1978) 2,1 no. 26 (pp 71-5); Ehrle-Liebaert no. 2c. A later date is argued for by Pratesi; see most recently *Palaeographica diplomatica et archivistica. Studi in onore di Giulio Battelli* (Rome 1979) 71-84.

6 See K. Dziatzko 'Zur Frage der Calliopianischen Rezension des Terenz' in *Commentationes Wölfflinianae* (Leipzig 1891) 221-6. The latter form of the subscription is characteristic of the γ MSS, the former of the δ MSS, though each is found by contamination in both groups.

7 R. Kauer *WSt* 22 (1900) 80 n 5 gives a list of interpolations in the Bembinus for *Hauton timorumenos*. For *Hecyra*, to take another play, note the following interpolations: *meum* (50), *se* (62), *diutius* (133), *post* (148), *nam* (161), *de* (172), *me* (215), *in ... meum* (264), *me* (298), *iudico* (343), *nunc* (355), *percepi* (363), *obsecrat* (390), *quantum* (417), *nuntiem* (436), *uxorem* (509), *et ingenio* (532), *se* (550), *esse* (555 and 585), *istinc* (629), *ideo* (712), *didigito* (ie *de digito*) (829); see also below pp 114, 175. A glance at any few pages of the OCT apparatus will show how frequently Σ was in error. I give a sample from the first half of *Eunuchus* (all giving unmetrical lines): 115 *audivisse* for *audisse*; 149 *parare* for *parere*; 157 *est dicta* for *dicta est*; 212 *quin* for *qui*; 257 interpolation of *aucupes*; 269 *eludere* for *ludere*; 287 *cursitet* for *curset*; 289 *videon* for *video*; 299 interpolation of *amare*; 302 *senem* for *senium*; 305 *ego* for *egone*; 349 *equidem ago* for *ago equidem*; 389 interpolation of *immo*; 494 *non* for *haud*; 510 *sese* for *se*; 530 interpolation of *est*; 545 interpolation of *sed*.

8 Scholars will naturally disagree on the contents of a list of common errors, but even the most conservative of critics will have an extensive list. Examples in *Hecyra* can be found at 84 *Philotis ubi* for *ubi Philotis*, 94 *illic* for *illi*, 246 *siet* for *sit*, 283 *cui* for *hui*, 334 *siet* for *sit*, 371 *praecurrit*

for *praecucurrit*, 430 interpolation of *nunc*, 438 *illic* for *illi*, 478 *cui* for *quae*, 537 *ex* for *de*, 560 *sensisti* for *sensti*, 649 *consequitur* for *sequitur*, 729 *possim* for *possiem*, 735 *obstet* for *obsiet*, 746 interpolation of *amicum*, 845 *dixisse* for *dixe*. See Jachmann 74.

9 P. Wessner *Gnomon* 3 (1927) 345 is sceptical about a Probus edition, Pasquali (357) is not. J.E.G. Zetzel *Latin textual criticism in antiquity* (New York 1981) 48 stresses the absence of any substantial evidence for a recension by Probus. On the nature of ancient editions see n 10.

10 One of the important points made by Zetzel in his book (above n 9) is that there is no basis to believe in ancient editions of Latin authors in our sense of the word: 'Such features as the order of plays or poems, arguments, lemmata and the like may without particular harm be ascribed to an "editor," but constitution of a critical text was surely not one of his tasks' (232). The agreement that is found in the Terence tradition with respect to scene division may on this view be accounted for by the activities of an 'editor' but little else. The term 'edition,' as used in this chapter, when it refers to one which existed in antiquity, should be seen in this light.

The unitary nature of a tradition as far as the text itself is concerned may often be explained by the paucity of ancient MSS which survived into Carolingian times. But for those authors where several ancient MSS survive (as is the case for Virgil) or where we must suppose them to have survived into the Carolingian period (as is the case for Terence) it is difficult to dispense with the supposed existence of a popular current text. The question then arises of why a particular MS apparently generated more copies than others: cf E. Courtney 'The formation of the text of Vergil' *BICS* 28 (1981) 26: 'We should accordingly in my view postulate the existence early in the fourth century of a manuscript of Vergil of such fame and splendour that its copies largely drove other texts out of existence.' This is not really a satisfactory answer but I know of no better or more specific one. The same is true for the apparent popularity of the 'Calliopian' text of Terence.

11 See *CLA* 10 no. 1537; Seider (above n 5) no. 41.

12 *Oxyrhynchus Papyri* 24 (1957) 110-23; Seider no. 41.

13 See O. Skutsch *RhM* 100 (1957) 53-68; Reeve (above n 1) 419.

14 See P. Lehmann 'Eine Palimpsesttudie (St. Gallen 912)' *SBAW* 1931.1; A. Gold and A. Allgeier *Der Palimpsestpsalter im Codex Sangallensis 912 ...* (Beuron 1933); *CLA* 7 no. 974.

15 L. Havet *Manuel de critique verbale appliquée aux textes latins* (Paris 1911) §§590ff points to the confusion of I and E in the copying of MSS written in capitals as being 'une des fautes qu'on a le plus souvent besoin

d'invoquer.' Contrast, however, S. Timpanaro *Die Entstehung der Lachmannschen Methode*[2] (Hamburg 1971) 100: 'könnte die Verwechslung von c und g, von e und i auf Verlesen in einer Majuskelvorlage zurückgehen, aber es könnten auch Vulgarismen der Aussprache sein; und deshalb wird man sie besser nicht weiter benutzen.' For the frequent interchangeability of E and I found in MSS see H. Schuchardt *Der Vokalismus des Vulgärlateins* 3 vols (Leipzig 1866-8) 1.244ff; 2.1ff. If a MS shows confusion of other letters which have similar forms in capitals but whose pronunciation is quite distinct, then it is likely that some at least of any examples of the confusion of I and E spring from misreading of the letters.

16 Barwick reads *sed sequentia non intellegunt*, Bentley *sententiam non intelligunt*. Possibly *sed sic 'quantum' intellegitur* = 'but *quantum* is understood in this way' (ie with *nimium*)?

17 Jachmann also concluded that Arruntius Celsus had only one *quantum* in his text. This is uncertain. Those whom he was criticizing could have read *GE. quid? nimium. DE. quantum? quantum dic ...* ; see Wessner (above n 9) 346-7.

18 J.E.G. Zetzel 'On the history of Latin scholia' *HSCP* 79 (1975) 335-54, esp 347ff.

19 F. Brunhölzl 'Zu den sogenannten codices archetypi der römischen Literatur' *Festschrift B. Bischoff zu seinem 65. Geburtstag* (Stuttgart 1971) 16-31; see also his 'Zur Überlieferung des Lucrez' *Hermes* 90 (1962) 97-104.

20 Cf the remarks of Virginia Brown 'The "insular intermediary" in the tradition of Lucretius' *HSCP* 72 (1968) 301-8, esp 305-6.

21 So in *Eun* cf *difficili* for *difficile* (209), *dicit* for *dicet* (441), *demet* for *demit* (627), *mirumne* for *mirumni* (711), *estimes* for *existimes* (758), *pellitur* for *pelletur* (1041); in *Haut* cf *vidisesse* for *vidi esse* (402), *ostenderes* for *ostenderis* (438), *nequed* for *nequid* (690), *recipies* for *receptes* (968); in *Ad* cf *indulgis* for *indulges* (63), *operire* for *operiere* (182), *inciperunt* for *inceperunt* (227), *mulieris* for *mulieres* (229), *coeperit* for *coeperet* (397), *referi* for *referire* (567), *nam illi* for *nam et illi* (602), *fortenprudens* for *forte inprudens* (711). It is possible that *some* of these errors may have been prompted by the similarity in pronunciation of E and I.

22 See *TLL* 5.52,37ff.

23 B for D and D for B occur in isolated spots in individual Carolingian or post-Carolingian MSS of Terence: *ad studio* for *ab studio* at *Ph* 2 in C; *adducit* for *abducit* at *Eun* 581 in E; *abduxti* for *adduxti* at *Eun* 949 in D. It is wrong, therefore, to think of such errors in MSS of the Carolingian period or later as being 'fossilized' corruptions which go back to

antiquity as is stated for errors in the 'second Medicean' MS of Tacitus by M. Zelzer 'Zur Frage der Vorlage des Tacitus-Codex Mediceus 68,2' *WSt* 86 (1973) 187 n 15.

24 J.D. Craig *Ancient editions of Terence* (London 1929) and in a series of articles: *CQ* 24 (1930) 65-73, 183-7; *CQ* 25 (1931) 151-5.

25 For criticism see L.W. Jones 'Ancient texts of Terence' *CP* 25 (1930) 318-27; cf J.E.G. Zetzel *Hermes* 102 (1974) 374 n 9.

26 Pasquali 363: 'A ogni modo l'originale delle illustrazioni è divenuto ora almeno un *terminus ante quem* per la datazione di γ.' Marti's remark (*Lustrum* 6 [1961] 120) – 'Den Bildarchetyp setzt man heute an den Anfang des 5.Jh.s, was für Σ einen *terminus ante* bedeutet' – also implies that the date of the original miniatures gives a date for an illustrated γ MS.

CHAPTER 2

1 See above pp 15ff.

2 Examples in *Eunuchus* include unmetrical lines caused by interpolation; so at 5 *sciat praesumat*, 257 *aucupes*, 289 *videon* for *video*, 299 *amare*, 389 *immo*, 426 *et*, 463 *pol*, 494 *non* for *haud*, 530 *est*, 545 *sed*, 572 *deducier* for *ducier*, 615 *bene*, 632 *reputo* for *puto*, 642 *est*, 684 *eo*, 692 *venistin* for *venisti*, 738 *video*, 748 *est*, 901 *pol*, 957 *facturum*, 1064 *nihil est*. The metre of other lines is disrupted by the use of the wrong form: so 115 *audivisse* for *audisse*, 149 *parare* for *parere*, 212 *quin* for *qui*, 287 *cursitet* for *curset*, 302 *senem* for *senium*, 328 *nostin* for *novistin*, 510 *sese* for *se*, 592 *hae* for *haec*, 743 *exspecto* for *exspectabam*. This is not a complete list and it should be said that in the number of unmetrical lines in the Calliopian archetype the *Eunuchus* is not untypical. In *Andria*, for example, where we do not have the evidence of the Bembinus for most of the play, I count approximately 30 unmetrical lines for Σ.

The examples given above include some where p (Paris, BN lat 10304) is not in error with the other Calliopians. In some instances p may have retained what was in Σ, but these do not significantly alter the situation.

3 See Wessner *Gnomon* 3 (1972) 344; Reeve (above ch 1 n 1) 413; Rufinus *GL* 6.565,1 Keil; Priscian *GL* 3.418,8; 3.422,28; 3.426,11.

4 See Grant *TAPA* 105 (1975) 123-53, esp 127-8.

5 The illustrated Leyden MS, Voss Q 38 (N), has a δ text for most of *Andria*, *Eunuchus*, and *Hauton timorumenos*, but the illustrations are the artist's own creation and are independent of the miniatures in the other MSS; see Jones and Morey 2.133, 147.

6 See Grant *TAPA* 105 (1975) 141ff.

7 See ch 1 n 24.

8 Described in detail by Jones and Morey.

9 F. Leo 'Die Überlieferungsgeschichte der terenzischen Komödien und der Commentar des Donatus' *RhM* 38 (1883) 316-47, esp 335ff; cf also *GGA* 1903, 996.

10 C. Robert *Die Maske der neueren attischen Komödie* (Halle 1911) 87ff, 108. Kurt Weitzmann *Ancient book illumination* (Cambridge, Mass 1959) 85 also thought that MSS of Terence and of other authors were furnished with illustrations at a fairly early date.

11 K. Engelhardt *Die Illustration der Terenzhandschriften* (Diss Jena 1905). He was followed by T. Birt *Die Buchrolle in der Kunst* (Leipzig 1907) 109.

12 R. Kauer *JAW* 143 (1909) 201.

13 K.E. Weston 'The illustrated Terence manuscripts' *HSCP* 14 (1903) 37-54.

14 E. Bethe *Buch und Bild im Altertum* (Leipzig 1945) 61; see also the *praefatio* of the reproduction of the Terence Ambrosianus (H 75 inf) p 64.

15 G. Rodenwaldt '*Cortinae*. Ein Beitrag zur Datierung der antiken Vorlage der mitteralterlichen Terenzillustrationen' *NGG, Philologisch-historische Klasse*, 1925.33-49.

16 A.W. Byvanck 'Antike Malerei, II: Das Vorbild der Terenzillustrationen' *Mnemosyne* 7 (1939) 115-35.

17 2.45, 117, 200.

18 See Jachmann 18-19 and below pp 25-6. On the miniature at *Eun* 923 see below in the appendix to this chapter.

19 Jachmann 27ff. On this point he argued against the view of Kauer (above n 12) 210, who did not think that the illustrations were originally connected with the scene headings. He believed that they were first drawn beside the section of the text which they depicted and were later moved to the beginning of the scenes (see next note).

20 In the non-illustrated MSS exceptions to the order of names being given in the order of speaking most commonly occur when two *senes, adulescentes, servi,* etc appear in the same scene. In those instances where the two characters do not speak immediately one after the other, the name of the second is nevertheless placed immediately after that of the first; so in the Bembinus at *Eun* 643 (IV.3; the *ancillae* Pythias and Dorias, first and third speakers respectively); 1031 (V.8; the *adulescentes* Chaerea and Phaedria, first and fifth – there is no scene division in the Bembinus or in D at 1049); *Haut* 723 (IV.4; the *servi* Syrus and Dromo, third and fifth speakers); *Ph* 713 (IV.5; the *senes* Demipho and Chremes, first and third); 894 (V.8; the same two characters, again speaking first

and third); *Ad* 265 (II.4; the *adulescentes* Aeschinus and Ctesipho, first and third speakers); 447 (III.4; the *senes* Hegio and Demea, first and third speakers). The only exception to this in the Bembinus appears to be at *Ph* 485 (III.2), where the *adulescentes* Phaedria and Antipho are named first and third, the order of speaking, although in this instance the Victorianus (D) adheres to the principle of grouping together the same types. Such grouping should therefore be regarded as the norm.

The coincidence between the order of figures in the miniatures and the order of names in the scene headings is too great to accept Kauer's hypothesis (see previous note) that the miniatures were originally independent of the scene headings. There are 141 scene-miniatures. Of these, however, 13 contain only one figure and have to be excluded from any reckoning (*Eun* IV.1, IV.2; *Haut* II.1, IV.2; *Ad* I.1, III.3, IV.4, IV.6; *Hec* II.3, III.3; *Ph* I.1, IV.2, V.4). Of the remaining 128 I count only 27 examples where the order of figures deviates from the normal order and in almost every case the deviation can be explained by the stage action or by the position of the figures in the preceding miniature. Examples of the latter occur at *An* 432 (II.6), 481 (III.2), 872 (V.3, though the preceding miniature has been lost), *Eun* 549 (III.5), and *Haut* 242 (II.3). The miniature at *An* 459 (III.1) provides a good example of the artist's having considered the stage action. To reflect this Mysis and Lesbia have to be placed together, although they speak first and fourth respectively. For some less clear reason Davos and Simo are also drawn in the reverse order of speaking. Simo speaks before Davos, but is on the extreme right of the miniature, further away from the women than Davos. The reason is perhaps that the artist thought Simo had difficulty in hearing the words of the women; cf his words *quid dicit?* at 459, words which are in fact exclamatory rather than interrogative. The miniature, however, seems to represent the stage action at 467ff, when the two women are just about to leave the stage and the artist may have drawn Davos first because he speaks first after the women exit; see also J.C. Watson, 'The relation of the scene-headings to the miniatures in manuscripts of Terence' *HSCP* 14 (1903) 76. Other examples of where the stage action has influenced the artist to depart from the normal order of speakers in the headings are *An* 412 (II.5), 904 (V.4); *Eun* 454 (III.2), 668 (IV.4), 771 (IV.7), 1049 (V.9; cf 1068); *Haut* 242 (II.3, where the order of the figures agrees with the order of the names in the Bembinus), 614 (IV.1), 723 (IV.4), 829 (IV.7); *Ad* 155 (II.1), 265 (II.4, agreeing with the Bembinus), 447 (III.4, agreeing with D), 540 (IV.2), 899 (V.7); *Ph* 348 (II.3; the preceding miniature may have been influential here), 441 (II.4), 606 (IV.3), 713 (IV.5), 894 (V.8).

The order in two miniatures, *Eun* 643 (IV.3) and *Ad* 958 (V.9), is difficult to explain. At *Ph* 231 (II.1) the order of figures is irregular but agrees with the order of names in the Bembinus and the Victorianus. At *Haut* 1045 (V.5) and *Ad* 776 (V.2) the order of figures is normal against an abnormal order in A and D. For discussion of the order of figures in the miniatures see Watson 55-172. While there is much of value in Watson's article the conclusion that the scene headings originated from the miniatures is unacceptable.

21 At *Eun* 629 the name of Dorias is missing from the heading in the non-illustrated MSS. At *Ad* 254, however, the name of Sannio appears in the heading in the Bembinus, as do the names of Demipho and Chremes at *Ph* 591, but all three names are missing in the δ branch of the Calliopians.

22 Quintilian's words at 11.3.178 suggest that he was familiar with productions of *comoediae palliatae*: *maximos actores comoediarum, Demetrium et Stratoclea, placere diversis virtutibus vidimus. sed illud minus mirum quod alter deos et iuvenes et bonos patres senesque et matronas et graves anus optime, alter acres senes, callidos servos, parasitos, lenones et omnia agitatiora melius.* Other phrases in the sections that follow (182, where *Eun* 46-8 are quoted, and 184) also appear to refer to the contemporary stage. A comment of Donatus at *An* 716 points to practices in the theatre of his time: *et vide non minimas partes in hac comoedia Mysidi attribui, hoc est personae femineae, sive haec personatis viris agitur, ut apud veteres, sive per mulierem, ut nunc videmus.*

The Terentian miniatures may have been inspired (directly or indirectly) by productions of New Comedy which continued to be put on in Greece and in the eastern Mediterranean well into the third century AD at least. See S. Charitonidis, L. Kahil, and R. Ginouvès *Les mosaïques de la maison du Ménandre à Mytilène* (Bern 1970 [*Antike Kunst*, Beiheft VI]) 105, and references there. See also A. Pickard-Cambridge *The dramatic festivals of Athens*[2] (Oxford 1968) 297ff. For theatre building in the Empire see M. Bieber *The history of the Greek and Roman theater*[2] (Princeton 1961) ch 14.

23 See above p 17 and ch 1 n 26.

24 The next few pages summarize what has been discussed in 'Γ and the miniatures of Terence' *CQ* 23 (1973) 88-103.

25 Unlike the major illustrated MSS the Bembinus and the δ MSS have no scene division at 1049, when Phaedria enters. The scene heading in these MSS serves therefore for 1031-94, but Thraso is still named before Gnatho.

26 In his edition (Saumur 1678) Faber assigns these words to Clitipho.

27 Watson (above n 20) 66 n 2 thinks that the artist had assigned 400b-1 to Clitipho.

28 W.M. Lindsay *CQ* 21 (1927) 190 n 1 states that Kauer had informed him that the variant *CLIT* for *CLIN* in the Valenciennes MS was by a Renaissance hand. On microfilm, however, it seems clear that the nota *CLIT* was written by the first hand of v. The final T of *CLIT* has been altered to N, written in a style very similar to how N is written by v^1.

29 For 'double' representations see the miniatures at *An* 481 (III.2), 684 (IV.2), 740 (IV.4); *Haut* 723 (IV.4), 874 (V.1 in P and F); *Eun* 454 (III.2); *Hec* 415 (III.4), 841 (V.4); *Ad* 776 (V.2).

30 C. Robert *Archaeologische Hermeneutik* (Berlin 1919) 189 also thinks that the miniature at *Haut* 381 is conflated but gives no details of how it came to occupy its present position.

31 It must be admitted that this would be an unusual position for a new 'scene' to be indicated. The beginnings of scenes usually coincide with the first words of an entering character or with an exit or with a change of metre. See *CQ* 23 (1973) 97-8 and the appendix to this chapter.

32 For the argument see *CQ* 23 (1973) 99ff.

33 See *CQ* 23 (1973) 91-3 for a longer discussion of this illustration.

34 In his recent edition of *Adelphoe* R.H. Martin cites Plaut *Merc* 557 for a similar usage of *rediero*. For the glossing of *rediero* cf *Ph* 243 where the δ MSS offer *veniens* or *reveniens* for *rediens*.

35 Contrast, for example, the comparatively greater divergence between the text of the *psalterium Gallicum* and that of the *Hebraicum*. In a persuasive article, 'The textual basis of the Utrecht Psalter illustrations' *AB* 25 (1943) 50-8, Dora Panofsky demonstrates that the illustrations in the Utrecht Psalter were created to accompany the text of at least these two versions, written side by side. The original artist sometimes chose the Gallican text, sometimes the Hebraic, depending on the scope each text provided for a concrete visual image. So 'when illustrating Psalm CXXXVI (137), v. 2, the artist had a choice between adorning his willow trees with harps (*citharae*) or pipe-organs (*organa*); and he very reasonably decided for the former alternative as suggested by the Hebraicum (*super salices in medio eius suspendimus citharas nostras*)' (53). What is interesting for our enquiry is that the illustrations now accompany only the Gallican version and there are clear discrepancies between the text and the illustrations (as in the example just cited). The text refers to pipe-organs but harps are depicted.

36 Menedemus must leave the stage at the end of 948 or 949. He should

not be given the words *quid eum?*, as in the OCT (see below pp 92-3). He must be given enough time to leave the stage and inform Clitipho of the situation before he returns with the young man at 954.

37 So also Watson (above n 20) 141: 'There can be little doubt that the tradition is correctly preserved in C.' Cf also what he says on p 81 of his article.

38 R.H. Webb 'An attempt to restore the γ archetype of Terence's manuscripts' *HSCP* 22 (1911) 55-110.

39 Included in the stemma are two important γ MSS, Y (Paris, BN lat 7900) and O (Oxford, Bodl Auct F 2 13). See ch 5.

40 See ch 5. Jachmann (136 n 82) expresses scepticism about the possibility of identifying separate classes among the γ MSS because of contamination, but he is excessively pessimistic.

41 R. Kauer (above n 12) 198.

42 For example the miniature that stands before *Haut* 512 (III.2) appears at the top of a page. On the preceding page, however, the last five ruled lines have been left blank after the final verse of the preceding scene.

43 So, for example, Engelhardt (above n 11) 71.

44 Above n 20 (near end).

45 See Watson (above n 20) 137: 'Where the only change consists in the exit of part of the characters, scene-division is not the rule, but the exception. In only seven of the 42 places of this nature are the MSS a unit in instituting new scenes.'

46 If the figures of Clitipho and Syrus in PF at *Haut* 874 were originally drawn to appear at 980, it would be necessary to postulate Ψ′ to allow for the conflation of miniatures before the whole miniature cycle was added to a γ MS.

47 In the Bembinus and in the δ MSS there is no new scene marked at *Eun* 943, but the action takes a new turn (and the metre changes) as Pythias begins her deceit. Wessner notes in his edition of Donatus (1.xlix) that a new scene is marked in the Donatus MSS at this point too. There is nothing in the scholia at this point, however, to confirm that Donatus knew of scene division at 943. The Donatus MSS may simply be reflecting the scene division in the γ MSS.

48 One may compare the drawing of Syrus at *Ad* V.7 (Jones and Morey no. 568), who exits at 916, and the figure of Parmeno, as drawn at *Eun* V.6 (Jones and Morey no. 298). Although the latter remains on stage during the next short scene when only Gnatho and Thraso speak, the artist clearly thought that he exited and then re-entered in V.8. (His

name does not appear in the scene headings in the Bembinus and D at v.7.)

49 Eugraphius' note suggests, though it does not prove, that he thought Pythias entered at 943: *dum egreditur Pythias, fingit adulescentem Chaeream intus captum et pro moecho deprehensum poenam ex consuetudine passum quo facilius Parmeno terreatur.*

50 The clear indication of an exit in the text at 921-2 makes it more likely that the original artist realized that Pythias left the stage at 922 and re-entered at 941. Although the artist did make some mistakes (as at *Ad* 364, and in the omission of some characters who were on stage but silent during a scene), he did at times pay close attention to the stage action beyond the individual scene. Thus he portrayed Laches in the miniature of *Hec* IV.2 (577) overhearing the conversation of Sostrata and Pamphilus because of Laches' opening words of the *next* scene (*quem cum istoc sermonem habueris procul hinc stans accepi, uxor*, 607), although there is no indication in the text of IV.2 itself of Laches' presence.

51 See above n 45.

52 If there were scene divisions at 918 and 923 in Ψ′, the failure of a scribe to leave space at the former position would not have caused problems, since the illustration at 918 in Ψ′, containing only Pythias, could simply have been omitted.

53 See Kurt Weitzmann *Late antique and early Christian book illumination* (London 1977) plate 7. Cf also plate 10 (no. XXVII from the Ilias Ambrosiana), plate 24 (no. 13 from the Vienna Genesis), plate 25 (no. 30 from the Vienna Genesis).

54 Cf Weitzmann (above n 53) 51 and also his *Illustrations in roll and codex. A study of the origin and method of text illustration*[2] (Princeton 1970) 85ff.

55 See F. Wieseler, *Theatergebaüde und Denkmäler des Bühnenwesens bei den Griechen und Römern* (Göttingen 1851) 73; Watson (above n 20) 141; Kauer (above n 12) 196.

CHAPTER 3

1 F. Umpfenbach 'Die Scholien des Codex Bembinus zum Terentius' *Hermes* 2 (1867) 337.

2 P. Wessner *Donatus: Commentum Terenti* (Leipzig 1902) 1.xlv-vi. R. Sabbadini 'Il commento di Donato a Terenzio' *SIFC* 2 (1894) 1-134 gives a survey of earlier views on the origin of the commentary in the first section of his work (4ff). His own view (14) is that the surviving commentary is a conflation of a continuous Donatus commentary ('un

solo commento originario'), equipped, however, with marginal notes, and of scholia which had been added to the margins of a Terence MS. Some of the latter had themselves been culled from Donatus, others had been added by unknown scholiasts.

3 H. Usener *RhM* 23 (1868) 496.

4 Sabbadini (above n 2) 22 n 1.

5 E. Löfstedt 'Die Bembinusscholien und Donatus' *Eranos* 12 (1913) 43-63.

6 The citations are taken from J.F. Mountford *The scholia Bembina in Terentium* (London 1934).

7 See Mountford 48.

8 J.E.G. Zetzel 'On the history of Latin scholia' *HSCP* 70 (1975) 335-54. That the Bembinus scholiast did not draw the scholia directly from a Donatus commentary is shown by the presence at *Ph* 1-59 of scholia which are misplaced or conflated or whose meaning is distorted. A significant example is the scholion which appears in the right margin beside verse 56, the first verse on fol 55ʳ: *ostenditur gratiarum actione ve⟨re necessariam fui⟩sse pecuniam*. This scholion, however, refers to line 54 (*amo te et non neglexisse habeo gratiam*) and in the surviving commentary the corresponding scholion is indeed attached to that verse. Originally, therefore, the scholion must have been added to a Terence MS to explain verse 54. Because of the later misplacement we may assume that it was written beside verse 56 with a reference sign to 54. (There may have been other scholia at this point which prevented its appearing at the correct verse.) In this earlier MS lines 54-6 must have been on the same leaf. In a copy of this MS lines 54 and 56 appeared on different pages. The scribe responsible for copying out the group of scholia from the exemplar wrote out this scholion as if it explained verse 56.

9 Sabbadini (above n 2) 22 n 1 and Leo (*RhM* 38 [1883] 328) drew the correct inference that the commentary known to Priscian was fuller than the extant one. Wessner (1.xlv) was wrong to deny this; cf also Zetzel (above n 8) 341.

10 *JAW* 188 (1921) 169.

11 *PhilWoch* 15 (1927) 433-8.

12 See Sabbadini (above n 2) 176; C.H. Beeson 'The text tradition of Donatus' commentary on Terence' *CP* 17 (1922) 284.

13 W.M. Lindsay 'The Donatus-extracts in the codex Victorianus (D) of Terence' *CQ* 21 (1927) 188-94.

14 Jachmann 89 n 20.

15 The agreement between D and the extant Donatus is all the more striking because of the corruption in the text of the commentary.

Wessner, following Bentley and Sabbadini, prints *EXISTIMAVIT pro existimarit*.

16 For a similar corruption cf *Eun* 364 where D offers *deducant* (*post rasuram*) for *deducam* or *ducam* of the other MSS (L has *deducantur*).

17 At *An* 745 in D there is a scholion *aliter litigant secundum Donatum* on *litigat* and over a of *litigat* the letter n has been added. In the Riccardianus (E) the gloss *vel exorem* appears above *exorem* at *Eun* 185. Thus it is by no means improbable that the reading *praesenserant* appeared in the exemplar of D, accompanied by a scholion which indicated the same form as a variant. Text and scholia were often copied separately.

18 Wessner (1.xxxviii-ix) suggests that the Donatus extracts in the Victorianus were added to it from a γ MS. I have argued that they must have been present in the exemplar of D and possibly even in D's 'grandfather.' The main support for Wessner's belief came from the Donatus extract on *occepi* at *An* 504: *vel 'occoepi' secundum Donatum*. The note in the commentary itself reads *'occepit' melius quam 'incepi,'* though the correct reading is perhaps *'occepi' melius quam 'coepi'* (the reading of the oldest Donatus MS is ... *qua incoepi*). Wessner thinks it probable that the point of the note was that the compound was preferred by Donatus over the form *coepi*. Since C and P, the two leading MSS of the γ branch of the tradition, alone of the Calliopians read *coepi*, he very reasonably suggests that the note must have first appeared in a MS which was related to them and which had the same reading.

It is barely possible that the Donatus extract related to the spelling of the compound verb, ie *occoepi* rather than *occepi*. In the surviving Donatus MSS, however, the reading is *occepi* and not *occoepi*.

19 Most of these appear in Wessner 1.viii, where the Greek in the scholion at *An* 149 is as given above. Cf, however, the critical apparatus *ad loc*.

20 See E.A. Lowe and E.K. Rand *A sixth-century fragment of the Letters of Pliny the Younger* (Washington 1922) 17 for a list of some eighth-century uncial MSS.

21 See L.D. Reynolds and N.G. Wilson *Scribes and Scholars*[2] (Oxford 1974) 81-2. Beeson also argues that two copies in insular script were made from the archetype.

22 F. Leo (above n 9) 326ff; Sabbadini *SIFC* 3 (1895) 340ff.

23 For discussion of the variants attested in Donatus see J. Marouzeau 'Les manuscrits térentiens de la bibliothèque de Donat' *Mélanges dediés à la mémoire de Félix Grat* (Paris 1949) 2.317-21.

24 F. Arens *De Terentianarum fabularum memoria in Aeli Donati quod fertur commento servata* (Westfalia 1910) 69.

25 See Arens (above n 24) 6ff for many examples of where the text in the

lemmata differs from that of our MSS. Usually the readings are inferior to those which have been transmitted in the MSS but there are exceptions: *An* 661 *me ducturum* (with Π^bp) against *me ducturum esse; Ph* 505 *usus venit* against *tibi usus venit* of all the MSS; *Eun* 98 *exclusti* (with p^1) against *exclusit; An* 358 *vidisse* against *vidisse se.*

26 Wessner brackets *nihil est* in his edition.

27 J.E.G. Zetzel '*Andria* 403 (II.3, 29)' *Hermes* 102 (1974) 372-6 suggests that 'the object of Servius' scorn … was presumably Donatus himself' (375).

28 Donatus certainly made use of earlier commentaries. He names Nigidius at *Ph* 190 and 233 and Asper at *Ad* 323 and 559 and frequently refers to views held and readings preferred by others: eg *Ph* 249 (on the case of *habendae compedes* after *molendum in pistrino, vapulandum*) *vitiosam locutionem servili personae dedit Terentius; nam integrum esset, si diceret 'habendas compedes.' unde quidam non 'esse' sed 'usque' legunt*; cf the scholia on *Ph* 485; *An* 44; *Ad* 532, 618.

When variants are cited, the tense usually employed is the present, as in the examples which have been given in the text (except for the scholia on *An* 1). In two other cases the perfect is used: *An* 236 *in aliis 'factu aut inceptu' fuit; Ph* 190 *'protinam' fuit* (⟨*in aliis*⟩ *'protinam' fuit* Koenighoff) *et sic Nigidius legit*. Possibily Donatus is here reproducing information which he found in earlier commentaries and is not giving evidence of the readings in contemporary MSS.

Two scholia refer to *veteres codices*: *Hec* 665 *in veteribus* (ventis *B* veris *V*, *om C*) *codicibus sic est 'remissan … reductan domum,' ut sit remissane … reductane* (so printed by Wessner: see the apparatus); *Eun* 307 *'qui vir sies' in veteribus invenitur*. At *Eun* 307 the Terence MSS offer *qui vir sies* and the point of the scholion is puzzling if it goes back to Donatus. At *Hec* 665 most of the Terence MSS offer *an reductan* for *reductan*. Should the last part of the Donatus scholion read *ut sit 'remissane … an reducta'*? Both of these examples may be much later than Donatus (in the early Carolingian period?).

Marouzeau (above n 23) 320 adduces the lemma and scholion at *An* 334 (*HABEO inveni. legitur et 'abeo,' ut merito illi dicatur 'resiste'*) as evidence for Donatus himself having examined several MSS. It would be extremely helpful to my argument if he were right. Unfortunately, he cannot be. *Inveni* must be an explanatory gloss on *habeo* (= *consilium inveni*). The two parts of the Donatus scholion may have been unconnected originally.

29 See above pp 4ff and ch 5. The possibility of a non-Calliopian MS being used in the Carolingian period is examined in ch 4.

30 The explanations of the meaning of this verse in the Donatus commen-

tary are wrong, being based on a misunderstanding of the sense of *satis.*

31 See P.W. Harsh *Iambic words and regard for accent in Plautus* (Stanford 1949) 70ff, 94ff for successions of iambic words in trochaic septenarii and in senarii. Harsh (13) points to *Men* 747 and 750 as examples of verses in which there is a succession of iambic words to create a special effect.

32 Kauer's suggestion, *neque id me,* noted in the apparatus of the OCT, would be my second choice. It has the attractiveness of going part way to explaining the variants in the tradition.

33 See O. Jahn *Berichte der Königlich Sächsischen Gesellschaft der Wissenschaften, Philologisch-historische Klasse,* 3 (1851) 364ff; Reynolds and Wilson (above n 21) 35-7.

34 Leo (above n 9) 323ff argues that Donatus based his commentary on a Calliopian MS and one which belonged to the δ class. This would place Σ considerably earlier than has been suggested here. The grounds for Leo's argument are these: first, the information given by Donatus in the *praefationes* of his plays agrees with that given in the *didascaliae* attached to the Calliopians; secondly, Donatus states that the *Eunuchus* was the third of Terence's plays to be produced (*Eun praef* 10) and reports that according to some the *Adelphoe* was the second play to be produced. Only in the δ branch do the *Adelphoe* and *Eunuchus* appear in second and third position respectively. Other explanations for the agreement between Donatus and the Calliopian *didascaliae* are possible, however, and the agreement between the alphabetic order of plays in the δ class and Donatus may be coincidental. Moreover, Donatus assigns *Hecyra* to fifth place, although this play appears last in the major δ MSS.

If Leo's thesis were right, one would expect to find errors in the δ MSS attested in the Donatus scholia. Some indeed can be found, as can errors of the γ MSS, although these are fewer in number. A list of the common errors is given below. Some of the agreements may have been prompted by the influence of the lemmata (eg *An* 88, 613) and one cannot be certain that all the scholia are authentic (eg *An* 950). The number is insufficient to support Leo's view.

Errors of the δ group attested in the scholia of Donatus are: *An* 88 *symbolum; An* 532 *obviam Chremen; An* 613 *pollicitus sum; An* 938 *mirando tanto hoc tam repentino bono; An* 950 *Pamphili; Eun* 445 *par pari referto* (Donatus at *Eun* 449); *Eun* 881 *tam; Eun* 1088 (?) *accede ubi vis; Hec* 590 *non; Ad* 402 *quem* (Donatus at *Ad* 560, but *qui,* correctly, at *Ad* 591); *Ad* 467 *etiam; Ad* 769 *fundes.*

Errors of the γ group attested in the scholia of Donatus are: *Eun* 803 *caput tuum* (correctly?); *Eun* 1093 *eloquentiam; Hec* 787 *vis; Ad* 507 *hoc.*

CHAPTER 4

1 K. Dziatzko (ed) *P. Terenti Afri comoediae* (Leipzig 1884).

2 Kauer and Lindsay, followed by Marouzeau, print *sum mactatum*, the former suggesting that the line might be a quotation from tragedy.

3 F. Ritschl 'De emendatione fabularum terentianarum' *Opuscula philologica* (Leipzig 1877) 3.293.

4 G. Prinzhorn *De libris Terentianis quae ad recensionem Calliopianam redeunt* (Diss Göttingen 1885). See Spengel *JAW* 68 (1891) 171-2.

5 F. Leo *RhM* 38 (1883) 325; Jachmann 126ff.

6 Jachmann 127.

7 J.D. Craig *Ancient editions of Terence* (Oxford 1929) 126, 127.

8 I confess my own adherence to this view: see *CQ* 23 (1973) 93. It should be pointed out, however, that unmetrical errors common to DGL outnumber such errors shared by C and P in the proportion 4:3. When unmetrical errors shared by DGLp are computed, the number is about the same as in C and P.

9 L.D. Reynolds 'Two notes on the manuscripts of Seneca's Letters' *CR* 7 (1957) 5-12, esp 7; M.D. Reeve (above ch 1 n 1) 415 n 25.

10 A. Fritsch *Philologus* 32 (1873) 446-60; O. Brugman *Neue Jahrbuch für Philologie und Paedagogie* 113 (1876) 420.

11 *CQ* 21 (1927) 190-1.

12 Similarly J. Andrieu *Mémorial des études latines ... offert ... à ... J. Marouzeau* (Paris 1943) 467.

13 T.F. Carney (ed) *P. Terenti Afri Hecyra* (1963) 1-2.

14 The possibility that a parent or grandparent of D was contaminated by a γ MS is indicated if one accepts Wessner's argument that the Donatus extracts in D were ultimately drawn from a γ MS (see above p 227 n 18).

15 In L the text of the *Hecyra* and almost all of the *Hauton timorumenos* has been drawn from a γ MS.

16 For the *Hecyra* L has a γ text and G lacks 1-194 and 310-880. I have considered only the section of the play common to D and G. This accounts for the paucity of γp agreements in this play.

17 I count the following γp readings against the δ MSS to be correct:
An: 356 *escendo*; 364 *nullam in aedibus*; 392 *nec tu*; 457 *est rei*; 516 *ais*; 551 *ni*; 562 *dein*; 577 *suadet*; 602 *erilem filium*; 621 *an*; 664 *satis scio fuisse iratos*; 688 *ait te*; 709 *incipit mi initium*; 728 *ad erum*; 742 *tum posuisti*; 743 omission of *hem*; 774 *magis dabit*; 882 omission of *hem*; 909 *qua re*; 935 absence of *tum*
Eun: 144 *ego eam*; 239 *contempsi prae me*; 277 *hos menses*; 300 *illum alterum*; 355 *dono contra*; 371 *deducam*; 384 *omnibus cruciant modis*; 402 *gestare*; 434

istac; 450 *iratus tu;* 454 *vocem visa sum;* 464 *adsunt tibi;* 469-70 *foras exire;* 485 *tibi;* 503 *adducito;* 515 *omnia ipsa* 521 *inde;* 526 *nata;* 532 *mihi insidias;* 563 *nempe opinor;* 599 *simul omnes;* 676 *est homo;* 738 *eccam;* 740 *atqui;* 740 *effodientur;* 748 *teque illaque;* 749 *tibi dono;* 756 *apage sis;* 777 *portes;* 786 *dari;* 811 *iam haec tibi;* 854 no displacement as in D[1]L[1]; 865 *hac contumelia;* 881 *ita;* 898 *posthac;* 938 *cibi;* 954 *factum;* 958 *velim;* 966 *esse ortum;* 999 *(e)venturum mali;* 1004 *ridiculo;* 1033 *subito;* 1073 *Phaedria;* 1085 *recipimus*

Haut: 29 *faciunt;* 79 *rectum est;* 301 *qui;* 572 *at;* 656 *animum;* 672 *me;* 676 *quid;* 723 *induxerunt;* 785 *scite poterat;* 948 *paret;* 982 *me;* 985 *id*

Ph: 32 *motus loco est;* 114 *eum;* 168 *ingenuam liberalem;* 262 *factum me esse;* 311 *at ego;* 351 *pro deum immortalium;* 373 *DE. Geta;* 379 *mihi ut;* 413 *item;* 566 *facies;* 642 *a primo;* 658 *istanc;* 698 *tu id quod;* 794 *ne;* 794 *adulescens mulier;* 820 *utut;* 840 *concrepuit;* 887 *siet;* 940 *quid id;* 1000 *hoc;* 1010 *fiunt;* 1013 *vilitas;* 1043 *iam*

Hec: 299 *in culpa*

Ad: 84 *quid fecit;* 184 *nunciam;* 187 *vah;* 189 *est orta;* 272 *scisse;* 281 *hercle te;* 286 *ego iam;* 301 absence of *se;* 325 *eloquere obsecro;* 329 *hoc;* 348 *mihi sum;* 371 *sane est;* 390 *haecine fieri;* 395 *ille somnium;* 492 *animus voster;* 497 *nitar;* 550 *huc prorsus;* 556 *quid ais;* 571 *quidem iam;* 583 *lacum;* 586 *bene sane;* 596 *accusant;* 597 *te;* 635 *dixi;* 636 *acta haec;* 656 *quid ipsae quid aiunt;* 765 *omnium rerum;* 769 *hic sapientia;* 777 *heus;* 809 *duo(s) olim;* 858 *putaris;* 892 *hodie iudicavi;* 950 *si;* 960 *aequom liberum;* 961 *bonus.*

18 At *An* 79 (*accepit condicionem, dehinc quaestum occipit*), which would be a parallel if *dehinc* were correct (it is printed by Kauer-Lindsay), the MSS are divided between *dein* (C) and *dehinc* (DGLEP). I prefer the reading of C.

19 H.C. Gotoff *The transmission of the text of Lucan in the ninth century* (Cambridge 1971).

20 See Gotoff 143ff.

21 J. Willis *Latin textual criticism* (Urbana 1972) 21-2.

22 To this list one might add a few more examples in which p agrees with E or with E and A: *An* 854 *audies; Eun* 275 *dicis; Eun* 1035 *scis me; Haut* 45 *si; Haut* 81 *est usus homini; Haut* 83 *ei mihi; Ph* 108 *in* omitted in the other MSS).

23 *WSt* 22 (1900) 81.

24 See H. Thesleff *Yes and no in Plautus and Terence* (Helsinki 1960) 26.

25 So also C and P in the γ group are shown to be less closely related than was once thought when other MSS are investigated. See the next chapter.

26 Bernhard Bischoff has dated P[c] to the ninth or tenth century and thinks

it was written in Milan (reported by Gotoff, above n 19, 19). This provenance fits nicely with the close relationship between P^c^ and Munich, Clm 14420 (the *commentum Monacense* of Terence), which was written at Brescia. See B. Bischoff 'Das Güterverzeichnis des Klosters SS. Faustino e Giovita in Brescia aus dem Jahre 964' *IMU* 15 (1972) 53-61; J.N. Grant 'The *commentum Monacense* and the MS tradition of Terence' *Manuscripta* 22 (1978) 83-90; C. Villa '"Denique Terenti dultia legimus acta ....": una "lectura Terenti" a S. Faustino di Brescia nel secolo ix' *IMU* 22 (1979) 1-44.

For V^b see H.J. Hermann *Beschreibendes Verzeichnis der illum. Handschriften in Österreich* (Leipzig 1926) 8,2 1-2, who points out similarities between V^b and MSS of Reichenau and St Gall in illumination.

N was once in Angers but was probably not executed there: see J. Vezin *Les scriptoria d'Angers au XIe siècle* (Paris 1974) 31, 43 n 24. Jones and Morey assign it to the Loire valley (2.149).

27 *TAPA* 105 (1975) 135-6.

28 *TAPA* 105 (1975) 133.

29 As happens in Lyon, Bibl mun 788, s ix (λ).

30 In this section of the text all the other δ MSS are written in prose with no regular indication of the verse division by capitals. One must conclude that the verse division in Δ was erroneous in this section of the text because of the errors of NLP^b.

CHAPTER 5

1 One problem concerns the source of the spurious ending of the *Andria* which does not appear in any of the major Calliopian MSS. The earliest MS to contain it is Oxford, Bodl Auct F 6 27, written in Germany in the tenth or eleventh century. Otto Skutsch has suggested (*RhM* 100 [1957] 58-9) that one of the later witnesses to the *exitus alter* (Bamberg, Staatsbibl class 49, a 1476) is descended from a non-Calliopian MS dating from the sixth century. If this is correct, some of the mixed MSS may also descend from this lost MS. But it is also possible that the influence of this archetype was limited to the spurious ending.

In his commentary on Terence, Pietro da Moglio, a friend of Petrarch, included a transcription of the *exitus alter* which he had found 'in vetustissimo codice' in the convent of S Domenico in Bologna. He states that this scene had been added to the text 'post perfectum opus' but that it was written 'antiqua valde littera.' The MS soon disappeared from the convent. See G. Billanovich *IMU* 17 (1974) 25; *IMU* 22 (1979) 380-1.

2 See Jones and Morey 2.28ff for discussion and earlier bibliography.

3 In his essay 'Hadoardus and the manuscripts of classical authors from Corbie' in S. Prete (ed) *Didascaliae: Studies in honor of Anselm M. Albareda* (New York 1961) 54 n 33 (= *Mittelalterliche Studien* [Stuttgart 1966] 1.59).

4 See also F.M. Carey 'The scriptorium of Reims during the Archbishopric of Hincmar' *Studies in honor of Edward Kenneth Rand* (New York 1938) 58; E. Bethe *Terentius. Codex Ambrosianus H 75 inf* (Leyden 1903) 13-14.

5 Jones and Morey 2.119 (Orléans); Bischoff, as reported by Reeve (above ch 1 n 1) 417 n 42, (neighbourhood of Rheims).

6 *AJA* 4 (1900) 310-38. For much of what immediately follows I am indebted to Hoeing.

7 Jones and Morey 2.89.

8 *HSCP* 22 (1911) 55-110.

9 Bischoff (above n 3) 53. It is possible that the Terence MS which is listed in the late eighth- or early ninth-century catalogue of the MSS of the court of Charlemagne (in Berlin, Diez B 66) was an ancestor of Y. The Terence entry in the catalogue is puzzling. It reads: 'Terenti Andria. libri multi / Incipit eunuchus. sic incipit thais meretrix / parmeno servus pamphilus adulescens. sostra/ta mulier. pamphilus aduliscens bachimeretrix / antichila mulier. clinia aduliscens. sirus servus.' The scene headings which appear in the entry relate to *Eun* I.2, *Hec* III.3, *Hec* IV.2, *Haut* II.4. It is a puzzle why these headings should have been chosen by the compiler of the catalogue – unless the leaves of the MS were in disarray. Read *libri mutili* for *libri multi*? Is it coincidence that in Y the *Eunuchus* begins at I.2? On the catalogue see B.L. Ullman 'A list of classical manuscripts (in an eighth-century codex) perhaps from Corbie' *Scriptorium* 8 (1954) 24-37; B. Bischoff 'Die Hofbibliothek Karls des Grossen' in *Karl der Grosse, Lebenswerk und Nachleben* (Düsseldorf 1965) 2.42-62 (= *Mittelalterliche Studien* [Stuttgart 1981] 3.149-69); L.D. Reynolds and N.G. Wilson *Scribes and scholars*[2] (Oxford 1974) 86-7. Ullman thinks that Y may have originated in Fleury.

10 Jones and Morey 2.96 suggest that *iacus* 'may well be a fancied cognate of *iacea*, attested as a medieval equivalent in France for *mentha* (mint).'

11 The text of F has not escaped contamination (see L. Havet *Manuel de critique* §1613A, with reference to *Ph* 748-832), but I doubt whether all the correct readings of F against CPYO can be imputed to this process.

12 There are a few errors which betray confusion of i and l; *unclatim* for *unciatim* (*Ph* 43), *nihi* for *nihil* (*Ph* 208), *ex illa* for *exilia* (*Ph* 243).

13 The three omissions in Y have arisen through homoeoteleuton. Such omissions are possible when a scribe is copying from prose but they

would have occurred much more easily and as often as they do if the exemplar of Y (or of its immediate exemplar) was written in verse. See Webb 91.

14 At *Ad* 470 *persusasit* for *persuasit* may have been prompted by confusion of a and u; *tam* for *tum* at *Ad* 851 was probably caused by the presence of *tum* at the beginning of line 849.

15 On λ see R. Kauer 'Handschriftliches zu Terenz' *WSt* 28 (1906) 111-37.

16 Jones and Morey also point to similarities in the labels which accompany the illustrations in P and O, but many of these could have been inherited from the hyparchetype of the two MSS. More weight is placed on one instance where the mistaken identification of the slave girl led by Parmeno in *Eun* III.2 as Pythias is imputed to the later minuscule labels in P. Certainly the name Pythias does appear under the slave girl in P, but the labels are *not* written in the order in which the characters are drawn.

17 So, for example, the preface at *An* II.5: 'Carinus recedens a pamphilo remisit servum suum birriam providere quid pamphilus de nuptiis ageret. in eundo ergo tacitus haec secum dicebat.' These prefaces occur in not a few MSS. What is peculiar about them in O is that they are preceded by the first words of the scene and sometimes a gloss. The preface of *An* II.5 is introduced by 'Herus me reliquid i. dominus meus Carinus.'

18 The MSS examined (excluding those mentioned in the text) are Barcelona, Bibl Centr 1743; Brussels, Bibl Roy 5329, 9705; Cambridge, CCC 231, Peterhouse 253; Erlangen 391; Leyden, Rijksuniv Lips 26, Voss lat O 31, Voss lat Q 38, BPL 109; London, BL Harl 2656, 2670, Roy 15 A VIII; Madrid, Bibl Nac Vitr 5-4; Milan, Ambros G 130 inf; Montpellier, Fac Méd 227; Oxford, Brasenose 18; Paris, BN lat 7901, 7902, 7903, 7904, 7905, 16235, 18544; Tours 924.

19 An exception is the MS from El Escorial in which *An* 804-53 were omitted by the first hand (see below.)

20 Compare what an artist of C did with the blank space which confronted him at *Haut* V.2 (see above p 39).

21 Jones and Morey (2.76ff) have argued that the miniatures in O share similarities with F against C and P and that the artists of O 'were employing, besides the manuscript which served them as principal model, a secondary source in the shape of an illustrated Terence MS of the μ-class' (81). If ω is substituted for O and if they are correct, there is a stronger case for believing in the authenticity of the miniatures in O. But the affinities with F and other illustrated MSS seem trifling to me and the number of alleged instances is very small. Presumably

the scribe of ω did not have access to an illustrated γ MS containing miniatures at *An* V.1 and V.2. If he did, would he not have used its text for *An* 804-53? Or was it written as prose?

22 For a detailed description of the MS see Y.-F. Riou in *Lettres latines du moyen âge et de la Renaissance* (Brussels 1978) 51ff. The Spanish origin of the MS, also suggested privately to me by Bernhard Bischoff, is disputed by Monique C. Garand, who thinks it to be Italian rather than Spanish: see *Scriptorium* 35 (1981), Bulletin Codicologique, p 79. The date of the MS may be somewhat earlier than the eleventh century.

23 E^s shares some readings with CPYO against E and v in the *Andria*: 268 *die* (with D); 353-4 *dare / hodie* (with G^1); 379 *culpam in te*; 504 *coepi*; 586 *habeo iam fidem*; 614 *necquidem me*; 712 omission of *ut* (*alterum*); 861 *rape hunc*; 916 *ita*; 950 omission of *id*; 958 omission of *sic*; 974 omission of *mihi*. The erroneous readings in this list need not mean that E^s has been contaminated by the Γ^b or Γ^c branch, though that is a possibility. The errors may also have been present in F and corrected by contamination in E and v.

24 No account of the γ tradition in the Carolingian period would be complete without mention of a Eugippius MS in the Bibliothèque Nationale (lat 2109.) The main text was written in St Amand before 828. On fol 1^r-1^v are found *Haut* 1-15, in rustic capitals, perhaps written at the same time or shortly thereafter: see E.K. Rand and L.W. Jones *The earliest book of Tours* (Cambridge Mass 1934) 68-70. The text is 'Calliopian'; it offers *simplici* (6), *esse voluit* (11), and *dicturus sum* (15) against the Bembinus. Only one reading provides assistance in assigning the text to the γ or δ branch; at line 1 it reads *sit vestrum* against *vestrum sit* of δE. It is not unlikely that it was copied from an ancient MS, itself written in rustic capitals. *DEDICEREM* for *dedicerim* may have been promoted by confusion of I and E. The interesting reading *QUAE SIT* for *quae esset* at line 7 may also have arisen from the same confusion. Other errors are *vestram* (9), *hoc* (13), *commodi* (14).

The most interesting feature of the passage is that the verses of the prologue are divided between two pages. On the first appear the first three verses of the prologue, followed, on a separate line, by *FINIT*. The twelve following lines on the page are left blank and verse 4 of the prologue begins on fol 1^v. This gives some manuscript support to those who have felt that the sequence of thought between verses 3 and 4 is intolerable and have postulated transposition, excision and lacunae to make sense of the first section of the prologue; see especially K. Dziatzko *De prologis Plautinis et Terentianis quaestiones selectae* (Bonn 1863) 7ff.

I am most grateful to M. Yves-François Riou for providing me with a transcription of the lines.

CHAPTER 6

1 It should be remembered that L has a γ text for *Hecyra* and almost all of *Hauton timorumenos*.

2 The replacement of an archaic by a modern form is of course more common: cf, for example, *istam* for *istanc* at *Haut* 994 (γ) and *Ad* 755 (Aδ); *horum* for *horunc* at *Hec* 172 (Σ except p); *sint* for *sient* at *Eun* 1061 (Aγ); *hae* for *haec* at *Eun* 582 (Σ) and *Hec* 790 (Σ); *ut* for *uti* at *Hec* 164 (Ap) and 390 (A).

3 Minton Warren 'On the enclitic *ne* in Early Latin' *AJP* 2 (1881) 50-82, esp 55ff. Warren received support from C.M. Mulvany *CR* 9 (1895) 15ff, and A.R. Anderson *CP* 9 (1914) 180.

4 See above pp 82, 115, 165.

5 Marouzeau and Prete print *exorent* without making any further change. This gives a doubtful trochaic septenarius.

6 See *CP* 79 (1984) 34-5.

7 See *TLL* 2.2173,19ff.

8 There are a few errors shared by CP and A: *ne* for *ni* at *Ph* 547; *maxumi* for *maxume* at *Ad* 501; and possibly *an* for *anne* at *Eun* 733. Each could have occurred independently.

9 See Laidlaw *The prosody of Terence* 53.

10 At the beginning of *Ad* 83 *siet* is iambic. Although often emended, it should be retained. The enjambment effectively reflects Demea's outrage.

11 If the licences admitted by the *loci Iacobsohniani* had been invoked by Terence, the line would scan with the final syllable of *diutius* being counted as *brevis in longo*. It is doubtful, however, whether these *loci* are observed by Terence: see C. Questa 'Ancora sui "loci Jacobsohniani"' *Maia* 20 (1968) 373-89; R. Raffaelli 'I longi strappati negli ottonari giambici di Plauto e Terenzio' in *Problemi di metrica classica. Miscellanea Filologica* (Genoa 1978) 179-222, esp 216ff.

12 C. Conradt *Die Metrische Composition der Comödien des Terenz* (Berlin 1876) 126-7 also thinks that *Ph* 182 is spurious but his reason is unconvincing. He takes *nostra audacia* to refer to the marriage which had already taken place and asks how that can be thought to have been kept secret. But *nostra audacia* surely refers to the way in which the marriage was facilitated.

13 An actor would be familiar with verse-endings comparable to *fingere fallaciam*.

14 *Ph* 114 *facere ait; Ph* 573 *audiveras; Ph* 661 *oppositus est; Hec* 220 omission of *est; Hec* 320 *celant; Hec* 609 *sit faciendum; Ad* 187 *modo aequi aliquid; Ad* 189 *est orta*.

SELECT BIBLIOGRAPHY

This bibliography lists only those articles and books which have been referred to in the text. It does not include many works of importance in Terentian and textual studies.

Allardyce, J.T. *Syntax of Terence* Oxford 1929

Arens, F. *De Terentianarum fabularum memoria in Aeli Donati quod fertur commento servata* Westfalia 1910

Barwick, C. *Flavii Sosipatri Charisii Artis Grammaticae libri v* Leipzig 1964

Beeson, C.H. 'The text tradition of Donatus' commentary on Terence' *CP* 17 (1922) 283-305

Bentley, R. (ed) *P. Terentii Afri comoediae* Cambridge 1726

Bethe, E. *Buch und Bild im Altertum* Leipzig 1945

Bethe, E. *Terentius. Codex Ambrosianus H. 75 inf. phototypice editus* Leyden 1903

Bieber, M. *The history of the Greek and Roman theater* 2nd ed Princeton 1961

Billanovich, G. 'Petrarca, Pietro da Moglio e Pietro da Parma' *IMU* 22 (1979) 367-95

Billanovich, G. 'Terenzio, Ildemaro, Petrarca' *IMU* 17 (1974) 1-60

Birt, T. *Die Buchrolle in der Kunst* Leipzig 1907

Bischoff, B. 'Das Güterverzeichnis des Klosters SS. Faustino e Giovita in Brescia aus dem Jahre 964' *IMU* 15 (1972) 53-61

Bischoff, B. 'Hadoardus and the manuscripts of classical authors from Corbie' in *Didascaliae. Studies in honor of Anselm M. Albareda* (New York 1961) 41-57

Bischoff, B. *Mittelalterliche Studien* 3 vols Stuttgart 1966-81

Brown, V. 'The "insular intermediary" in the tradition of Lucretius' *HSCP* 72 (1968) 301-8

Brunhölzl, F. 'Zu den sogenannten codices archetypi der römischen Literatur' *Festschrift B. Bischoff zu seinem 65. Geburtstag* (Stuttgart 1971) 16-31

Brunhölzl, F. 'Zur Überlieferung des Lucrez' *Hermes* 90 (1962) 97-104

Byvanck, A.W. 'Antike Malerei, II: Das Vorbild der Terenzillustrationen' *Mnemosyne* 7 (1939) 115-35

Carey, F.M. 'The scriptorium of Reims during the Archbishopric of Hincmar' *Studies in honor of Edward Kenneth Rand* (New York 1938) 41-59

Carney, T.F. (ed) *P. Terenti Afri Hecyra* Classical Association of Rhodesia and Nyasaland 1963

Charitonides, S., L. Kahil, and R. Ginouvès *Les mosaïques de la maison du Ménandre à Mytilène* Bern 1970 (*Antike Kunst* Beiheft VI)

Chatelain, E.L.M. *Paléographie des classiques latins* 2 vols Paris 1884-1900

Conradt, C. *Die metrische Composition der Comödien des Terenz* Berlin 1876

Courtney, E. 'The formation of the text of Vergil' *BICS* 28 (1981) 13-29

Craig, J.D. *Ancient editions of Terence* London 1929

Craig, J.D. 'Priscian's quotations from Terence' *CQ* 24 (1930) 65-73

Craig, J.D. 'Terence quotations in Servius Auctus' *CQ* 25 (1931) 151-6

Dziatzko, K. (ed) *P. Terenti Afri Comoediae* Leipzig 1884

Dziatzko, K. 'Zur Frage der Calliopianischen Rezension des Terenz' *Commentationes Woelfflinianae* (Leipzig 1891) 221-6

Dziatzko, K., and E. Hauler *Ausgewählte Komödien des P. Terentius Afer: Erstes Bändchen: Phormio* 4th ed Leipzig 1913

Dziatzko, K., and R. Kauer *Ausgewählte Komödien des P. Terentius Afer: Zweites Bändchen: Adelphoe* 2nd ed Leipzig 1903

Ehrle, F., and P. Leibaert *Specimina codicum latinorum Vaticanorum* 2nd ed Berlin 1927

Engelhardt, K. *Die Illustrationen der Terenzhandschriften* Diss Jena 1905

Faber, T. (ed) *P. Terentius Afer Comoediae* Saumur 1678

Fritsch, A. 'Zu den Terentiushandschriften' *Philologus* 32 (1873) 442-60

Gold, A., and A. Allgeier *Der Palimpsestpsalter im Codex Sangallensis* 912 Beuron 1933

Goldberg, S.M. 'Scholarship on Terence and the fragments of Roman Comedy' *CW* 75 (1981) 77-115

Gotoff, H.C. *The transmission of the text of Lucan in the ninth century* Cambridge Mass 1971

Grant, J.N. 'The *commentum Monacense* and the MS tradition of Terence' *Manuscripta* 22 (1978) 83-90

Grant, J.N. 'Contamination in the mixed MSS of Terence: a partial solution?' *TAPA* 105 (1975) 123-53

Grant, J.N. 'T and the miniatures of Terence' *CQ* 23 (1973) 88-103

Haffter, H. 'Terenz und seine künstlerische Eigenart' *MH* 10 (1953) 1-20,

73-102. Reprinted as a book with the same title (Darmstadt 1967). Translated into Italian as *Terenzio e la sua personalità artistica* Rome 1969

Harsh, P.W. *Iambic words and regard for accent in Plautus* Stanford 1949

Havet, L. *Manuel de critique verbale appliquée aux textes latins* Paris 1911

Hermann, H.J. *Beschreibendes Verzeichnis der illum. Handschriften in Österreich* 8,2 Leipzig 1926

Hoeing, C. 'The codex Dunelmensis of Terence' *AJA* 4 (1900) 310-38

Jachmann, G. *Die Geschichte des Terenztextes im Altertum* Basel 1924

Jachmann, G. 'P. Terentius Afer' *RE* 5A (1934) 598-650

Jachmann, G. *Terentius. Codex Vaticanus latinus 3868 picturis insignis, ex auctoritate procuratorum Bibliothecae Apostolicae Vaticanae phototypice editus* Leipzig 1929

Jahn, O. 'Über die Subscriptionen in den Handschriften römischer Classiker' *Berichte der Königlich Sächsischen Gesellschaft der Wissenschaften zu Leipzig, Philologisch-historische Klasse* 3 (1851) 327-72

Jocelyn, H.D. *The tragedies of Ennius* Cambridge 1967

Jones, L.W. 'Ancient texts of Terence' *CP* 25 (1930) 318-27

Jones, L.W., and C.R. Morey *The miniatures of the manuscripts of Terence prior to the thirteenth century* 2 vols Princeton 1931

Kauer, R. 'Bericht über die Terenzliteratur in den Jahren 1898-1908' *JAW* 143 (1909) 176-270

Kauer, R. 'Handschriftliches zu Terenz' *WSt* 28 (1906) 111-37

Kauer, R. 'Zu Terenz' *WSt* 22 (1900) 56-114

Kauer, R., W.M. Lindsay, and O. Skutsch (edd) *P. Terentius Afer. Comoediae* Oxford 1958

Keil, H. (ed) *Grammatici latini* 7 vols Leipzig 1857-80

Klose, D. *Die Didaskalien und Prologe des Terenz* Diss Freiburg 1966

Laidlaw, W.A. *The prosody of Terence* Oxford 1938

Lehmann, P. 'Eine Palimpseststudie (St Gallen 912)' *SBAW* 1931,1

Leo, F. 'Die Überlieferungsgeschichte der terenzischen Komödien und der Commentar des Donatus' *RhM* 38 (1883) 316-47

Leumann, M., J.B. Hofmann, and A. Szantyr *Lateinische Grammatik* 2 vols Munich 1965

Lindsay, W.M. 'The Donatus-excerpts in the Codex Victorianus (D) of Terence' *CQ* 21 (1937) 188-94

Lindsay, W.M. *Syntax of Plautus* Oxford 1907

Löfstedt, E. 'Die Bembinusscholien und Donatus' *Eranos* 12 (1913) 43-63

Lowe, E.A., and E.K. Rand *A sixth-century fragment of the Letters of Pliny the Younger* Washington 1922

Marouzeau, J. 'Les manuscrits térentiens de la bibliothèque de Donat' *Mélanges dediés à la mémoire de Félix Grat* (Paris 1949) 2.317-21

Marouzeau, J. *Térence. Comédies* 3 vols Paris 1947-9
Marti, H. 'Terenz 1909-1959' *Lustrum* 6 (1961) 116-47; 8 (1963) 5-101, 244-7
Martin, R.H. (ed) *Terence. Adelphoe* Cambridge 1976
Mountford, J.F. *The scholia Bembina in Terentium* London 1934
Panofsky, D. 'The textual basis of the Utrecht Psalter illustrations' *AB* 25 (1943) 50-8
Pasquali, G. *Storia della tradizione e critica del testo* 2nd ed Florence 1952
Pickard-Cambridge, A.W. *The dramatic festivals of Athens* 2nd ed Oxford 1968
Pratesi, A. 'Appunti per la datazione del Terenzio Bembino' in *Palaeographica diplomatica et archivistica. Studi in onore de Giulio Battelli* (Rome 1979) 1.71-84
Prete, S. (ed) *Didascaliae. Studies in honor of Anselm M. Albareda* New York 1961
Prete, S. *Il codice di Terenzio Vaticano Latino 3226* Vatican City 1970 (*Studi e Testi* 262)
Prete, S. 'La tradizione del testo di Terenzio nell' antichità' *SIFC* NS 25 (1951) 111-34
Prete, S (ed) *P. Terentius Afer. Comoediae* Heidelberg 1954
Prinzhorn, G. *De libris Terentianis quae ad recensionem Calliopianam redeunt* Diss Göttingen 1885
Questa, C. 'Ancora sui "loci Jacobsohniani"' *Maia* 20 (1968) 378-89
Raffaelli, R. 'I longi strappati negli ottonari giambici di Plauto e Terenzio' *Problemi di metrica classica. Misc Filologica* (Genoa 1978) 179-222
Rand, E.K. 'Early mediaeval commentaries on Terence' *CP* 4 (1909) 359-89
Rand, E.K., and L.W. Jones *The earliest book of Tours* Cambridge Mass 1934
Reeve, M.D. 'The textual tradition of Donatus's commentary on Terence' *Hermes* 106 (1978) 608-18
Reeve, M.D. 'The textual tradition of Donatus' commentary on Terence' *CP* 74 (1979) 310-26
Reynolds, L.D. (ed) *Texts and transmission. A survey of the Latin classics* Oxford 1983
Reynolds, L.D. 'Two notes on the manuscripts of Seneca's Letters' *CR* 7 (1957) 5-12
Reynolds, L.D., and N.G. Wilson *Scribes and Scholars* 2nd ed Oxford 1974
Ribbeck, O. *Scenicae romanorum poesis fragmenta* 2 vols 3rd ed Leipzig 1897-8
Ribuoli, R. *La collazione poliziano del codice Bembino di Terenzio* Rome 1981
Ribuoli, R. 'Per la storia del codice Bembino di Terenzio' *RFIC* 109 (1981) 163-77
Riley, H.T. (ed) *Gesta Abbatum Monasterii S. Albani* 3 vols London 1867
Riou, Y.-F. 'Essai sur la tradition manuscrite du Commentum Brunsianum des comédies de Térence' *RHT* 3 (1973) 79-113

Riou, Y.-F. 'Gloses et commentaires des comédies de Térence dans les manuscrits de la bibliothèque du monastère San Lorenzo el real de l'Escorial' in *Lettres latines du moyen âge et de la Renaissance* (Brussels 1978) 5-55

Ritschl, F. 'De emendatione fabularum terentianarum' *Opuscula philologica* 3 (Leipzig 1877) 281-300

Robert, C. *Archaeologische Hermeneutik* Berlin 1919

Robert, C. *Die Maske der neueren attischen Komödie* Halle 1911

Rodenwaldt, G. '*Cortinae.* Ein Beitrag zur datierung der antiken Vorlage der mittelalterlichen Terenzillustrationen' *NGG, Philologisch-Historiche Klasse,* 1925, 33-49

Rubio, L. (ed) *P. Terentius Afer. Comedias* 3 vols Barcelona 1957-66

Sabbadini, R. 'Biografi e commentatori di Terenzio' *SIFC* 5 (1897) 289-327

Sabbadini. R. 'Il commento di Donato a Terenzio' *SIFC* 2 (1894) 1-134

Sabbadini, R. *Storia e critica di testi latini* Catania 1914. Reprinted as *Medioevo e umanesimo* 11 (Padua 1971)

Schlee, F. 'Jahresbericht über Terenz von 1889-1896' *JAW* 93 (1897) 116-64

Schlee, F. *Scholia terentiana* Leipzig 1893

Schuchardt, H. *Der Vokalismus des Vülgarlateins* 3 vols Leipzig 1866-8

Seider, R. *Paläographie der lateinischen Papyri* Stuttgart 1972-

Shipp G.P. (ed) *Andria* 2nd ed Melbourne 1960

Skutsch, O. 'Der zweite Schluss der Andria' *RhM* 100 (1957) 53-68

Spengel, A. 'Jahresbericht über Terentius und die übrigen scenischen Dichter ausser Plautus für 1884 (zweite Hälfte) bis 1888' *JAW* 68 (1891) 171-92

Sydow, K. *De fide librorum Terentianorum ex Calliopii recensione ductorum* Berlin 1878

Thesleff, H. *Yes and no in Plautus and Terence* Helsinki 1960

Timpanaro, S. *Die Entstehung der Lachmannschen Methode* 2nd ed Hamburg 1971

Ullman, B.L. 'A list of classical manuscripts (in an eighth-century codex) perhaps from Corbie' *Scriptorium* 8 (1954) 24-37

Umpfenbach, F. 'Die Scholien des Codex Bembinus zum Terentius' *Hermes* 2 (1867) 337-402

Umpfenbach, F. (ed) *P. Terenti comoediae* Berlin 1870

Vahlen, J. *Ennianae poesis reliquiae* 2nd ed Leipzig 1903

Vezin, J. *Les scriptoria d'Angers au XIe siècle* Paris 1974

Villa, C. '"Denique Terenti dultia legimus acta ... ": una "lectura Terenti" a S Faustino di Brescia nel secolo ix' *IMU* 22 (1979) 1-44

Warren, M. 'On the enclitic *ne* in early Latin' *AJP* 2 (1881) 50-82

Watson, J.C. 'The relation of the scene-headings to the miniatures in manuscripts of Terence' *HSCP* 14 (1903) 55-172

Webb, R.H. 'An attempt to restore the γ archetype of Terence manuscripts' *HSCP* 22 (1911) 55-110

Weitzmann, K. *Ancient book illumination* Cambridge Mass 1959

Weitzmann, K. *Illustrations in roll and codex. A study of the origin and method of text illustration* 2nd ed Princeton 1970

Weitzmann, K. *Late antique and early Christian book illumination* London 1977

Wessner, P. 'Bericht über die Erscheinungen auf bem Gebiete der lateinischen Grammatiker ... für 1908-20' *JAW* 188 (1921) 34-354

Wessner, P. (ed) *Donatus. Commentum Terenti* 3 vols Leipzig 1902-5

Wessner, P. *Gnomon* 3 (1927) 339-47 (review of Jachmann *Die Geschichte der Terenztextes im Altertum*)

Wessner, P. 'Zu den Donatauszugen im cod. Victorianus (D) des Terenz' *PhilWoch* 15 (1927) 443-9

Weston, K.E. 'The illustrated Terence manuscripts' *HSCP* 14 (1903) 34-54

Wieseler, F. *Theatergebaüde und Denkmäler des Bühnenwesens bei den Griechen und Römern* Göttingen 1851

Willis, J. *Latin textual criticism* Urbana 1972

Zelzer, M. 'Zur Frage der Vorlage des Tacitus-codex Mediceus 68,2' *WSt* 86 (1973) 185-95

Zetzel, J.E.G. 'Andria 403 (II.3.29)' *Hermes* 102 (1974) 372-6

Zetzel, J.E.G. *Latin textual criticism in antiquity* New York 1981

Zetzel, J.E.G. 'On the history of Latin scholia' *HSCP* 79 (1975) 335-54

GENERAL INDEX

INDEX OF MANUSCRIPTS